Taming the Corporation

Taming the Corporation

How to Regulate for Success

Robert Baldwin and Martin Cave

OXFORD
UNIVERSITY PRESS

Great Clarendon Street, Oxford, OX2 6DP,
United Kingdom

Oxford University Press is a department of the University of Oxford.
It furthers the University's objective of excellence in research, scholarship,
and education by publishing worldwide. Oxford is a registered trade mark of
Oxford University Press in the UK and in certain other countries

First Edition published in 2021

Impression: 1

Published in the United States of America by Oxford University Press
198 Madison Avenue, New York, NY 10016, United States of America

British Library Cataloguing in Publication Data
Data available

Library of Congress Control Number: 2020941054

ISBN 978-0-19-883618-6

Printed and bound in Great Britain by
Clays Ltd, Elcograf S.p.A.

Preface

Our goal in writing this book is to set out how positive regulation can work in a way which is beneficial to firms and investors and to citizens and consumers. We have combined an account of how positive regulation can and should work with extended case studies of climate change regulation and the regulation of traditional physical networks and of modern digital platforms. In doing so we discuss how regulators can get things right, or how they may fail to 'regulate for success'. We have also included a number of shorter illustrations of success and failure, and a chapter on how regulators can seek to avoid the latter.

This book is not about economic and social policy or its making, which is the preserve of legislatures or governments, but about the more technical aspects of regulation that are commonly undertaken by independent agencies within broad policy frameworks set by governments. Thus strategies for implementing or enforcing given policies are central to our concerns. This is seen, for example, in our discussion in chapter 6 of regulatory activity designed to support climate change objectives; our objective is not to discuss governmental objectives but to outline how regulation can best achieve them.

Robert Baldwin is chiefly responsible for Chapters 1–5 and 10–11; Martin Cave for Chapters 7–9. Chapter 6 is a joint production. The views expressed belong to the authors alone and not to any organizations with which they are affiliated.

The book aims to highlight the strategic relevance of many messages gleaned from scholarly and practitioner analyses of regulation. For a more detailed discussion of a wider range of regulatory issues, scholarship and operational experience see R. Baldwin, M. Cave, and M. Lodge, *Understanding Regulation: Theory, Strategy, and Practice* (2nd ed., Oxford University Press, 2012).

We are grateful to many people for help and advice, including in particular: Peter Alexiadis, Sean Ennis, Rob Nicholls, and Tim Tutton.

Contents

List of Figures and Tables

Figures

Tables

PART I

REGULATING FOR SUCCESS

1
Positive Regulation

Politicians and commentators often protest: 'Why regulate? Why not leave matters to the market?' They complain about the restrictiveness of regulation, the way that it interferes with economic activity and increases the costs of doing business. They see regulation in negative, 'red light', terms—as mainly about stopping healthy entrepreneurial activity.

Case in point: Taking the brakes off

In July 2015 the UK Government launched an initiative to cut red tape in the energy, waste, agriculture and a number of other sectors.

  Business Secretary Sajid Javid said: 'I am determined to take the brakes off British businesses and set them free from heavy-handed regulators. The government's pledge to cut £10 billion in red tape over the course of this parliament will help create more jobs for working people, boost productivity and keep our economy growing. For the first time, these reviews will look not only at the rules themselves but the way they are enforced.'

This book adopts a more positive view and argues that regulation is part of the process for creating economic wealth and social welfare. Positive regulation is pro-business and pro-society. Using regulation to tame the corporation is about harnessing corporate capacities and motivations so as to maximize the excess of benefits over costs—taking both economic and social factors into account. We stress here that regulation has a strong enabling, or 'green light' role. It is a respectable activity!

  Laws and regulations, after all, actually enable markets to operate. Property laws are the building blocks that support systems of rights and allow these to be traded in an efficient manner. Without the protections offered by legal rights the actors in markets would have to take other, far more burdensome, steps in order to create the levels of security that would induce them to trade.[1] Property laws provide readily available, pre-packaged and secure regimes for allocating rights, and for enforcing these. They create low-cost frameworks for buying and selling. As Joseph Singer has stressed: 'Neither private property nor the free market can exist without regulation.'[2]

There is, accordingly, no opposition between free markets and regulation. Laws allow markets to operate. We may object to examples of bad regulation, to controls that impose costs unjustifiably, but these examples make no case for seeing regulation negatively—any more than a few poor meals should lead us to see food as an unnecessary evil.

It is also misguided to see markets as processes that somehow exist in states of nature, and which are interfered with by regulators. Markets only exist and sustain over time because there are general laws and more specific regulatory regimes that make this possible. Take, for example, the use of radio frequency bands (or spectrum) for mobile telephony. A range of frequencies is divided into segments which can be assigned, traded, and used by companies to supply services to end users. It is the relevant regulatory regime (a mixture of general property laws and more particular laws dealing with telecommunications issues) that makes use of the frequency bands possible in this way and which provides a controlled environment in which the market can operate to the consumer advantage. Regulation, in this context, is logically prior to the market and is enabling.

Companies and entrepreneurs need regulation in order to create wealth. A first reason for this is consumer and investor confidence. Few travellers would buy a ticket for a potentially dangerous activity (e.g. travelling by air) unless they felt that there was a regulator whose actions would ensure their safety. When consumers think about buying a pension plan they want to know that there is a competent financial regulator to protect their important investment. For the airlines and the pensions providers, the regulators act to promote the purchase of their products as much as their own marketing divisions. The regulators foster economic activity just as forcefully.

On the larger scale, inward investments have to be underpinned by regulatory regimes that create confidence. Take, for example, a train operating company's decision to spend millions of pounds in setting up its business. Before it invests, that company will want to know that it will have

---

[1]   See generally J. Singer, *No Freedom Without Regulation* (Yale University Press, 2015).
[2]   Singer, *No Freedom Without Regulation*, p. 2.

reasonable access to some other provider's infrastructure (the railway track) at a reasonable and predictable price. It will, accordingly, need to know that issues of infrastructure access and pricing are properly controlled by a regulator so that it will not be vulnerable to the self-serving actions of the infrastructure provider.

Case in point: Pensions

In a 2018 speech Andrew Bailey, Chief Executive of the Financial Conduct Authority spoke about the need to support individuals' decisions to save for retirement. He argued: 'We have to do all that we can do enable individuals to take these decisions, and we have to be prepared to intervene early, while the market is still developing. The benefits of doing this will come if we avoid unwanted practices becoming entrenched and over time consumers have confidence in their pensions.'

Whether markets operate domestically or internationally, investors in an enterprise will want assurance that they will be trading on a level playing field and that they will not be put out of business because competitors operate to lower standards of behaviour and, accordingly, lower costs. Thus, those funding a manufacturer will want regulation to protect it from being exposed to competition from operators who operate cheap, unsafe, and inefficient systems. That desire may be driven by ethical considerations but also economic factors—failing to match the low-grade systems would place the manufacturer at a competitive disadvantage but matching them would increase costs when accidents involve liabilities, interruptions of operations, reputational and other losses.

At the international level similar considerations apply. Thus, the rational investor would not put money into, say, a British pig farming enterprise if they feared that the animal welfare standards that they adopt will not be matched by overseas competitors who will both undercut them in the market and behave unacceptably. That investor would need to know that there will be no prejudicial race to the bottom on welfare standards—that there will be a regulatory regime that will protect them from this.

Businesses can also need regulation in order to provide structural management of the industry. This will often be necessary when the regulator is better placed to steer broad-scale industry changes than the operators they regulate. Thus, there are examples from around the world (e.g. the UK and Thailand) of communications regulators being better positioned to manage the change from analogue to digital delivery than the broadcasting companies they control. Transaction costs explain this—if there are a few hundred small, local broadcasting operators in a country it is difficult for them to come together at acceptable cost and agree a plan to move to digital. It is far easier for the single centrally placed regulator to manage the technological switch-over. When they act in this role the regulators act directly as wealth creators and service providers. There is little that is 'red light' about this.

A further major reason why companies and entrepreneurs need regulation in order to generate wealth is that markets require information—and, often, this will not be forthcoming without regulation. The pharmaceutical industry is a case in point. If company A spends twenty million pounds to develop an arthritis drug together with the information that it is both safe and effective, it can only recover that investment in research if it is given a protected position in the market by a regulator—otherwise competitors will free-ride on A's valuable information by copying the drug, using A's information, and under-selling A. Fear of such free-riding would stop any company from engaging in research on new drugs. There would be no new drugs, or pharmaceutical industry, as we know it, without regulation.

For all the above reasons, it makes little sense to stick to the 'red light' notion of regulation. Adopting a positive model does not, of course, mean that we have to forget about the differences between good and bad regulation. Much of this book is about ways to achieve high quality 'positive' regulation and methods of avoiding unjustifiable costs when regulating. Taming the corporation involves using positive regulation so that corporate capacities to self-regulate are used to the maximum extent and so that, when regulation is needed, it is the lowest cost, most effective method of control that is used to achieve the outcomes a society desires.[3] Some corporations, of course, need 'taming' more than others and at the heart of positive regulation lies an emphasis on responding intelligently to variations in regulatory targets—a theme that runs through the chapters below.

---

[3] Regulators usually do not pick their goals themselves but have these set out in primary regulation. Statutory objectives often include social or distributional aims—concerning, for example, the protection of particular groups of customers, such as those on low incomes.

The Elements of Positive Regulation

How can a positive approach to regulation be reflected in regulatory strategies? The argument here is that there are two key elements in positive regulation. First, its **predisposition**, which is to maximize the degree to which regulatory objectives (substantive and procedural) can be achieved by harnessing firms' capacities to behave well. This means that, other things being equal, the regulator should err on the side of employing instruments that are enabling rather than restrictive. Thus, the inclination should be to choose from the left hand side of Table 1.1 when selecting control strategies.

Table 1.1 Enabling versus restrictive approaches

Enabling	Restrictive
Incentives	Prohibitions
Self-monitoring	External inspections
Principles	Detailed rules
Negotiating, informing, and educating	Prosecuting and sanctioning
Self-regulation	State regulation

The second element of positive regulation is a **delivery framework** that involves *awareness, intelligence*, and *dynamism* across the key tasks of regulation (see Table 1.2)—as is further explained in Chapter 2.

Table 1.2 The elements of positive regulation

Predisposition	Harness firms' self-regulatory capacities. Favour enabling rather than restrictive intervention tools.
Delivery framework	Show *awareness, intelligence*, and *dynamism* in discharging the tasks of regulation.

Why Regulate at All? Social and Economic Rationales for Regulating

A central aim of positive regulation is to use controls in a manner that maximizes overall benefits to society and businesses. But why regulate at all? Why not leave matters to markets?

As seen above, the need to enable and foster business activity provides a cluster of reasons for regulating but there are other justifications for regulatory interventions. Here it is useful to distinguish between social and economic rationales for regulating. These differ markedly, as the following example shows. A company operates a large factory that makes wooden furniture. The five hundred staff use circular saws, lathes, band saws and other tools to produce tables and so on. The band saws have no guards on them, however, and the workforce lose, on average, twenty fingers per year in the blades. The issue is whether there should be a regulation demanding the fitting of guards—which will slow down production and reduce profits by £20,000 per year. In addressing this issue, an economic approach would focus on producing outcomes that are efficient, and maximize the total sum of wealth in society. Thus if fingers are worth £1100 the answer would be to fit the guards so that society as a whole is £2000 better off than would be the case without guards. If the fingers are worth £900 the message is to cut the fingers off and compensate victims—again society as a whole is £2000 better off than in the alternative scenario.

A social approach to the band saw issue would yield a different message—fit the guards whatever the value of a finger because it is morally wrong to allow factory owners to grow rich by operating unsafe systems of production that slice off the fingers of workers. This is the implied approach of UK Health and Safety law. It instructs employers to ensure that, where practicable, access to cutters or dangerous parts of a woodworking machine is prevented by guards. It does not say: 'But you can use unguarded band saws if you make enough profit to compensate the losers'.

Social and economic justifications may differ but they both play a role in regulatory decision-making around the world. Sometimes policy-makers, legislators, and judges focus on efficiency considerations. Thus, they will demand that potential polluters spend the efficient amount of money on avoiding pollution. This happens when a factory is induced to spend up to £100 on filtration in order to avoid £100 worth of damage to the adjacent river. (From an efficiency perspective it is undesirable to spend £101 to avoid a harm of £100.) At other times, legislators will adopt the social stance—they will impose £20,000 costs on businesses to save fingers worth only £18,000 because this is the right thing to do.

A social approach would thus suggest that there are a number of good reasons for regulating other than that of fostering efficient markets. It has been argued, notably by Tony Prosser,[4] that regulation is often needed to

---

[4] T. Prosser, The Regulatory Enterprise: Government Regulation and Legitimacy (Oxford University Press, 2010), pp. 11–20.

protect human rights and to further social solidarity. In doing so, he takes issue with the assumptions that markets provide the best ways to allocate goods and services, and that 'non-market' rationales for regulating are essentially arbitrary. He also questions the idea that market allocations are 'technical' whereas social justice issues are 'political'. What can be said as a matter of description, says Prosser, is that environmental regulators, and those in many other sectors, can properly be seen as seeking to further social objectives, rather than as simply acting to correct market failures. Even where markets are involved, regulatory laws, on such a view, are not limited to merely correcting the market but often serve to provide the frameworks of rights and processes that allow markets to work, and to protect markets from fragmentation. In many contexts, accordingly, regulation can be seen as prior, not secondary, to the market and as a first-choice method of organizing social relations.

Consistent with such social rationales are examples of regulating for reasons of distributional justice, rights protection, and citizenship—as, for example, where regulated utilities are obliged to apply geographically averaged tariffs or to meet universal service obligations (so that, for instance, utility services are provided to isolated farms that are uneconomic to supply). Governments, indeed, regulate on a host of matters simply in order to further social policies such as the prevention of discrimination based on race, sex, or age.

'Market Failure' Reasons for Regulating

Before the rise of the 'social' approach, the often-cited reasons for regulating were strongly influenced by economists' ways of thinking and were mainly seen in 'market failure' terms. Markets could fail in two senses. There might be the absence, in a sector, of a healthy, competitive market, with plenty of buyers and sellers and good information flows, or there might be a healthy market that was not delivering the outcomes that society might desire (as where that market failed to provide a continuous service due to seasonal or other factors). The role of regulation was to fix both kinds of market problems and to foster efficient markets. Standard texts on regulation would thus identify around ten reasons to regulate.[5]

---

[5] See e.g. S. Breyer, *Regulation and its Reform* (Harvard University Press, 1982); R. Baldwin, M. Cave, and M. Lodge, *Understanding Regulation: Theory, Strategy, and Practice* (2nd ed., Oxford University Press, 2012).

Monopoly Power

Monopolists tend to maximize profits by restricting outputs and setting prices above marginal cost. The task of the regulator is to avoid the emergence or sustaining of a monopoly by using competition (or antitrust) laws to conduce to a competitive business environment. An alternative situation occurs when a market or sector is 'naturally monopolistic' because it can be served at lowest cost by one provider (thus, competition would be wasteful with, say, railway track provision). Here the role of the regulator is not to encourage competition but to set prices near incremental cost (the cost of producing an additional unit) in order to encourage the monopolist to expand output to the level that would have been induced by competitive conditions. A further regulatory task is often to identify those parts of a process that are naturally monopolistic so that these can be regulated while other aspects are left to the influence of competitive forces.

Windfall Profits

A firm earns a windfall profit (an 'excess profit' or 'rent') when it comes across a source of supply that is significantly cheaper than that available in the marketplace—e.g. it locates a rich seam of a valuable mineral that is easily extracted. Central issues are whether there is a need to control the firm's enjoyment of the windfall and whether it is necessary to share the benefit between the firm, the relevant consumers, and taxpayers. Two main arguments are often used in favour of the firm. First, there may be a need to incentivize investment and research and development (e.g. into new drugs).[6] Second, it can be contended that leaving windfalls with the firm demonstrates respect for the bundles of property rights that the firm has exploited and that emphasizing the security of such rights is generally good for business.

Externalities

An externality (or 'spillover') is a cost (or benefit) imposed on a party beyond the immediate transaction. Thus, for example, a car tyre

---

[6] The Pharmaceutical Pricing Regulation Scheme and the patent law regime exemplify forms of regulation that incentivize research into new technologies.

manufacturer sells a tyre for £50 but pollutes the river to the extent of £5 damage for each car tyre produced. The price does not reflect the total cost to society of production and the reason to regulate is to eliminate the waste of under-spending on filtering out the pollution and to protect affected third parties (angling clubs etc.). A law prohibiting this pollution thus internalizes the spillover costs on 'polluter pays' principles and the price of £55 per tyre pays for the filtration system.

Information Inadequacies

Markets only operate healthily if consumers have good information. Markets, however, may not always supply good information to consumers. First, as noted, information might cost money to develop (e.g. regarding the safety and efficacy of a new drug) and the unregulated market might not allow for the recovery of such costs. Second, suppliers may collude to deprive consumers of information about a relevant matter (e.g. a product's dangers) or the suppliers may merely be under-incentivized to provide this information. Finally, consumers may lack the experience or expertise to counter the suppliers' incentives to falsify information.

In such cases it may be justifiable to regulate in order to generate information flows. A relevant consideration here may be the kind of product that is at issue and the associated vulnerability of the consumer. Three different varieties of product have been said to lead to different cases for regulating. With *search* goods (e.g. fresh fish) the consumer is generally well-placed to evaluate quality and risks before they purchase. The case for protective regulation may be weak in the absence of high risk levels. With *experience* goods (e.g. restaurant meals) consumers have to experience the product in order to evaluate it and they are, therefore, ill-placed to self-protect. The case for regulating is greater here and becomes stronger the greater the risk. With *credence* goods, any evidence of quality, value, or risk may be absent or uncertain (e.g. the benefits of glucosamine sulphate pills). The case for protective regulation may be all the greater here as self-protection is not feasible.

Continuity and Availability of Service

Sometimes even healthy markets will not provide the socially desired levels of continuity and availability of service. Thus, with passenger air transport to a summer holiday island, even if numbers of operators compete on the route, none of the competing airlines may provide a winter air service in spite of this being desirable for the social development of the island. Regulation, accordingly, may be used to sustain services through supply troughs—for example, by attaching 'minimum winter service' conditions to annual route licences. The subsidizing of off-peak by peak travellers will, however, raise issues of equity to be considered alongside questions of social policy.

Anti-Competitive Behaviour and Predatory Pricing

Markets may be deficient not merely because competition is lacking; they may produce undesirable effects because firms behave in a manner that is not conducive to healthy competition—as when they engage in predatory pricing. This occurs when a firm prices below costs, in the hope of driving competitors from the market, achieving a degree of domination, and then using its position to recover the costs of undercutting the opposition and to increase profits at the expense of consumers. Preconditions for a rational firm to engage in predatory pricing are that: it must be able to outlast its competitors once prices are cut below variable costs; and it must be able to maintain prices well above costs for long enough to recover its prior losses. The costs of entry to and exit from the market must, accordingly, allow it this period of comfort before new competition arises. The aim for regulators is to sustain competition and protect consumers from the ill-effects of market domination by outlawing predatory or other forms of anti-competitive behaviour.

Public Goods and Moral Hazard

Some commodities, e.g. security and defence services, may bring shared benefits and be socially desired. It may, however, be very costly for those paying for such services to prevent non-payers ('free-riders') from enjoying the benefits of those services. As a result, the market may fail to encourage the production of such commodities, and regulation may be required—often to overcome the free-rider problem by imposing taxes.

Similarly, where there is an instance of moral hazard—where someone other than the consumer pays for a service—there may be excessive consumption without regard to the resource costs being imposed on society.

When governments bail out the banks, the latter will tend to embrace too much risk. Or, if medical costs are not met by the patient, but by the state or an insurer, there may be excessive consumption of medical services. In such cases, regulatory constraints may be required in the public interest.

Unequal Bargaining Power

If bargaining power is unequal, regulation may be justified in order to protect certain interests. Thus, if unemployment is prevalent it cannot be assumed that workers will be able to negotiate effectively to protect their interests, and regulation may be required to safeguard such matters as the health and safety of those workers. These inequalities may be the products of relative positions in the marketplace, but they may also stem from asymmetries of information. Workers, for instance, may be poorly placed to secure health protections from their employers because they lack information about relevant risks.

Scarcity and Rationing

When an essential resource (e.g. diesel) is in short supply, the market will allocate this to the highest bidders (e.g. power-boat racers not ambulance operators). Public interest objectives, however, may demand that regulatory rather than market mechanisms are used for such allocations so that social priorities will trump economic considerations.

Rationalization, Coordination, and Planning

In many situations, it is extremely expensive for individuals to negotiate private contracts so as to organize behaviour or industries in an efficient manner—the transaction costs would be excessive. The firms in an industry may be too small and geographically dispersed to bring themselves together to resolve issues efficiently. (This might happen when small fishing concerns in a sparsely populated area fail to make collective marketing arrangements.) Enterprises may, moreover, have developed different and incompatible modes of production. In these circumstances, regulation may be justified as a means of coordinating the market and rationalizing production processes (perhaps standardizing equipment in order to create effective networks).

With regard to planning issues, markets may ensure reasonably well that individuals' consumer preferences are met, but they are less able to meet the demands of future generations or to satisfy altruistic concerns (e.g. the quality of an environment not personally enjoyed). Many people, moreover, may be prepared to give up some of their assets for altruistic purposes only if they can be assured that a large number of others will do the same. Regulation may be required in order to further such altruistic desires and to cope with free-rider problems.

Conclusions: Choosing to Regulate Positively

Regulation contributes to the creation of wealth and socially desirable outcomes and fostering business activity looms large among the reasons for regulating. Taming the corporation is, accordingly, as much about the successful aligning of corporate and social objectives as about constraining business activity. Here we offer a positive approach to steering corporate power in productive and useful directions.

Positive regulation focuses on devising the best configurations of influences for achieving desired outcomes at lowest cost. It is delivered by regulators who are aware, intelligent, and dynamic across the range of regulatory tasks. We turn now to what this involves.

2
Positive Regulation and Success

There are familiar examples of regulatory systems that seem to have failed—the financial crisis of 2007–8 offers an instance of a hugely costly failure of regulation and government. What, though, does successful regulation look like?

What is Regulatory Success?

Regulatory success is achieved when a regulator delivers the right outcomes (for businesses, consumers, and society) by acceptable procedures at the lowest feasible cost. When this occurs, regulation is at its most positive. Claiming success through positive regulation is not free from contest, however. The 'right' outcomes and 'acceptable procedures' are not matters beyond argument.

Those arguments, and ways to deliver regulatory success, can be unpacked by restating the three core tasks that regulators have to perform well. First, they must be clear about their objectives—a precondition for the effective pursuit of acceptable outcomes and processes. Second, they must deliver the right substantive outcomes and, third, they must operate procedures that satisfy the expectations of parties affected by their decisions and policies—through being properly accountable, open, fair, rational, and transparent (see Table 2.1). They must discharge all three tasks at non-excessive cost.

Table 2.1 Core regulatory tasks

1. Setting objectives
2. Delivering outcomes
3. Meeting procedural expectations

As noted, there are considerable challenges to be faced both in delivering on these matters and in demonstrating success to relevant parties.

Identifying objectives, for instance, is no simple matter. If regulators look to their legally mandated objectives they will find that these are stated in the broadest of terms. Ofcom, the UK's communications regulator, for instance, has principal duties: 'to further the interests of citizens in relation to communications matters; and to further the interests of consumers in relevant markets, where appropriate by promoting competition'. What this means in detail is, of course, open to contest and different stakeholders will have different interpretations of this mandate—in spite of any statements of exposition offered by the regulator or any associated statements of strategic priorities that may be issued on behalf of the Government.

With most regulators their mandated objectives will be stated in very broad terms—this is what gives them the flexibility to deal with new problems as they arise. Regulators, after all, have generally to exert influence over operators in a constantly shifting world in which new markets emerge, new services are developed, fresh operators come on to the scene, costs are constantly moving up or down, and so on. The effect is that it is seldom, if ever, the case that regulators can demonstrate beyond contention that they are pursuing the 'right' objectives—some sets of interested parties will always contest the conception of the mandate that is offered.

Related challenges arise in delivering the right substantive outcomes. As with conceptions of mandates and objectives, which outcomes are 'right' will turn on the viewpoint of the stakeholder concerned. It is likely, for instance, that large upstream producers and small retailers or consumers will have quite different ideas about desired outcomes.

As for operating procedures that meet procedural expectations, it will also be the case that different stakeholders will vary in their notions of the procedures that are reasonable and protect their interests. Small enterprises and multinational ones will, for example, diverge on the forms of explanation and communication that they think it right for the regulator to use in dealing with them.

Regulators, in short, have to satisfy a variety of expectations on a number of fronts. That is their first major challenge. Their second fundamental difficulty is that most of the ways in which they can appeal for stakeholder support are subject to contention.

Those ways of seeking support (or claiming to be a good regulator) can be seen as five-fold. The regulator can claim to be delivering on the mandate, it can claim to be expert, it can suggest that it is properly accountable, it can assert that it is fair and open, and it can urge that it is efficient. The regulator's overall claim can be seen as the collective force of these five arguments (which are commonly used around the globe, albeit under potentially different labels). Weaknesses on any of these fronts will tend to undermine claims to be a good regulator—thus, if a regulator cannot persuade stakeholders that it is properly accountable or fair (in decisions or procedures) those stakeholders will withdraw support.

As said, though, all five claims tend to give rise to contention. Claims to be delivering on the mandate are contentious because, as noted, different readings of the mandate will be found with different stakeholders. Claims to be a trustworthy and 'expert' regulator tend to stumble because few stakeholders will be prepared, in the modern world, to trust blindly in the work of experts—they will want explanations and reasons for actions and decisions. They will expect regulators to be able to collect and process evidence in an expert manner—and will withdraw support if such expectations are not satisfied. They will not, though, tend to accept that even the most competent regulators can be left to make unexplained decisions. In short, they will want a good deal of accountability.

The difficulty a regulator has in persuading parties that it is properly accountable is that, again, different views are taken across the body of stakeholders. Each of these has to be convinced that the regulator is accountable to persons who represent their own interests. They have to be happy also that such representatives have the power to exert influence over the regulator so as to protect their interests. Similarly with regulators' arguments that they are fair in their actions and decisions and that their procedures are fair—on such matters there will be different conceptions and expectations across the stakeholder population.

As for the claim that a regulatory body performs well because it is efficient, the meaning of this claim turns on the notion of efficiency used. If a regulator asserts that its actions conduce to allocative efficiency, or the maximization of wealth or welfare in society, the objection likely to be made is that this behaviour is at odds with the regulator's mandate—which will often involve the pursuit of social rather than economic ends. If the regulator makes the more modest claim to be acting efficiently in the sense of non-wastefully (i.e. at lowest feasible cost) the difficulty is that stakeholders will see such efficiency as necessary but not sufficient as a basis for conferring approval. Thus, they will tend to withdraw support if a regulator is seen as wasteful but a lack of profligacy will not be seen as an adequate reason to give approval—there may be other flaws that make the regulator a poor performer.

Delivering Success through Positive Regulation

How then, does a positive regulator do the best job in discharging its core tasks and in demonstrating that it has performed well? An examination of the most successful regulators around the world suggests that success is associated with certain key qualities.[1] When the most positive regulators approach their key tasks (setting objectives, delivering outcomes, and meeting procedural expectations) they are *aware*, *intelligent*, and *dynamic*.

Being *aware* is being conscious of the challenges faced as a regulator. Thus positive regulators will know about (and often anticipate) the key problems and risks that have to be attended to. They will be conscious also of the variety of possible options for responding to these challenges—the strategic possibilities and mixes of approach that could be adopted. They will be aware of the various opportunities and constraints that flow from their regulatory positioning—that is the institutional, legal, governmental, and other settings in which they operate. Such awareness will not be seen in poor regulators who will be slow to identify challenges, will not review the range of potential response options, and will fail fully to appreciate what they can and cannot get done within their regulatory environment.

Being *intelligent* means that a regulator will establish a data collection and evidence processing system that provides it with all of the information it needs to discharge its key functions. Thus, the positive regulator will not merely be aware, when setting objectives, that different stakeholder groups will have different views on the mandate, it will have extensive information on what those different views are. It will, similarly, have information on the different stakeholder expectations regarding accountability and fairness in procedures. Intelligence thus provides the basis for not only delivering outcomes but for being able to meet expectations by explaining to stakeholders why certain actions have been taken. This is what provides the positive regulator with a basis for making the strongest feasible claims to support.

Being intelligent also involves performance sensitivity. The positive regulator will have information on those respects in which its strategies and interventions are achieving desired objectives and those respects in which there is a lack of success and adjustments will need to be made. Poor regulators will lack such sensitivity, they will merely adopt a strategy and hope that it works.

[1] See C. Coglianese, *Achieving Regulatory Excellence* (Washington DC: Brookings Institution, 2016).

Being *dynamic* is marked by abilities to deal with issues swiftly and administratively efficiently. It involves being able to adjust strategies or processes when a need to revise its current approach has been identified. The dynamic regulator will accept that the world is liable to change constantly; it will use its information systems to pick up such changes so that it can act on that information. Poor regulators will tend to assume that the world is fairly static and they will be caught out by changes.

Table 2.2 offers a framework for delivering positive regulation. Positive regulators tend to be aware, intelligent, and dynamic across all of the core regulatory tasks.

Table 2.2 Hallmarks of the excellent regulator

	Aware	Intelligent	Dynamic
Setting objectives			
Delivering outcomes			
Meeting procedural expectations			

In **setting objectives**, the positive regulator will be *aware*, as noted, that different stakeholders have different expectations and views about objectives/aims/mandates. That regulator will investigate whether some expectations and views are difficult to ascertain or are under-explored. It will be conscious of areas where there are important divergences of expectations and views and it will recognize the value of different approaches to the identification of objectives. It will take on board the different institutional constraints that impact on the framing of objectives, such as governmental expectations as well as budgetary, legal, and bureaucratic factors (such as agency structures). The positive regulator will be aware of its position within government, of respective institutional responsibilities and capacities and it will be conscious of the challenges and opportunities that stem from the division of institutional roles. It will be heedful of any needs to redraw boundaries of responsibility.

In setting objectives, the *intelligent* regulator will develop and apply information systems that gather data on different expectations and views on objectives/aims/mandates. It will, moreover, generate the information that allows it to explain and justify its conceptions of aims and objectives to the various stakeholders. It will promote performance sensitivity by gathering information on its success or failure in securing approval for its own conceptions of objectives/aims/mandates. It will be *dynamic* in dealing responsively with discovered changes in the various expectations and views about objectives/aims/mandates.

In **delivering outcomes**, being *aware* involves recognizing that different stakeholders have different expectations and views about appropriate outcomes. It also involves appreciating the nature of trade-offs between delivery on different outcomes. The aware regulator will take heed of the different potential methods of effective delivery and it will recognize and deal with resource and institutional constraints. It will realize that different kinds of firms will react differently to the same tools of regulatory intervention. Being *intelligent* involves the expert gathering and analysis of evidence so that decisions and policies are well-grounded. The intelligent regulator will have systems to identify key risks or problems and it will be able to coordinate agency actions around these. Such a regulator will have the level of information on regulated firms that allows it to match intervention strategies to types of firm. Positive regulation also demands the gathering of information on agency success in delivering appropriate outcomes in a cost-effective manner. Intelligence, in addition, provides the information that allows the agency to explain and justify its delivery of outcomes. Being *dynamic* is marked by an ability to act on its awareness of needs to change by adjusting processes and strategies accordingly. It will also involve the fostering of innovations and the delivery of different outcomes as these are prioritized in response to changes in expectations and the regulatory environment.

Finally, in **meeting procedural expectations**, the *aware* regulator will know that different stakeholders have different expectations and views about processes for making decisions and policies and for offering explanations. It will be conscious of the array of possible ways to explain and justify agency actions. It will take on board the different institutional/ legal constraints that impact on its abilities to explain and justify— including the challenges presented by shared responsibilities. The *intelligent* regulator will develop information on the nature of different expectations regarding the agency's need to explain and justify and the processes used to satisfy that need. It will gather information on its success or failure in explaining and justifying its actions, and it will develop the information that allows it to explain and justify its activities to the various stakeholders. Being *dynamic*, the positive regulator will deal responsively with discovered changes in the various expectations and views about agency processes for making decisions and policies and offering explanations/rendering account.

Running through all three of the core regulatory tasks is the need to carry these out at non-excessive cost. Positive regulators will set objectives, deliver outcomes, and meet procedural expectations without wasteful use of resources and their awareness, intelligence, and dynamism will foster this result. Thus, they will be aware of resourcing issues, and needs for cost-effectiveness, at all stages of the regulatory process, they will have relevant information on resources and will be able to deal rapidly with changes that have cost and resource implications.

Success and Win-Win Outcomes

Regulating for success, as noted, involves the use of positive regulation to maximize the excess of social and business benefits over costs. If, therefore, a regulatory strategy can further both social and business interests (a 'win-win' result) there is a very attractive route to success.

At first sight, however, it might not seem to require a regulator to accomplish a win-win outcome. The people involved should be able to work out how to ensure that result themselves. In cases, like the example described below of a utility company helping its customers to get the money together to pay their own utility bills, failure to take the necessary steps looks like a managerial deficiency or a behavioural error.[2]

Greater difficulties arise where, in order to persuade consumers to accomplish the win-win, the firm must contract with them. Thus, an energy network may realize that if it persuades some of its customers to reduce their electricity consumption at peak times, the company will save on costs, so that both it and the customers will benefit. Such action to deliver a mutually advantageous outcome should clearly go ahead, but in some circumstances this will not happen—as when the bargain is too complicated for the numerous parties to bring into action or when one side is too greedy. There are thus reasons to suppose that win-wins which have not already been exploited may face difficulties.

So when can 'win-win' outcomes be prompted by regulators? The message of the 'Porter Hypothesis'[3] is that 'properly crafted' environmental

---

[2] Behavioural science would put many such errors down to a series of identifiable heuristics. Corporations as well as consumers can make such mistakes—as can regulators, a matter discussed in Chapter 9.

[3] See M. Porter and C. van der Linde, 'Toward a New Conception of the Environment–Competitiveness Relationship', *Journal of Economic Perspectives* 9(4) (1995): 97–118; S. Ambec, M. A. Cohen, S. Elgie, and P. Lanoie, *The Porter Hypothesis at 20* (Washington, DC: Resources for the Future Discussion Paper No. 11-01, 2011).

regulation can commonly lead to two results: the spurring of innovations (the 'weak' version of the hypothesis); and to innovations that will often offset costs (partially or fully) and increase competitiveness (the 'strong' version of the hypothesis).

Case in point: Dyestuffs

In 1992 it was reported that Ciba-Geigy's dyestuff plant in New Jersey had re-examined its wastewater streams because of the need to meet new environmental standards.

It made two notable changes in its production process—replacing iron with a different chemical conversion agent that avoided the formation of solid iron sludge; and redesigning systems in a way that eliminated the release of potentially toxic products into the wastewater stream.

These changes not only boosted yield by 40 per cent but also eliminated wastes, resulting in annual cost savings of $740,000.[4]

There are a number of cited reasons why regulation can stimulate desirable innovations in processes and technologies. For a start, regulatory actions may 'signal' potential innovations or new efficiencies to firms—the regulators may point out, for example, the arrival of newly efficient waste-reduction technologies. Corporate awareness can thus be enhanced, corporate inertia can be combated, and regulators' interventions can counter the adverse incentives of some senior managers—such as inclinations to stay with current operating systems in order to reap the short-term gains that will serve their own financial and reputational interests. Regulators can stimulate investments in new technologies by reducing corporate fears that spending on cleaner technologies will render first-movers vulnerable to undercutting by competitors. (If a change has to be made by all operators in the sector this keeps the playing field level and removes the option of obtaining a market advantage by staying with the current, dirtier, technology/process.) Regulators may even counter the tendency of comfortable firms to stay with established operational systems by mandating that a move is made to new (say, cleaner) production processes.

[4] M. Dorfman, R. Warren Muir, and C. Miller, *Environmental Dividends: Cutting More Chemical Wastes* (New York: INFORM, 1992) cited by Porter and van der Linde, 'Toward a New Conception of the Environment–Competitiveness Relationship'.

Why may investing in such innovations lead to offsetting reductions of firm costs? In the first place, competitive advantages may result from the innovations that are introduced. The advice, information, or prompting of the regulator may drive new efficiencies in the firm, regulation may lead to lower compliance costs, and may create first mover advantages—as where those who are first to adopt new technologies prove to be best-placed to exploit evolving markets. Products and procedures may be improved, more creative (and profitable) uses of waste products may be driven forward, and waste-disposal costs lowered as firms respond to regulation.

Case in point: Helping customers out of debt

Customers of essential services such as energy or water sometimes fall into debt. In such cases there are strict regulatory rules on disconnection. Utility companies who provide services to indebted customers are encouraged by these rules to offer special help lines to assist such customers.

With such processes the companies can offer advice on financial management, and can seek to agree feasible repayment schedules. They can also provide advice on any further benefits to which members of the relevant household might be entitled.

These services serve regulatory objectives, benefit the utility companies, and help to free customers from the burden of debt.

Rewards for firms that are induced to innovate can also come from consumers, who may be attracted by virtuous behaviour—as where purchasers choose those products that are produced by cleaner technologies. The employment market may similarly reward virtue—as when the cream of potential recruits will be attracted to firms with the best environmental reputations.

At the industry-wide level, regulation can produce positive results by ensuring that the reputation of the sector, service, or product is protected (which will encourage consumers) and by coordinating technological step-changes where it would be difficult for numbers of competing operators to come together to make such a move. On the international stage, domestic producers can be shielded from the actions of international competitors which may undercut them on standards or undermine consumer confidence in the product.

Indirect social gains may also flow from regulatory actions. Thus, consumers' costs of locating virtue may be reduced by regulation—potential purchasers know that if goods are manufactured in a properly regulated manner there is no need to spend resources on searching out those that are made to the ethical or quality standards that they espouse. The social price for dealing with the by-products of industry may also be reduced where regulation lowers social clean-up costs.

The win-win argument should not, however, be overstated. The Porter Hypothesis does not contend that regulation *always* involves offsetting gains and it is predicated on the use of 'properly crafted' regulation. Here 'properly crafted' favours intervention instruments that are flexible enough to allow or encourage firms to innovate. Thus, trading mechanisms and taxes tend to be preferred to restrictive commands. If a firm pays a certain tax on each unit of pollution it puts into the river, it will arguably have a strong incentive to buy or develop an innovative filtration technology that will lower its tax bill. This contrasts with the position in which 'command' laws mandate the use of a stipulated technology.

Crafting regulation to maximize win-win outcomes would, according to Porter and van der Linde, involve: maximizing opportunities to innovate; using regulation to drive *continuous* improvement; and minimizing uncertainty while maximizing clarity and consistency. Regulators would coordinate with businesses in order to foster buy-in to innovation and they would both educate firms regarding innovative opportunities and assist them to transition to newer systems.

Whether 'win-win' is possible in a given situation is, however, difficult to predict because the occurrence of 'innovation offsets' is highly dependent on the specifics of operations and markets. In general terms, moreover, there are a number of potential hurdles to win-win.

In some sectors or markets it may be that there is a direct trade-off between imposing a more expensive production processes and gaining a socially desired objective. In other instances, the regulatory costs of trading or taxes will have the principal effect of chilling incoming investment, diverting funds from production and reducing innovation.

A central issue in any given context is whether regulation will drive innovation at all.[5] A key factor here is the availability of an innovative technology. Some sectors are 'innovation dynamic' but, in others, there

---

[5] See generally, N. Ashford, C. Ayers, and R. Stone, 'Using Regulation to Change the Market for Innovation', *Harvard Environmental Law Review* 9(2) (1985): 419–66.

may be no new process or technology that is discoverable or fiscally feasible.

Political and cultural constraints may also be an issue. Current technologies and practices may be embedded by political or cultural factors that the regulator is poorly positioned to overturn. It may also be the case that the major operators in the sector have a degree of influence that may approach or constitute capture of the regulator. In such circumstances, there will be pressure on the regulators to preserve the comfort of the incumbent operators and to act in order to control existing risks rather than to drive forward more radical innovations.

Knowledge is also a consideration. If a regulator is to drive innovation it will need to develop information on the technological innovations that are feasible and desirable in the sector. This is especially the case where the regulator selects the change that is to be made and stipulates the technologies that firms must use. It may want to do this, and sacrifice the use of flexible incentives, in order to counter the comfort of incumbents who are wedded to old systems, or to coordinate the sector's change to a new technology and avoid fragmentation, increase inter-operability and prevent the undercutting of those who first comply with the demand for change. The challenge here is that the regulator has to have the awareness and intelligence system, as well as the expertise and resources to identify the optimal course for the sector to take (and to do so without blocking future innovations). It will have to amass the evidence that makes the case for the stipulated innovation and may have to justify adopting a precautionary approach. Even if this is possible, some stakeholders and commentators may object that technological innovations are far better driven by properly incentivized firms and by markets than by government regulators.

If, on the other hand, the regulator is content to leave choices of innovative direction to incentivized firms (as in a pollution tax regime) the challenge is to set incentives at the appropriate level. An incentive regime, such as a pollution tax, offers a choice to a firm: to innovate in abatement approaches so as to pay less tax than currently; or to adhere to the known production and abatement processes and pay the tax. The regulator's overall aim will be to set the tax so that it induces firms to spend on abatement up to the point when the value to society becomes less than the business costs of further abatement.

This last point raises the notion of 'properly crafted' regulation and its limits. The difference between 'flexible', innovation-driving intervention tools and 'command and control' strategies is easy to overstate. The idea of a 'command' tends to be associated with the stipulation of a technology, process, or a mandated technical standard. A command, however, may incorporate a variety of standards and these may vary in flexibility and technology-forcing effects. *Technological or design* standards do tend to lock firms into a given technology since they stipulate the particular equipment or process to be used. A command, however, may incorporate a *performance or output* standard (e.g. a cap on the amount of pollution that can be emitted per day). This leaves the firm free to choose its technological route to the cap, although it does not incentivize the firm to 'go beyond compliance' and lower pollution below the cap. Where a command uses an *outcome* standard (e.g. do not kill fish in the river) this links the command more directly to the regulator's desired outcome (preservation of the fish stocks) but, again, there is no incentive to go beyond compliance.

A command can, however, incorporate a *principle* (as where it mandates firms to take all reasonable steps to develop and use the best technologies to avoid polluting). This is a 'command' but, given high-capacity regulated firms, it brings higher technology-changing potential than commands of other kinds.

In some circumstances, moreover, even the most restrictive forms of commands may provide the best ways to stimulate innovation—as in the discussed situation in which the industry is overly-attached to the old technology and the regulator has to mandate that an operational sea-change must be made and a new technology adopted.

As for the capacity of trading mechanisms and taxes to drive innovation, it is possible to exaggerate these. As noted above, firms have a choice, for example, to innovate or to pay the appropriate tax or the price of an emissions permit. It has been argued that this can sometimes dampen incentives. To take an emissions trading example: firms that currently use fairly advanced technologies but want to expand production can: (a) spend money on researching new clean-up technologies, or (b) buy more emissions permits from low-tech operators who have lower abatement costs than itself. The first course of action involves a host of uncertainties regarding the costs of research and the potential yields from this. The second route is far more certain—the costs are known. Such firms are thus likely to eschew innovation in favour of buying permits from less technologically advanced operators. This may lead to cost-effective abatement (by those using lower technology production methods) but it does not force cutting-edge technological change until the whole sector reaches the same stage of technical development.

It can also be argued that in some sectors, especially those marked by established incumbents who are wedded to old technologies, any substantial innovations will have to come through the introduction of new operators who will deploy new technologies and production processes. A worry may be that the costs associated with regulation will often make life difficult for start-ups and may hinder the entry of new operators into markets—a tendency that is aggravated because regulatory costs tend to impact more heavily on new entrants than on industry incumbents.

Nor can it be assumed that all firms will respond equally well to different kinds of regulatory stimuli. Low-capacity, poorly managed firms may not react quickly or positively to, say, the incentives imposed by regulators. (These, however, may be exactly the kinds of firm that are causing most of the problems for the regulators.) In such cases, the success of regulation may turn on the amount of resource that the regulator is able to apply in building such capacities and on the receptiveness of the firms to such measures. In the absence of such resources, or receptiveness, it may be a mistake to seek to stimulate innovations through incentive mechanisms—commands may be more effective.

As for high-capacity firms, the danger is that those of these who are self-serving will use their skills to capture the regulator or to play the system to their advantage. Porter and van der Linde argue that 'properly crafted' regulation will involve coordination with businesses in order to secure approval for innovations but there are risks here that powerful incumbents will use such coordination processes to turn regulation to their advantage by shoring up their established, comfortable, positions and by resisting the prospect of destabilizing innovations.

Other perverse effects may also arise. In favour of the Porter Hypothesis it can be argued that consumers' inclinations to reward virtuous firms will lead to innovation offsets. A risk may, however, be that consumers will seek out short-term gains (paying less for a product) rather than act to stimulate innovations (by purchasing products made with new, cleaner technologies). On the international stage a related danger is that of 'pollution havens'. Thus, regulators in one jurisdiction may incentivize firms to adopt newly high standards but those firms may outsource or move the relevant processes to other jurisdictions with known lower standards. Consumers may not always be inclined to punish firms who engage in such actions.

Nor is it a given that a drive to innovate will create optimal market conditions for firms. 'Properly crafted' regulation, it is suggested, should foster *continuous* improvement and innovation. The danger here is that pressures to innovate constantly may produce uncertainties for firms because the lifespan of a given technology is difficult to predict. Such ongoing uncertainty may make it more difficult to attract inward investment.

What are the implications of the 'win-win' hypothesis for regulatory design? As noted, it is difficult to predict those circumstances in which win-win outcomes can be secured[6] but positive innovations and innovation offsets are most likely to arise when the above-discussed challenges either do not arise or can be dealt with.

Win-win is thus more likely when there are innovations available at feasible cost; when a sector is innovation dynamic; where there are numbers of potential new market entrants; and where there is a lack of secure, powerful, and traditionalist incumbents. It is also more achievable where regulators are well-resourced, highly informed, and free from capture; where innovation uncertainties can be controlled; and where industry conditions allow for investments in innovative processes and technologies. As for regulated firms and their customers, win-win is more probable where the sector's firms are sufficiently high capacity (and well-intentioned) to be able and inclined to react positively to incentives; where consumers will search out and reward virtuous firms; and where consumer or social objectives do not put regulatory costs into the background (see Table 2.3).

Table 2.3 Win-win possibilities: nine questions

- Are innovative processes/technologies available?
- Are there potential new market entrants?
- Will there be resistance from secure and traditionalist incumbents?
- Are regulators well-resourced and informed and free from capture?
- Can innovation uncertainties be contained?
- Do industry conditions allow for investments in innovation?
- Are firms sufficiently high capacity (and well-intentioned) to react positively to innovation incentives?
- Will consumers reward virtue?
- Do consumer or social objectives put regulatory costs into the background?

---

[6] See e.g. S. Albrizio, E. Botta, T. Koźluk, and V. Zipperer, *Do Environmental Policies Matter for Productivity Growth? Insights from New Cross-Country Measures of Environmental Policies* (Paris: OECD Economics Department Working Papers No. 1176 (2014) (ECO/ WKP(2014)72))—finding no empirical evidence that environmental policy tightening has a long-term effect on productivity.

When thinking about regulatory strategies, win-win theory provides a useful prompt, that, other things being equal regulators should:

- Facilitate innovation with flexible instruments (when industry has the capacity and inclination to respond to these) and avoid using controls that lock in technologies.
- Reduce the uncertainties and transition costs involved in innovating.
- Foster innovation by building capacities as well as by incentivizing and mandating.

Conclusions

Regulating for success involves using positive regulation to secure the right outcomes by acceptable processes at lowest cost. It favours using the least intrusive, least expensive forms of regulation that will get the job done and this means that opportunities for win-win should be sought out and embraced when they are identified. Such opportunities, however, may be limited in many market settings and win-win, accordingly, provides no easy answer to many regulatory challenges.

Positive regulation is most likely to be achieved by regulators who are aware, intelligent, and dynamic in setting objectives, delivering outcomes, and meeting procedural expectations. The chances of regulatory success, however, will always be affected by the levels of resource available to the regulator and by the capacities and dispositions of the firms that are being controlled. The discussion next turns to regulatory strategies and their enforcement and a good deal of that discussion will emphasize how the aware, intelligent, and dynamic regulator will tailor its approaches with reference to these key factors.

3
Strategies for Success

Positive regulation involves using the appropriate intervention strategy, or mix of strategies, to deliver desired results (substantive and procedural) at lowest cost. If, say, there is a pollution issue, choices have to be made between responses such as commanding polluters to desist, taxing polluters, and naming and shaming them. Or between asking firms to self-regulate, setting up emissions trading regimes, and providing state assistance for clean-up technologies. Governments can even rely on private parties to control firms by creating rights to clean air or water that are enforceable in the civil courts.

The Supposed Evils of Command and Control Approaches

The command and control method is typically a law that demands that firms avoid certain behaviour (e.g. polluting above a certain level), or instructs them to do certain things (e.g. to use a certain clean-up technology). The command is backed up with the threat of a sanction, such as a fine, for non-compliance. Often that sanction will be applied by regulatory inspectors and prosecutors through the criminal justice process.

In recent decades politicians and commentators around the word have urged that a move has to be made away from such 'command' strategies and towards 'less-restrictive' or 'incentive-based' or 'light-touch' or 'business-friendly' methods of control.

But what is so bad about the 'command' method? Criticisms centre on a number of allegations. The first of these is that commands rely on detailed prescriptions that are unduly restrictive of businesses and stand in the way of those who would develop innovative ways of dealing with problems. This claim is easily overplayed. As noted in the last chapter, commands can be linked with restrictive 'design' or 'technology' standards but they can also be used to enforce highly flexible principles that are far more amenable to managerial freedom and innovation.

Case in point: Imaginative thinking

In 2003 the UK Government's Better Regulation Task Force (BRTF) recommended that each UK Government Department should have an Executive Board member with a specific objective to promote better regulation and the consideration of alternatives to classic 'command' based regulation within their Department.

The alternatives discussed were: incentives, no regulation, information and education, and self-regulation and co-regulation.[1]

Command and control methods supposedly render the regulator vulnerable to capture (whereby regulation serves the interests of the regulated firms rather than those of the public or consumers). The accusation is that the processes of writing and enforcing rules bring the regulators too close to the firms that they regulate. Regulators often rely on firms for the information needed to set standards and this renders them open to capture. When, moreover, matters such as 'compliance' with the rules are negotiated, the regulators and firms arrive at shared visions of reasonable behaviour. As this process continues, the argument runs, the regulators see 'compliance' through the same eyes as the firms and the interests of the wider public or consumers are left in the background. Various 'capture theories' suggest that regulators who rely on enforced commands tend to become increasingly vulnerable to accusations that they are imposing unreasonable costs and legal demands on firms—and that this vulnerability produces capture as regulators become more intimidated. This process is exacerbated whenever regulatory rules multiply and there are business protests about red tape and form-filling.

Setting the standards for use in command regimes is said to be a resource intensive activity that results in ponderous and costly control systems, and the kinds of standards incorporated within commands are another source of criticism. 'Design' or 'technology' standards, as noted, are said to be too inflexible and innovation-unfriendly as well as being intrusive in managerial decisions. Performance standards (e.g. caps on the permissible amounts of pollution) are criticized as overly blunt instruments. Thus, if employers are permitted to expose workers to no more

---

[1] BRTF, *Imaginative Thinking for Better Regulation* (London: Cabinet Office, 2003).

than 80 particles of a substance per cubic metre (pcm) of air, there are two main difficulties. Firms that can filter out particles very cheaply (low-cost abaters) could easily go 'beyond compliance' and reduce particles to 20 pcm but if the official standard is 80 pcm they may not choose to do so. A second problem is that, as shown below, this approach may fail to identify the most efficient combination of reducing emissions and keeping down service prices to consumers.

Commands, of course, usually have to be enforced through the criminal justice process and this prompts the criticism that this is expensive—and all the more unproductive when, as is common, the fines meted out to errant firms tend to be insufficient to create broader or even firm-specific deterrent effects (a matter returned to in Chapter 4). Such enforcement is also said to foster antagonistic relationships between regulators and firms so that, instead of working together to produce low-cost but effective controls, there are costly and often legalistic contests that serve neither public nor private interests.

A final worry about command regulation is that, if certain issues have to be dealt with by transnational networks of regulators (as is common in, for example, the environmental sector) command styles of regulation can be ill-suited. This is because it may be hard to design technical standards that will be acceptable to all the participants in the network and it may be difficult in the transnational context to establish a secure authority for issuing and enforcing binding commands. Other more diverse mixes of strategy, influence, and responsibility may have to be adopted in such contexts.[2]

Overall, then, command regulation is faced with a lengthy charge sheet. In looking at the main alternatives to commands, however, it is worth flagging that many of the criticisms of the 'command' style are easily overstated and that numbers of 'alternative strategies' either rely on commands to a degree or encounter challenges that echo or differ from those found with commands. It is, accordingly, understandable and right that other options are considered, and comparative advantages of 'commands' and 'alternatives' are likely to vary from case to case.

Incentives

Regulators or governments can use positive or negative incentives to influence behaviour. Thus, they can give tax breaks for expenditures on filtration systems or they can tax polluters for each litre of effluent they discharge.

---

[2] See V. Heyvaert, *Transnational Environmental Regulation and Governance* (Cambridge University Press, 2019), chapter 4. On transnational issues see Chapter 10 in this volume.

Taxation brings a number of supposedly attractive features. Taxes can operate in a low-discretion, low-intervention manner. Thus, when, say, tobacco is taxed, the consumer's price sensitivity limits consumption without any on-site enforcement action in the tobacconist's shop—purchasers simply react to the price signal and taxes are collected upstream in the supply chain. This limits the intensity of interactions between the regulators and the targets of control and reduces the dangers of capture.

It may seem sensible and straightforward to use the command and control method to set a quantitative limit on the amount of carbon, say, which can be emitted per unit of output of an industrial process. But that might automatically rule out of contention firms which are costly abaters, but which also incur low non-carbon costs of production—whose continued presence in the market might benefit customers.

A tax per unit of carbon set at the optimal level, where the marginal cost of abating emissions equals the marginal benefit of doing so, would ensure that each firm pays the full social cost of its production, but it would allow each firm some flexibility in choosing how much abatement to purchase. A firm whose cost of emission was high would be handicapped, but not automatically thrown out of the market, as would be the case with a simple quantitative limit. For any given level of carbon emissions, this more sophisticated form of control could reduce overall non-carbon production costs, which should benefit customers.

With a tax system a prediction has to be made at the outset of the cumulative level of abatement that the tax will generate. This may be an important issue if there are certain thresholds that should not be crossed—such as levels of total pollution that will kill river life. Where many firms are involved, such forecasting may be quite difficult. If, however, a potential catastrophe is involved (e.g. the wiping out of a rare salmon strain) the need to avoid this outcome stands in the way of a trial and error strategy and the taxation method may be ill-advised. A way round this problem which preserves the greater efficiency of taxes over command and control is to auction tradable emission permits.[3]

There are further caveats about the use of taxes. Tax laws do not escape the need for rules and enforcement and it is easy to exaggerate the difference between a firm being fined £1000 for polluting and its paying a £1000 tax bill for polluting. (Those who cheat on their pollution tax returns still have to be prosecuted and field enforcers still have to assess compliance.) Tax laws are

---

[3] This method is discussed later in this chapter, and considered further in Chapter 6 in relation to climate change.

not known for their simplicity and where officials and firms have repeated conversations about liabilities, these interactions may come to resemble those that, in association with commands, are alleged to lead to capture.

Incentive regimes, moreover, depend on there being a rational response to an incentive. The trouble is that the 'regulatory paradox' applies—the parties that the regulator most needs to influence (the mischief creators) tend to be the parties *least likely* to be influenced. With taxes, it is likely to be the badly managed, low capacity companies (routinely the major polluters) who will least respond to either positive or negative incentives.

Finally, it should be noted that taxation approaches may bring presentational difficulties—as when the green pressure group asks: 'Does this mean that a firm can pollute as much as it wants provided that it just pays the tax?' ('Yes, but the tax is set at a level which is optimal, given the damage which the particular emission causes.') In contrast, a strength of the 'command' approach is that it clearly designates some conduct as unacceptable. It should not be forgotten, though, that a tax does generate revenue which can be recycled for other public purposes.

Disclosures

Governments and regulators possess a good deal of information and they can influence the behaviour of corporations by disclosing firms' actions or by using more pronounced naming and shaming strategies. Thus they can reveal firms' compliance records or publish league tables of, say, the best or worst polluters. Such processes allow the consumers of products (or even voters more generally) to decide on the acceptability of firm behaviour. This is a control strategy that is low-cost and low-intervention. It does not regulate the production process, the prices charged for goods, or the standard of product.

The potential weakness of disclosure regulation is that it relies on consumers or members of the public to use their purchasing or political power to discipline firms. This brings a number of difficulties. Consumers, for instance, may buy the cheapest products and ignore the costs to society of producing the item at issue. They may also lack the expertise or time to process and use the information disclosed. Behavioural science warns us that purchasers' responses (and their risk calculations) may be flawed especially if they are drawn to the attractiveness of products, or giving in to temptation. Similarly, they may behave in a lazy and unthinking manner or may be excessively influenced by advertising or marketing strategies, or the behaviour of others.

Case in point: Naming and shaming the polluters

In March 1999 Britain's worst corporate polluters were named for the first time in a 'hall of shame' league table compiled by the UK Environment Agency.

The table was based on the previous year's prosecution figures and included household names such as ICI, Shell, BNFL, five water companies, and a number of sewage, energy, construction, and chemical firms. By far the heaviest fines were imposed on ICI Chemicals for polluting ground-water and releasing chemicals that killed birds, fish, and vegetation on marshland.

The worst five water companies were prosecuted twenty-three times, with Welsh Water heading the list. Three of the worst offenders were waste disposal companies whose remit was to clear up pollution.

The costs of processing the information, moreover, may be excessive. Thus, if food safety was controlled by information disclosures instead of command regulation, a visit to the supermarket would involve a very lengthy process of scrutinizing labels. It might, in many circumstances, be far more efficient for consumers to rely on the expertise and protection of public regulators and inspectorates, rather than depend on their own individual assessments of risks.

In relation to some activities or products the risks may be so great that it is inappropriate merely to inform consumers or others about these, and command methods may be called for. Finally, there is the issue of accuracy of information. Especially with significant risks it will be necessary to control the quality of the information disclosed. This increases the costs of disclosure-based regulation and the procedures used to control information quality will often resemble those used to enforce commands—namely systems of inspection and prosecution for non-compliance.

Disclosure strategies thus bring a number of challenges, they may be combined productively with other controls but tend to be most useful where risks and potential harms are low, where the information is easily processed and used by lay persons, and where the accuracy of disclosures can be assured at low cost. The users of disclosures must also be willing and capable of acting on disclosures. In the energy sector, for instance, disclosures on relative prices will have only limited value if end users find it difficult to compare pricing frameworks or if they find it burdensome to change suppliers.

Direct Action and Design Strategies

Governments can use their resources to achieve desired results by taking direct action. Rather than using commands and enforcing standards on, say, dust extraction levels in factories, public bodies can build properly ventilated premises and lease these to private manufacturers. Public funds can thus be used to achieve desired results where firms, particularly small ones, might not invest in the required measures.

A degree of subsidization may, by such means, be effected and public resources can be used to assist firms to reduce harms rather than to fund command regimes or to apply penalties that take money away from the enterprises that are asked to spend on avoiding undesired consequences.

Such subsidization, however, may give rise to questions about the fairness of, say, access to subsidized premises, and subsidies may produce undesirable distortions of competition. Where, moreover, there is public funding of an element of a production process, this may encourage firms to build operations around the funded element. This stands in the way of market-based pressures to innovate. Thus if the well-ventilated manufacturing premises are publicly owned and there are no other controls on dust levels in the air, there is little incentive for the private sector to devise new, more efficient ways to control dust.

A final concern about direct action approaches is that it cannot be assumed that where the state provides a solution, this will remove the targeted mischief unproblematically. The reality may be that the state may fall down on its ongoing obligations just as badly as the private sector. It cannot be assumed, for instance, that, in the above example, the state's dust extraction systems will be perfectly maintained and effective over time. Public bodies' failures to renew filters and maintain machinery may be as pronounced as those of private firms.

Another way in which the state can use its resources to eliminate problems is through the use of design solutions. Thus, rather than regulate the mischief, the state can 'design out' problems in a variety of ways. These include constructing the physical environment in a certain manner—as where parking is controlled by concrete bollards or road speed is governed by chicanes or bumps.

The labels of 'techno-regulation', 'architecture-based', and 'code' approaches are attached to such design strategies and some commentators make a case for dealing with some of the most daunting regulatory challenges in this way. Thus Lawrence Lessig suggests that the most feasible way to regulate cyberspace is through control of the software code that shapes the structure of cyberspace and dictates access to and participation in that space.[4]

Allocating Rights

Command regimes routinely use criminal justice processes to impose sanctions on non-compliers. Governments, however, can also allocate civil law rights and these can be used to control behaviour. Rather than threaten the potential polluter with a criminal fine, the state can give out rights to clean water that can be enforced in the civil courts. Deterrence is provided where the potential polluters anticipate that they will have to pay out damages for infringing such rights.

Case in point: Grantham Angling Association

In 2016 Grantham Angling Association secured a £36,000 settlement from a farmer responsible for polluting the River Witham near Grantham with approximately 6000 litres of liquid fertilizer.

The fertilizer spill was estimated to have killed over 2000 wild brown trout—some up to 24 inches in length and up to 4 lb in weight—and countless fish of other species in the Witham.

The effect of allocating civil law rights is to privatize the enforcement process—the party with a right to clean water has to bring a civil action against the polluter. This reduces costs to the state but such private enforcement tends to under-deter potential polluters for a number of reasons that are seen in the following example. Let us suppose that, if filters are not fitted, a potential polluter will do £10,000 worth of damage to river users (in fish deaths, corrosion of boat hulls, etc.). The efficient level of

---

[4] See L. Lessig, *Code and Other Laws of Cyberspace* (Basic Books, 1999); A. Murray, *The Regulation of Cyberspace: Control in the Online Environment* (Routledge-Cavendish, 2006).

deterrence would be established where the polluter anticipates having to pay out £10,000 in damages. This gives an incentive to spend up to £10,000 on filters. Under-deterrence occurs because, say, it will cost the river users (anglers, sailing clubs, etc.) £2000 in legal fees and time off work to secure the £10,000. They would accordingly settle for £8000. When their lawyers tell them that there are issues of evidence and proof and that they have a 50 per cent chance of winning a lawsuit, their prospects further diminish. (They would settle for £4000 now.) At this point half of the rights-holders give up the pursuit of damages and bear the loss. The remainder will now settle for £2000. Assuming that the potential polluter knows the above there is huge under-deterrence.

Could a judge act to ensure efficient levels of incentive to abate by awarding punitive damages to the resolute pursuers who win their legal claims? The problem, in practice, is liable to be that a judge has difficulty calculating the right punitive element of the damages award—because different victims of the pollution are liable to come at different times to make their claims, and because arrivals of future claims, and their sizes, are difficult to predict.

A further problem in some cases may be that of 'shallow pockets'. Some companies or people (e.g. car drivers) may have a capacity to do harm that exceeds their wealth. They, accordingly, cannot be threatened with a level of damages (or, indeed, a fine) that matches the harm and which creates the desirable level of incentive to take care. Liability rules, in such cases, have to be reinforced with commands that require compulsory insurance.

Tradable Permits

The best-known systems of permit trading are used to control emissions of pollutants. Thus, since 1991 the US Environmental Protection Agency (EPA) has sought to control sulphur dioxide emissions by allocating tradable emission permits to coal-burning electric power plants, and the EU launched its Emissions Trading System (ETS) in January 2005. By 2007, the Stern Review had advocated the broad use of trading mechanisms to combat climate change.[5]

In typical regimes, the public agency issues a given number of permits and each of these allows a polluting discharge of a fixed amount. Following

---

[5] N. Stern, *The Economics of Climate Change: The Stern Review* (Cambridge University Press, 2006).

the initial allocation, permits may be traded and this allows, say, a generating company to switch to cleaner fuels and sell its excess allowances to other firms. In a 'cap and trade' system, the regulator sets a cap on the total allowable level of permitted discharges and it distributes permits up to this level—which it may do by allocation or auction. In a baseline and credit regime, companies are given performance targets or 'baselines' (often set with reference to business as usual projections) and they can generate credits by beating their emissions targets. Such credits may then be traded on the open market. With cap and trade, there is a fixed supply of permits for trading, whereas in baseline and credit the supply of credits for trading depends on the performance of permit holders in generating credits by reducing emissions below baselines.

The main advantages claimed for permit trading are, first, that the incentive to reduce harmful behaviour can, as in taxation regimes, operate down to zero, since the process of abatement will release permits for resale until the point where no harm is being done at all. As with taxation, managers are free to decide both how to abate and the right balance between abatement and paying for permits. A second advantage of trading is that those with the lowest costs of avoiding pollution tend to sell permits to the higher cost abaters to whom the permits are worth more. This is efficiency-enhancing as abatement tends to be carried out by those parties who can do so at lowest cost. Third, it is far easier to predict the outcome of the regime than it is with, say, a taxation system—in a river pollution example the regulator knows, for instance, that (provided there is no cheating on permits) the river will suffer from a pollution level that is capped and which is consistent with fish life. It can also be said that, with a trading system, the regulatory playing field is kept level as there is a common, market-driven price for emitting a unit of pollution. This places competitors on an equal footing.

A further point is that regulatory discretions (and dangers of capture) are low because markets rather than bureaucrats are imposing restraints, and a further attractive feature is that trading mechanisms can solve difficult political problems. Thus, it has been seen with the European ETS that its introduction can be welcomed by both the green lobby (because it compels powerful polluters to pay for their sins) and the powerful industrial concerns (because it allows them to carry on producing and often entrenches their positions). Finally, regulatory costs are low since, once established, the market in permits runs of its own accord.

The problems to be anticipated with permit trading are, however, numerous. The kinds of enforcement actions that would be associated with command systems still have to be carried out to prevent non-permit holders from creating harms and to stop permit holders from exceeding the terms of their permits. Inspectorates and prosecution processes, accordingly, require funding.

Permits, moreover, do not provide the resources needed to compensate the victims of harmful conduct and, politically, permits may create difficulties with electorates, since they may be seen as 'licences to pollute'. The system, in addition, demands that there be a healthy market in permits—which calls for such factors as a large number of potential buyers possessed of adequate information. If the market is deficient (perhaps because of uncertainties or lack of information), the value of permits may be low and the incentives to desist from harmful conduct may be weak.

A further issue is that markets in permits may allow hoarding and the creation of barriers to enter into certain markets. This will be more likely where conditions favour collusion between powerful firms. The effects may be generally anti-competitive and may be unfair to less well-resourced firms. In markets that rely on new entrants to drive innovations, an effect of trading may be to entrench the positions of the established players and thereby to stifle what may be desirable changes.

There is another argument why trading mechanisms may impede innovation. As noted in Chapter 2, firms have a choice: to engage in innovation through research or to buy permits from low-cost abaters. If the former involves higher levels of uncertainty than the latter, firms will tend to postpone innovating until they have exhausted opportunities to buy relatively cheap permits.

A further issue concerns the results of trading. Nothing in a trading mechanism reduces the level of pollution—it is lowering the cap that does that. Trading simply ensures that the cap is arrived at by the lowest-cost route. As for the driving of efforts to abate, a first worry is that uncertainties will chill these. This may happen especially in baseline and credit regimes. Experience with the EU ETS has shown how, in a baseline and credit system, excessively generous initial allocations of allowances can produce volatilities in the price of emissions. Parties considering investing in research and development into abatement technologies may be discouraged by such volatility and the uncertainties of any potential returns on their investment. The associated worry is that where initial allowances are excessive, this drives down the prices of permits and undermines incentives to abate so as to avoid permit costs. It has, for instance, been argued that the price for emitting a tonne of carbon in the EU ETS has never approached the level that would induce desirable levels of abatement.

Fairness is also a serious issue. A problem with market-based systems of distribution is that they incorporate an inherent bias in favour of those parties who possess wealth and they tend to remove power from those who lack resources. The results of trading may be claimed to be cost-effective but this does not ensure fairness.

A special difficulty with trading systems is that, if they are to overcome the political hurdles of inception, they tend to have to 'grandfather' existing operators into the system. If, however, permits to pollute are allocated on the basis of historical or current emission levels, polluters will not 'pay'. They will be rewarded for their records of pollution and will be well positioned so as to be able to maximize their rewards by exploiting their informational advantages and abilities to manipulate data to their advantage. Nor do fairness issues disappear if permits are allocated by auctioning rather than by free allocation. Auctioning favours those incumbents who have the existing resources to make successful bids. The principled objection here is that it is unfair that incumbent polluters—who have accumulated wealth at the cost of the environment—should be better positioned in such auctions than non-polluters or new entrants to the field.

At the international level, a key issue is the development effect of trading systems. Internationally, emissions trading solutions have been accused of bringing a double injustice. The effects of existing emissions are felt disproportionately by the less developed nations and they restrict development over coming years.

The charge, then, is that historically based allocations allow currently high emitters to impose environmental damage on other countries and to lock the less developed nations into lower levels of development. The linked concern is that in the early years of trading, the mechanism allows existing industrialized users to meet their targets at lowest cost and to avoid making reductions in home emissions. When, however, developing countries become faced with emissions targets themselves, the cheapest forms of emissions abatement will have been exhausted and only more expensive high-tech forms will be left—at which time industrialized countries will be unwilling to invest abroad. In short, industrialized countries will have gained preferential use of lowest cost abatement methods and reaped a competitive advantage while suppressing development. Supporters of emissions trading might argue that such considerations can be taken into account when allocations are negotiated; but this response makes assumptions about the bargaining power and positions of developing countries (or the altruism of developed countries) that may be unrealistic—a matter to be returned to below.

A central concern regarding global fairness is that developing countries cannot reasonably be expected to restrict their future emissions without being assured of a fair allocation scheme that will not impair their ability to develop. This demands, it can be said, not historically based or auction based distributions but allocations based on equal rights to the atmospheric commons for every individual.

A further argument, however, suggests that, from a development point of view, it is not enough to allocate emissions rights on a per capita equal rights basis. The effect of this would be to allow existing wealthy polluters to purchase, from poor permit holders, sufficient allocations to allow them to continue to trade at profit maximizing levels. There would be a one-off transfer of wealth to poorer firms but these less wealthy players would be paying a price for that transfer—in the form of forfeited opportunities—an effect that informational asymmetries would be likely to exaggerate.

To take an example, let us suppose that it is decided internationally to cap pollution from air travel and to do so by establishing a trading scheme in which all companies are allocated x hours of flights per year (size of allocations to reflect numbers of employees). Wealthy Company A, from a developed country, engages in a great deal of air travel as it trades in global markets. It would, accordingly, purchase the emissions allowances of less technologically advanced companies B, C, and D who are based, and trade, in certain less developed countries. Would the price paid reflect the true wealth generating potential of those allowances? It is unlikely to do so because Company A has both greater capacity to develop that potential and superior information about that potential.

Companies B, C, and D, moreover, are likely to suffer from non-informational factors that will further undermine their abilities to strike satisfactory deals with Company A. Notably they are likely, if sited in less developed countries, to be competing, as sellers of allowances, with firms that are less well-informed, less rational, and more desperate to sell. The overall effect of allowances trading on Companies B, C, and D is that they receive a one-off payment (a sub-optimal one) and, being excluded from air travel (at least until they use their resources to buy allowances) they will have restricted development potential and are likely to be left ever further behind in the marketplace by Company A.

According to Stern, one of the major advantages of emissions trading systems is that they allow efficiency and equity to be considered separately.[6] The hope may be that developed countries will show leadership in tackling

---

[6] Stern, *The Economics of Climate Change*.

emissions, transferring technology, supporting capacity building, and financing the incremental costs of emissions reductions. The difficulty is that emissions trading and re-allocative policies pull in opposing directions and such a tension may be so severe as to lead cost-effectiveness concerns to swamp those of equity—which negates Stern's argument that emissions trading conveniently allows equity and efficiency issues to be considered separately. Thus, it has been argued that: 'Emissions trading may conflict with the post-Rio developed country leadership principle in several ways. Most obviously, it allows developed countries to claim that they are meeting their reductions obligations through trading and to "double count" trades as both domestic reductions and assistance to developing countries.'[7]

Emissions trading exaggerates the effects of inequalities in wealth distribution and offers up wealth creating opportunities to the currently wealthy (and often polluting). Re-allocative policies, when linked to emissions trading, may look transparent and worthwhile, but three points are worth stressing. First, any re-allocative virtues will be due to distributional decisions and restrictions that are placed on the trading mechanism—not to the trading mechanism itself. Second, any protections for the less well off, less powerful, less developed, and less well-informed will be operating within a system that is intrinsically skewed in favour of wealth holders. Finally, it can be argued that, as far as fairness is concerned, there are grounds for doubting whether emissions trading systems match up to the performance of command or taxation regimes.

On the question of enforcement, a concern is that under some conditions emissions trading systems may render enforcement particularly difficult. Within an international greenhouse gas trading regime, for instance, an enterprise within a developed country will look to buy allocations as cheaply as possible. The very lowest prices are likely to be those offered by those firms in developing countries whose governments are poorest at monitoring and enforcing. (This will be the case because the selling firms will anticipate that, thanks to poor enforcement, they can sell their allowances but still carry on emitting at the usual levels.) The invisible power of the market may thus place hopes for abatement in those locations where delivery on those hopes is most unreliable.

As for the areas where markets in permits can be used, some harms or pollutants may have to be prohibited absolutely and, accordingly, the tradable permit system will be inappropriate. Finally, it should be cautioned that

[7] E. Richman, 'Emissions Trading and the Development Critique: Exposing the Threat to Developing Countries', *Journal of International Law and Politics* 36 (2003): 133–76.

democratic accountability and influence may be low once the system is up and running, since the market (and its degree of genuine competitiveness) will govern the price to be placed on pollution. Where markets are imperfect, it is also likely that information flowing into the public domain is below optimal levels.

Overall, it can be said that, in divergent contexts, trading regimes display very different potential—both in absolute terms and in comparison with other regulatory instruments. Thus, with relatively small numbers of well-resourced emitters and continuous emissions monitoring devices—as in the US Acid Rain Program—the problems faced are not of the same scale as those encountered in a decentralized and international greenhouse gas system with large numbers of differently resourced emitters and daunting challenges regarding monitoring and enforcement. It is often difficult, moreover, to pinpoint the extent to which observed difficulties are inherent in the trading device or can be explained as teething troubles (as with the EU ETS) or as implementation failures (that might or might not afflict other regulatory instruments). Some problems (e.g. of accountability and transparency) may, furthermore, be pointed out in trading regimes but may be readily addressable through supplementary controls. That said, it is to be expected that the difficulties associated with emissions trading regimes will tend to be the greater when they involve such factors as: high numbers of regulated organizations or regulators; decentralized regimes; cross-jurisdictional applications; and high variations in resources and competencies across regulated enterprises or regulators. Further such factors include: complexities in the allowances traded; inequalities of wealth or pollution records that raise contentious redistributive questions; serious enforcement and monitoring issues; stringent emissions targets; and high levels of incumbency power.

Nudging

A regulatory strategy that purports to offer a user-friendly and a low intervention alternative to traditional controls is 'nudging'. This approach is highly influential in many government circles following the publication of Thaler and Sunstein's 2008 book *Nudge*.[8] Nudging involves presenting citizens and others with decisions in a manner that encourages them to act in ways that are beneficial. Thus, placing fruit rather than confectionery

---

[8] R. Thaler and C. Sunstein, *Nudge: Improving Decisions about Health, Wealth, and Happiness* (Harvard University Press, 2008).

next to the supermarket till will induce healthier eating without any need to ban confectionery. Common nudge tools might include: default arrangements (presumed consent and opt-out cards for organ donation); design approaches (placing raised lines on roads at decreasing intervals before roundabouts); and public information health warnings or campaigns (see Table 3.1).

Table 3.1 Common nudge tools

Tool	Example
Defaults	• Systems of presumed consent for organ donation plus opt-out card.
Physical designs	• Placing the stairs, not the lifts, next to the office doors.
Information/warnings	• Reminders to fill in tax forms.
Campaigns/social norms	• Requests that include reports of widespread compliance by others.
Shocks	• Horrifying photographs of smoking-related symptoms.
Low transaction costs	• One-click systems for donation.

Studies in the fields of decision-making and behavioural science suggest that people tend to make poor choices for a number of reasons.[9] They process information in shorthand ways, they are biased by immediate concerns, they succumb to temptations and inertia and so on (Table 3.2). Nudges often exploit such behavioural limitations in order to steer choices.

Table 3.2 Common behavioural limitations

Inertia	• We are lazy and do not always make the effort to do what will realize our settled intentions.
Social norms	• We are influenced by other people's opinions and attitudes.
Affect/dread	• Emotional reactions bias our thinking and actions.
Immediacy	• The immediacy of events influences our attitudes to these.
Availability/anchoring	• Our calculations are biased by the information that is available to us and we reason and estimate with reference to what is most familiar.
Temptation	• We give in to temptation against our better judgement.
Thinking fast	• We think in shorthand ways due to cognitive limitations and we act on simplified analyses of the world.

[9] As we discuss in Chapter 9, 'people' in this case includes regulators, who are also prone to cognitive failures

Nudging uses 'choice architectures' to encourage sensible decision-making but nudging purports to leave the target person or firm free to choose to take the non-sensible course of action ('The opt-out should always be easy'). In its ideal form, therefore, the approach, dubbed 'libertarian paternalism', cleverly combines an element of paternalism with the preserving of freedom of choice.

It is arguable, however, that there are three different kinds, or degrees, of nudge and that some are more worrying than others. 'First Degree nudges' respect the decision-making autonomy of the individual and enhance reflective decision-making. Typical First Degree nudges involve the supply of simple information to individuals or the sending of reminders ('There are three weeks left to complete your tax return'). Such nudges differ from two other, more intrusive, kinds of intervention.

A 'Second Degree nudge' typically builds on behavioural limitations so as to bias a decision in the desired direction. Thus, a default rule with an opt-out can be used to shape decisions—as where there is presumed consent to organ donation, or the physical environment can be designed to apply influence (as where the office smoking zone is placed at a distance from the work area). Both of these examples nudge individuals' decisions by relying on human inertia: the smoker's laziness will mean that he or she will not make the walk to the smoking zone each time they have a craving. The Second Degree nudge involves a greater impact on individual autonomy than the First Degree nudge since the targeted individual's behavioural or volitional limitations and 'automatic' responses will in practice lead him or her to accept the nudge with limited awareness, resistance, and reflection. The target of the nudge could, on reflection unearth the nudge—but is unlikely to do so because of cognitive or volitional limitations.

A 'Third Degree nudge' offers an intrusion on autonomy that is a degree more pronounced because it involves behavioural manipulation to an extent that other nudges do not. Framing devices can be used to shift the preferences of an individual in a manner that is difficult to resist. A Third Degree nudge will often rely on affect or dread to produce its result. Typically, there is use of the behavioural scientists' finding that people are influenced by novel, personally relevant, or vivid examples of, say, a harm. In such instances the message receiver will be motivated emotionally in a manner that stands in the way of reflection. Thus, the cigarette pack would show a graphic display of a cancerous growth. The element of 'manipulation' stems from the use of a level of emotional power that makes it difficult to go back to the status quo. The target is influenced but resisting the nudge is blocked—often because preferences have been permanently shifted. The difference between a Second and a Third Degree nudge is that, with the former, the message receiver has the potential to uncover the nudge, and assess its extent, by the exercise of reflection, whereas in the latter, it is a step more difficult to neutralize the nudge.

Will nudges be effective? As with other control mechanisms, nudges can be expected to work with degrees of success that vary according to the nature of targets. Thus, confirmed and determined smokers may not react as significantly to health warnings on packets as persons who aspire to healthier lifestyles.

On many matters there is evidence of success—positioning raised lines at diminishing intervals on roads does reduce speeds in the approaches to roundabouts. Some issues—such as the problem of obesity in Western societies—may, however, be due to more structural causes than individuals' decisions to grab candy bars when at supermarket tills. Many decisions, moreover, may be taken by groups, boards, and committees and may be difficult to influence with individual nudges. As for corporations, it has been suggested that they can be nudged to 'do the right thing' by harnessing their concerns for reputation and brand by, for example, publishing their compliance records (a broad interpretation of 'nudge'). For such a strategy to work, however, the corporation has either to value high standards in their own right, or anticipate that consumers will punish it for poor compliance rather than care mainly about product price, or be led by corporate advertising and promotion. A problem here may be the regulatory paradox: the firms that care least about reputations, and are least responsive to consumer opinions are likely to be the firms who are causing most of the problems.

As for the use of other nudges on corporations, different levels of success might be anticipated—as indicated in Table 3.3.

Even if nudges achieve results, there are other potential concerns. In the medical literature it has been argued that if patients suspect that doctors are manipulating them by exploiting their cognitive or volitional limitations, this is likely to undermine the trust relationship that is essential to treatment.

The notion of 'libertarian paternalism' may also be subject to question. The liberality of nudging turns on the statement that the 'opt-out has to be easy'. It is difficult, however, to claim both that Second and Third Degree nudges really work and that opting out is easy. The reason why the raised lines leading to the roundabout are effective is that humans do have cognitive limitations that mean that *in practice* opting out is not really an option. With a preference-shifting Third Degree nudge it may be almost impossible to revert to the position held before application of the nudge. A danger with nudge is that the centrally important issue of opt-out can be seen by proponents as a small and relatively uncontentious matter. This approach, the objectors would say, sows the seeds of an illiberal system of control.

Table 3.3 Nudge tools and corporations

Tool	Likely effect on corporations
Defaults	• Some effect on less organized firms who fail to act to avoid the default.
Physical designs	• Some potential as where road designs influence firm decisions on e.g. locations.
Information/warnings	• Nudges, such as reminders, may influence firms, especially those of lower capacity.
Campaigns/social norms	• Name and shame strategies that impact on reputations and brands may work under certain conditions (see the discussion of *disclosures* above).
Shocks	• Less effective–it may be more difficult to shift the corporate psyche than an individual's preferences.
Low transaction costs	• Some potential, as where steps are taken to facilitate compliance.

A further worry is related: that the processes of nudging are value-laden yet low in transparency. Nudge sceptics may argue that whether a nudged-for outcome is 'good' or 'beneficial' is not always obvious. The evaluation of an outcome's merits may reflect the nudger's conception of the good rather than the nudge target's, or it may, simply, be an outcome whose merits are debatable and contested. Nudging, the objection goes, is not a device that is easily confinable to the pursuit of uncontentious benefits. In response, Thaler and Sunstein suggest that nudges are inevitable (all choices are structured) and so they might as well be made benignly. Sceptics would, however, say that this response misses a key point. Some manipulations of decisions, and control systems, are more open than others. If a government issues a law that prohibits citizens from smoking in public places, this is a mode of control that is open, discussed, and implemented after representative processes have been followed. If nudging is used, the process used to effect a nudge may be far more hidden from view—the nudge may flow from an administrator's decision on how to design a public building: a decision not subjected to advanced disclosure or debate.

The danger of nudging is that, under the banners of neutrality and easy opt-out, control regimes become less overt, less accountable, and more paternalistic.

Such concerns about the accountability and openness of nudging are not necessarily assuaged by Thaler and Sunstein's comments about the occasions when nudging will have the most potential for good. The authors suggest that nudging will be most useful where the nudgers or 'choice architects' have high levels of expertise and the nudge targets face difficult decisions on which they have poor feedback and few opportunities for learning. Nudge opponents would immediately voice worries that systems in which 'experts' manipulate the choices of less well-informed parties are exactly those scenarios in which there are the greatest dangers that regulatees' and citizens' preferences will be overridden in the name of expert judgements of a spuriously neutral nature.

A major defence of governmental nudging contends that citizens are constantly bombarded with nudges by practitioners of advertising and marketing—so we may as well use nudges to push people in sensible directions. If there is no freedom from nudging, we may as well use the device for worthwhile ends. The counter to this argument is that, in a world where we have to battle constantly to make a decision on an un-manipulated basis, the last thing we need is a tranche of governmental nudges (especially of the Second and Third Degree) to add to all the others. There lies the route to nudge fatigue and a world in which we are infantilized by those who see us as sheep to be steered in 'sensible' directions. In any event, the sceptics may say, we expect advertisers to play tricks on us but we expect better from our elected governments.

To conclude, in the appropriate form and location, nudging offers a useful means of regulating social and corporate behaviour. It is wise, however, to distinguish between different degrees of nudge. Second and Third degree nudges pose issues that First Degree nudges do not. Care, moreover, should also be taken in treating nudge as 'just another' control to add to the regulation toolkit. Second and Third Degree nudges involve a different, and more contentious, relationship between state and citizen than, say command laws.

Self-Regulation and Meta-Regulation

Positive regulation, as noted, is predisposed to harness firms' capacities to control risks themselves. This avoids the need for expensive and intrusive regulation. The term 'self-regulation' can be used to refer to controls that operate within firms and 'industry self-regulation' to denote systems involving external, non-state controls over firms, e.g. by trade associations. In processes of 'meta-regulation' the state regulator will delegate the front-line task of control to the corporation but will generally engage in a degree of oversight—which may involve a variety of arrangements, from monitoring compliance records to scrutinizing risk management systems. ('Meta-regulation' is thus akin to what has been called 'monitored self-regulation'.) Advantages of self-regulation and meta-regulation include the benefit to the public purse in delegating controls; the harnessing of firms' specialized stocks of expertise in devising controls; and the opportunities for firms to devise customized lowest-cost methods of control that will best dovetail with their operational needs. Firms are liable, moreover, to see their own systems as more reasonable than externally imposed rules (which enhances compliance) and self- or meta-regulation allows controls to be established where the regulator lacks the resources or information to control directly—which may be a special problem in complex and heterogeneous, new and dynamic industries. Speed and flexibility may be further advantages of meta-regulation.

Advocates of meta-regulation tend to place a good deal of emphasis on the need for law, legal institutions, and regulators to *motivate* firms to self-control and self-monitor. This can be done together with mechanisms of oversight such as accountability procedures that establish standards against which the law can judge responsibility, companies can report and stakeholders can debate.

Christine Parker suggests that there are two main ways to use attributions of liability to increase a company's commitment to self-regulation. First, liabilities and sanctions can relate to the quality of the company's self-regulation programme and its disclosures regarding this.[10]

A second strategy is to give courts or regulators powers to require or encourage a company to implement a self-regulatory system when a breach has been alleged or has occurred. Thus, a company might be placed on 'probation' until it has instituted such a system in satisfactory form.

Rewards and incentives can also be used to encourage corporations to develop newly-effective risk management and compliance approaches. State authorities can, for instance, encourage good risk management systems by granting public recognition to high-performing corporations (e.g. through

---

[10] See generally C. Parker, *The Open Corporation: Effective Self-Regulation and Democracy* (Cambridge University Press, 2002).

certification processes or publications of best practice or league tables). Regulators may also reward trusted firms by reducing inspection fees or giving freedom from inspection and detailed regulatory oversight (subject to satisfactory performance).

Case in point: Southern Water penalized after Ofwat investigation

In 2019 an Ofwat investigation resulted in Southern Water agreeing to pay £126m in penalties and payments to customers following serious failures in the operation of its sewage treatment sites and for deliberately misreporting its performance.

Ofwat found that Southern Water had failed to operate a number of wastewater treatments works properly, which led to equipment failures and spills of wastewater into the environment.

Ofwat also found that Southern Water manipulated its wastewater sampling process which resulted in it misreporting information about the performance of a number of sewage treatment sites. This even extended to tankering polluted water away from certain sites ahead of inspections, in order to avoid penalties under Ofwat's control regime.

The £126m package will see Southern Water pay a rebate of £123m to customers through their bills and pay a fine of £3m.

What, though, are the conditions under which self-regulatory and meta-regulatory systems are likely to prove successful? A first consideration is the profile of the sector in issue. Let us suppose that, in a hypothetical sector, some operators are well-intentioned and are highly disposed to comply and to deal in a constructive manner with rules and regulators. Others are less well-intentioned (even ill-intentioned) and see regulation as something to be resisted or gamed to selfish advantage. Operators, moreover, vary in capacities. Those of high capacity tend to be well-managed and to possess good knowledge about regulatory requirements. Low capacity operators tend to be slack in management and to have scant knowledge of relevant regulations. Different mixes of intention and capacity thus produce four basic models of firm, as shown in Table 3.4.

If the overall (simplified) profile of the sector is as in Table 3.4, the question arises: which operator types will self- or meta-regulatory systems tend to work well with? Type One firms offer some hope, they are competent, they will devise good risk management systems and will communicate well with the monitoring regulator. Type Two firms are more problematic as they are not good at designing their own control systems, they do not communicate well, and are not very aware of their obligations. They will, however, respond reasonably positively to instructions and assistance from overseeing regulators. Type Three firms are difficult because they are not inclined towards compliance, they will use their considerable skills for self-advantage and will be expensive to control. Their positive feature is that if they are convinced that they need to produce a good regime of control so as to further their own interests (e.g. because there is a penalty to be paid for failure) they have the competence to deliver such a control system.

Table 3.4 Four models of firm

Type of firm		Percentage of such firms in the sector
1. Well-intentioned	High capacity	10
2. Well-intentioned	Low capacity	40
3. Ill-intentioned	High capacity	20
4. Ill-intentioned	Low capacity	30

Type Four firms are a real problem as they are not good at designing their own control systems, they do not communicate well, and are not very aware of their obligations. Nor will they respond positively to instructions and assistance from regulators.

Experience with self-regulatory procedures in the British food safety and the health and safety sectors suggests that firms of either ill-intention or low capacity, and most small and medium enterprises (SMEs), are very likely to do nothing about designing control systems or compliance procedures until they are prompted by the government regulator. They are essentially reactive.

The managers of SMEs are likely to see compliance not as an ongoing obligation but as a periodic negotiation with an inspector. They will, accordingly, tend to think of themselves as compliant until they are told otherwise by an official. SMEs, moreover, will tend to dislike meta-regulatory systems and see them to be more difficult to comply with than prescriptive regimes. They will, understandably, be less compliant under a meta-regulatory regime than under a prescriptive 'command' regime or one involving an interventionist 'educative' approach.[11]

---

[11] R. Fairman and C. Yapp, 'Enforced Self-Regulation, Prescription and Conceptions of Compliance within Small Businesses', *Law and Policy* 27 (2005): 491–519.

Where the firms regulated are small in size and numerous, it may thus be more effective to rely on government officials to enforce rules than to rely on firms to develop the needed risk management expertise. Similarly, there may be advantages in centralized regulation where the accumulation of expertise in a government body is likely to lead to more rigorous controls than would emerge from the firms themselves.

In the USA there are indications that firms' performances can be patchy when overall guidelines for firm-based self-regulation are set down by the industry itself.

Case in point: Responsible Care

The Responsible Care programme was set up by the US Chemical Manufacturers Association (CMA) in 1988 in the wake of the Union Carbide chemical disaster at Bhopal in 1984. Under this programme, firms make commitments to uphold certain environmental, health, and social values. These values are elaborated on in a series of practice codes, which are broad in terms and allow firms to devise their own targets and ways of meeting these.

By 2007 the CMA was requiring that members obtain third party certification for their environmental, health and safety systems and disclose their environmental and safety records.

Research findings suggest that some firms take their obligations under the programme far more seriously than others, with some studies reporting that CMA members have performed less well than firms who are not in the Responsible Care programme.[12]

In contrast with Responsible Care, however, are more successful instances of self-regulation, such as the regime of the Institute of Nuclear Power Operations (INPO), a body set up by the nuclear industry in the wake of the Three Mile Island accident of 1979. As in Responsible Care, INPO sets down general standards and non-mandatory statements of good practices that leave firms to set their own objectives. INPO conducts inspections and makes recommendations. It also publishes rankings that

---

[12] See C. Coglianese and E. Mendelson, 'Meta-Regulation and Self-Regulation', in R. Baldwin, M. Cave, and M. Lodge (eds.), (Oxford University Press, 2010), pp. 154–5.

place members in a range of performance categories—this is the most serious consequence of non-compliance. Most analysts cite INPO as a success and it has been argued that this may be explained by a number of factors. The nuclear industry is marked by a greater homogeneity and smaller size than the chemicals sector. There are also tighter interdependencies between firms; more common interests and shared concerns for the reputation of the industry. In the nuclear sector there is also a greater threat that state regulation will replace a poorly performing regime of self-regulation.[13]

The above considerations suggest that, when considering the use of self- and meta-regulatory mechanisms, attention has to be paid to the profiles of the industries involved; to the broader sets of constraints that reinforce inclinations to self-regulate; and to the levels of resources that may be needed in order to bring firm capacities up to the levels required to make self-regulation work. Selective application of self-regulation and meta-regulation does, of course, bring an advantage yet to be mentioned. Where firms such as those of Type One (Well-Intentioned and High Capacity) can be controlled through self-regulation, this will free regulatory resources to deal more intensively with firms in the other categories.

Self-regulatory systems have historically faced considerable hurdles in generating public confidence. There have been worries over the years that processes of self-regulation and self-reporting on performance can lack rigour and can contribute to capture.

A more general challenge involved in delegating regulatory tasks to corporate managers is that of persuading corporate managers to see the world in anything like the same way that regulators view it. A fear is that, at least with some firms, the views that business managers take of regulatory responsibilities differ in kind from the visions of regulators and do so to a degree that rules out effective dialogue. Managers may see regulatory liabilities as risks to be managed, not as ethically reinforced prescriptions. Compliance is an option, but another potential response is to side-step liability through a series of steps, which may include: shifting risks by outsourcing; developing public relations systems that can limit any reputational losses caused by regulatory sanctioning; or increasing insurance arrangements to cushion liabilities. Alternatively, firms may seek to block regulatory actions by restricting activities that are liable to give rise to sanctions (e.g. by silencing whistle-blowers).

---

[13] Coglianese and Mendelson, 'Meta-Regulation and Self-Regulation', pp. 155–6.

Case in point: The Boeing 737 MAX worries

In March 2019, aviation authorities around the world grounded the Boeing 737 MAX passenger airliner after two new 737 aircraft crashed within five months, killing all 346 people aboard.

It later emerged that, before these crashes, Boeing staff had sent internal messages that revealed staff efforts to deceive regulators about safety matters and contained the phrase: 'This airplane is designed by clowns who in turn are supervised by monkeys'. One email described regulators viewing Boeing presentations as: 'Like dogs watching TV'.

A Times investigation of July 2019 noted major concerns that:

- Boeing had allegedly been given too much unmonitored scope to self-certify equipment as safe.
- Staff of the regulators (the Federal Aviation Administration) had been 'too cosy with' or 'captured by' Boeing.

In November 2019 the FAA announced plans to revise its regulatory approach in favour of a more 'holistic' strategy that involved closer FAA involvement in the design of new aircraft. It stated that it would not allow Boeing to self-certify and sign off on the safety of the 737 MAX.

In 2020 the US House Committee on Transportation stated that the FAA's oversight of Boeing had been 'grossly insufficient' and it had 'failed in its duty' to both uncover critical problems and make sure that Boeing fixed them.

In moving from meta-regulation and self-regulation within firms to 'industry self-regulation' the focus shifts to instances in which the state delegates regulatory functions to non-state assessment organizations, industry associations, or professional bodies. What is clear is that many governments see an increasing reliance on industry self-regulatory mechanisms as the way to foster lower-cost, less-interventionist, yet effective systems of control. Thus, when a group of UK regulators and the Cabinet Office worked to produce *The Regulatory Futures Review* in 2017, they proposed a 'general shift' towards what they called 'regulated self-assurance'. These are systems that put the challenge of designing an effective compliance regime substantially in the hands of the regulated businesses or of intermediary assurance or certification bodies (as in the Red Tractor assurance scheme seen in the food industry).[14] Self-assurance was distinguished

---

[14] Cabinet Office, *Regulatory Futures Review* (London: Cabinet Office, 2017).

from 'pure' self-regulation as it still placed a responsibility on the regulator to ensure that regulations are adhered to.

The posited advantages of industry self-regulation and regulated self-assurance regimes are, first, that the design of control mechanisms lies in the hands of those who have direct experience and expertise in the relevant activity. This can produce leaner, more efficient, and better-targeted control systems than those emanating from the state. The expenses and strictures of command and control regimes can be replaced by systems that are cheaper and more effective because corporations are given the freedom and incentives to work out what, for their mode of operating, is the best way to avoid the given mischief and to manage their reputational risks. Non-uniform approaches to compliance can thus produce better results than across-the-board rules, which unduly restrict some firms yet are too lax in the case of others. Managers are, moreover, said to be more likely to innovate and to improve controls than under a standard-setting instrument and regulated firms are more likely to attune their own standards of behaviour to the expectations of society when they are given the responsibility to govern their own behaviour, rather than being dictated to with a rule.

The public purse is also protected as industry self-regulation and regulated self-assurance systems reduce the need for on-site inspections by government regulators. Another advantage is that cooperation between the state regulator and those providing controls or assurance can lead to intelligence-sharing and better quality controls. In the case of self-assurance, competition between providing bodies has been said to hold out the prospect of more efficiency in the control system.

There are potential issues with industry self-regulation and regulated self-assurance systems. The bodies that offer control and monitoring functions are funded by the industries they supervise and they may prioritize the economic well-being of the regulated firms or the industry over the welfare of consumers or society. Such systems tend to owe much to the influence of powerful firms in the sector and this may lead to worries that they become captured and protective of 'grandfather' interests with controls designed to limit industry competition and to shore-up established methods of production or technologies. Ensuring the input and influence of a balance of interests may be a challenge here, as may the facilitation of new entrants to markets. Those bodies that offer controls or assurance, moreover, may be highly focused on achieving the elements of formal compliance and may not have the same eye on overall outcomes and objectives as the governmental regulator.

Where, in addition, the regime is voluntary this means that consumers are not protected from providers who are not covered by any assurance mechanisms. There may, indeed, be incentives for firms to stay outside the self-regulatory regime so as to keep their costs low and free-ride on the reputational advantages that the industry as a whole earns through self-regulation and assurance.

On costs, it may be rash to assume that the compliance costs that assurance systems impose on firms will be lower than those charged by state regulators and, where charges are made for assurance services, businesses may not welcome a shift away from taxpayer-funded regulators' inspections. There may be further worries about levels of charging for assurance services. Private assurance bodies may be able to set prices from highly protected positions in the markets that they serve. Where, moreover, control responsibilities are shared between two layers of institutions (assurers and regulators) there may be issues, not only of coordination and consistency of policies and approaches but of duplication, uncertainty, and multiple regulatory burdens.

As for public confidence and regulatory effectiveness, there have been repeated issues with both the standards set by self-assurance bodies and their enforcement processes.

Case in point: Red Tractor

In 2012, Red Tractor, Britain's largest food standards assurance scheme was condemned in the press for offering the lowest animal welfare standards of any quality mark. It was said to do little more than meet legal requirements and to allow such practices as the docking of pigs' tails without anaesthetic.

In 2017 the House of Commons Environment Food and Rural Affairs Committee reported on allegations of malpractice at the Red Tractor accredited 2 Sisters poultry plant in West Bromwich. This followed undercover footage obtained by the Guardian and ITN which showed workers at the plant changing slaughter dates on crates of poultry. The Committee was alarmed by the 'patchwork nature of the accreditation process' in which it was: 'simple for someone to game the system and hide infractions'.

In 2018–19 a number of different media stories exposed cruelties at Red Tractor assured farms.[15]

---

[15] See e.g. https://www.theguardian.com/environment/2019/jun/25/footage-chickens-big-uk-producer; https://www.independent.co.uk/news/uk/home-news/footage-pigs-injuries-wounds-red-tractor-fir-tree-farm-animal-equality-tesco-a8391231.html.

On the accountability of industry self-regulators, the critics are likely to point to a lack of holding to account through normal democratic channels and to the strong hold that the industry, rather than consumers or the public, exerts on policy and practice. The complaints managing regimes of self-regulated industries and professions have been especially prone to criticisms. This has been exemplified in the legal sector. It was lack of confidence in the solicitors' complaints system that substantially prompted the wholesale regulatory reforms that were effected with the Legal Services Act 2007. Worries about the fairness of processes will be all the more pronounced if the area is not populated with strong consumer organizations, non-governmental bodies, and others who can seek expression for aggrieved parties' concerns.

As for regulatory expertise, there is a narrow path to tread. If an industry self-regulatory system lacks this, confidence will be undermined. If there is a high level of skill and specialization, there are dangers that governmental expertise in this area will diminish and there will be insufficient oversight of the industry bodies.

Collaborative Regulation

The self-regulatory capacities of firms can be harnessed to an ultimate degree by 'collaborative' regulatory systems in which regulators and firms work together to improve performance. In such systems, which include those termed 'supportive' or 'co-regulatory' and 'cooperative', there are often elements of self-regulation and self-assessment but they are marked by a movement towards support for desirable behaviour, building trust relationships between regulators and firms, and working collaboratively to improve performance. There is a philosophical shift away from an emphasis on using regulatory deterrence to achieve compliance from untrustworthy corporations. When things go wrong, the emphasis is on helping firms to ensure that things are put right rather than on placing blame.

Ethical Business Regulation (EBR) is a prime example of the collaborative approach.[16] EBR involves an open relationship of trust between businesses and regulators—one founded on shared understandings that each will fully cooperate to control risks according to society's rules. Such a system builds on: support for ethical behaviour; consistent, transparent, and ethical regulation; and business evidence of commitment to fair and ethical behaviour.

---

[16] See C. Hodges and R. Steinholtz, *Ethical Business Practice and Regulation* (Hart, 2017).

It also embraces: a learning rather than a blame culture; collaborative regulation to maximize performance, compliance, and innovation; and proportionate responses to non-compliant or unethical behaviour.

Case in point: Civil Aviation Authority safety regulation

The CAA is responsible for economic, safety, and environmental regulation in the UK aviation sector. In the safety regime pilots and air traffic controllers self-report near misses and incidents, on a 'no blame basis'. The training and qualifications of pilots are managed by 'approved entities' overseen by the CAA. Aircraft maintenance schedules are submitted by the operators themselves and approved by the CAA and then audited by the CAA. There is a degree of earned autonomy in inspection regimes and the CAA relies heavily on self-reporting, approval and audit of airlines' own safety management systems, and allowing third party entities to assure the training and quality of pilots.

The cited advantages of collaborative systems are that they escape the inabilities of deterrence regimes to change behaviour effectively in the face of adversarial relationships and adverse cultural pressures. They focus on improving not only levels of compliance but on outcomes, business cultures, and general ethical standards in firms. This means that win-win opportunities can be pursued effectively and it avoids the expenses and frictions of adversarial relationships between regulators and firms. Collaborative systems foster the taking of actions before harms occur rather than punishing after the event. Openness, good information flows, and the exposure of problems are also encouraged rather than cover-ups. Mistakes are dealt with and learned from, and uncertainties are reduced as firms develop informed understandings of compliance requirements. The EBR strategy also distinguishes between the culpabilities of those who try to do the right thing and make an error, those who make little effort to control risks properly, and those who deliberately flout the law.

Consistent with an EBR strategy are regulatory efforts to promote corporate social purpose—as exemplified in recent steps taken by the UK water regulator, Ofwat.[17] In Ofwat's strategy for 2020 onwards a central

---

[17] See Ofwat, *Time to Act Together: Ofwat's Strategy* (Ofwat, October 2019) and R. Fletcher, 'Regulators and the Social Contract', Beesley lecture, 16 October 2019. https://www.ofwat.gov.uk/wp-content/uploads/2019/10/RF-Beesley-Lecture-16-October-2019.pdf.

aim is to encourage water companies to provide greater public value by delivering more benefits for consumers, society, and the environment. The target here is cultural change throughout regulated water companies so that opportunities to improve public value are taken in all decisions made across the corporate business. Corporate processes would reflect such cultural change with fresh corporate thinking on how firms can give citizens a voice and how they can provide the transparency that will allow stakeholders to hold them to account. In addition, companies would strive to find win-win solutions that are lower cost, or no higher cost, than traditional methods, but deliver greater public benefits. They would also aim to go beyond the standards and norms set by regulators where this was the right thing to do.

A corporate culture that has a clear purpose of providing greater public value has been said by Ofwat to bring a host of benefits to regulated firms. It allows the water companies to build legitimacy in the eyes of the public and to enlist the support of customers and other partners in tackling ongoing challenges. It enhances their abilities to recruit the skills they need to address their business challenges and to retain and get the best from their staff. This improves financial performance. When a company has a clear purpose of promoting public value this also improves abilities to attract new sources of finance (especially those from ethical funds) and it reduces the risks of developing a toxic culture that can lead to a variety of corporate failings.[18] In addition, it helps to avoid those perceptions of corporate unethical behaviour that can lead to losses of market share or government interventions such as proposals of renationalization.

In promoting the corporate social purpose strategy, Ofwat introduced revised binding principles of Board Leadership and Governance into the licences of all the water companies in 2019. The first principle requires each Board to set a purpose for the company that recognizes the needs of its wider stakeholders as well as its shareholders, and to ensure that corporate culture aligns with that purpose.

Other regulatory measures to promote social purposes have been canvassed by Ofwat. It will consider whether to offer a differentiated price control process to those with a proven track record in delivering against the public value agenda and it will look to join forces with other regulators, such as the Environment Agency to bring reputational incentives to bear on those who are slow to act.

---

[18] Ofwat, *Time to Act Together*.

Further regulatory measures that have been mooted include: imposing an overarching public value licence condition on all companies; placing a more formal 'fit and proper' test on future owners; and introducing a senior managers regime in which executives are held directly accountable for their conduct and competence. Ofwat has said that it will keep these options in mind and will also pay increased attention to measuring the extent to which water companies serve social purposes.[19] Such measurement, it has suggested, would allow Ofwat to include social and natural capital outcomes in future price controls.

Consistent with the theory of positive regulation, Ofwat has stressed the need to develop its intelligence on companies' corporate cultures—on the footing that an improved understanding of such cultures would allow Ofwat to assess such key issues as: corporate abilities to translate purposes into improved outcomes; the levels of risks that a company poses; the degrees of regulatory scrutiny a company needs; and whether a particular company should be controlled with rules rather than principles.

The EBR approach can be seen as taking on board one of the criticisms of 'responsive regulation' that was made by advocates of 'smart regulation'.[20] The latter argued that, rather than respond to non-compliance by simply imposing more severe sanctions, it will often be better to work with firms to fix problems and tackle challenges—to break away from ever more punitive responses. EBR also stresses, more than responsive regulation, the degree to which decisions to invoke sanctions should turn on culpability. EBR does not espouse a blame culture but it does hold that strong sanctions should be applied where firms or individuals deliberately or recklessly break the law—a response that contrasts with the supportive strategies to be used for those who breach laws by mistake.

Sceptics are liable, however, to argue that collaborative approaches, such as EBR, are likely to come up against many of the difficulties discussed above in relation to self-regulatory and meta-regulatory systems. Critics of EBR might concede that trust-based and supportive strategies are likely to be worthwhile with well-intentioned and reasonably capable firms but they would suggest that far less success is to be anticipated with less well-intentioned firms. Of these firms, those with high capacity are likely to possess cultures that stand in the way of trust relationships—strong and

---

[19] Ofwat, *Time to Act Together*.
[20] See Chapter 4; see also I. Ayres and J. Braithwaite, *Responsive Regulation: Transcending the Deregulation Debate* (Oxford University Press, 1992); N. Gunningham and P. Grabosky, *Smart Regulation: Designing Environmental Policy* (Clarendon Press, 1998).

adverse industry cultures have been said by many to have undermined the financial regulatory system in the lead-up to the financial crisis of 2007–8. Those with ill-intention and low capacity are unlikely to respond to regulatory support and will not be able to develop the kind of convincing reporting systems that would create the necessary trust for this kind of regulation. The critics might add that corporate managers in general may not readily see themselves as surrogate regulators or philanthropists whose mission is to go beyond the rules on risk control, or to pursue social values. Regulators' efforts to shift corporate cultures, therefore, may be akin to encouraging the carnivores to eat grass—though a way forward (as seen with Ofwat) is to seek to persuade corporations that when they are seen to pursue social value and virtuous outcomes this will serve their commercial interests.

Advocates of EBR have conceded, as noted, that strong sanctions have to be applied to those who deliberately or recklessly break the law. This admission, however, points to a central challenge for EBR—to identify those firms who will respond constructively to the supportive regulatory approach and those who will not. Critics, moreover, might argue that, if a sector contains both trustworthy and untrustworthy firms, advocating a general shift away from punishment and blame, towards trust and support is overstating the case for EBR—as is abandoning all messages about the need for 'credible deterrence'.

The EBR strategy faces other challenges beyond those posed by the inclination of the less well-intentioned and capable to do nothing in advance of regulatory action. The operation of a highly discretionary control mechanism renders it vulnerable to accusations of differential and unfair treatments. These will be difficult and expensive to defend against through mechanisms of confining, structuring, and checking discretions. The close relationships that are central to EBR will, moreover, render the regulators vulnerable to allegations of capture and to reductions in public confidence—echoing reactions to the FAA's reliance on self-certification processes in the Boeing 737 MAX affair.

Collaborative arrangements, in addition, are liable to face the criticisms made in relation to 'ecological modernization'—a theory stressing that the best way to improve environmental quality is to use government-industry dialogues, consensus-building, and continuous learning to exploit industry's capacity to innovate. The worry is that, even if such approaches do not produce full-scale regulatory capture, they will often stand in the way of the kind of transformations that are needed to serve the public interest on such issues as sustainability. Industry collaborations, the critics say, will tend to produce a focus on reducing the risks associated with current operational methods and will not readily contemplate fundamental changes in systems.[21]

The procedures for building the trust relationships for EBR are also potentially problematic. They turn on the supply by firms of a constant stream of data that offers assurances of good behaviour and trustworthiness. Even if it is assumed that firms are willing and able to provide this data, there are considerable costs to businesses in doing so and governments around the world are nowadays calling constantly for regulators to demand less form-filling and data from businesses.

For regulators there are very considerable costs involved in collaborative systems. Not only does all the above data have to be analysed for each firm but, as is conceded by proponents of EBR, the regulators have to leave their desks and engage with operations on the ground in order to understand the particular businesses involved and to make suggestions—as would a non-executive director. This is a hugely resource-intensive process. It might be feasible with generous funding and a relatively small number of well-disposed and capable firms but is far less workable where there are large numbers of firms who range across the scales of intentionality and capacity.

The measurement of success within EBR is also a considerable challenge. Within the Ofwat regime, for instance, it might be asked how the delivery of improved corporate culture or social value is to be evaluated. A central thrust of EBR is to go beyond the rules and 'do the right thing' but when the rules are left behind, when regulatory mandates are vague, and when the regulator, individual corporations, and different stakeholders have their own conceptions of the public values that should be recognized and are priorities for attention, those who seek to evaluate performance will have to look hard for a method of assessment that can command broad support. In the case of Ofwat, for instance, its portrait of the 'Value in the Round' to be promoted by water companies involves no fewer than twenty headings, ranging from 'carbon footprint' and 'damage to wildlife' to 'flood and climate risks' and 'river pollution'. It may be necessary to rank these twenty factors in importance. A further, and contentious issue,

---

concerns the balance that should be sought between delivering social value and delivering the substantive and procedural outcomes that are mandated in legislation. Once again, it can be expected that different stakeholders will have quite divergent views and this is another matter that will render the evaluation of success a fraught activity.

Closely related is another issue—that of the regulator's role in encouraging the pursuit of social value. A regulator can fairly easily act as 'cheerleader' in encouraging the companies that it regulates to be mindful of sources of public value, but it is another thing to use regulatory incentives and prescriptions to encourage corporate pursuit of public value. A key issue in such cases will be the need to justify actions and to demonstrate equality of treatment between different firms. That will be very difficult, time consuming, and expensive when the reference points are not laws and rules but a large collection of social values that compete for resources and attention.

Defenders of EBR might respond to the above concerns by pointing out that the use of EBR will be selective because adopting EBR has to be 'a voluntary choice' by business. This concession leads to the prospect that EBR may be a minority activity to be enjoyed by the best-intentioned and most capable firms. It would follow that EBR has limited potential as an across-the-board approach to regulation. It also raises doubts about the impact of EBR. The regulatory paradox stresses that those firms who are the least likely to volunteer for, or respond well to, EBR are those firms that are most likely to be causing the most problems.

None of the above rules out the value of collaborative regulation—the harnessing of firms' self-regulatory capacities is central to positive regulation. A valuable point made by proponents of EBR is that, where possible, regulators should work collaboratively with firms to encourage the development of healthy corporate cultures that conduce to ethical behaviour. They can do this, amongst other things, by such measures as laying down clear principles for guiding conduct, and striving to remove perverse incentive structures. The above discussion, however, emphasizes that the real key to positive regulation lies in using regulatory methods that are aware of, and attuned to, the kinds of firms being dealt with—that developing intelligence on the character of the firms within a regime (and the risks that their activities involve) is a matter of central importance. Some firms will respond well to collaborative regulation and others will need to be dealt with more firmly, or even punitively. The trick lies in the tailoring of strategies through awareness, intelligence, and dynamism.

Personal Liabilities

Why not tame the corporation by holding individual decision-makers personally liable through criminal or civil liability rules?

Case in point: Social media

In December 2019 the UK Government announced plans to make senior managers in social media companies personally liable to criminal fines for breaches of their duties of care to service users.

Under those plans US technology companies such as Facebook and Google would have to appoint a British-based director who would be accountable for breaches of duties of care and Ofcom would draw up legally enforceable codes of practice covering the protection of users from harmful content. Matters covered would include terrorism, child abuse, cyber-bullying, self-harm, harassment, violence, and pornography.

In early 2020, however, the Government responded to concerns from the technology giants by signalling an amended approach that emphasized 'naming and shaming' executives rather than imposing personal criminal liabilities.

It has often been suggested that the minds of senior managers will be concentrated wonderfully by the prospects of personal criminal liability and that deterrence will work well when directed at key individuals in a firm. A further posited advantage of individual liability is that it leaves risk evaluation and risk spreading to those who are best placed to select optimal control strategies.

There are, however, problems in attempting to secure desired outcomes by targeting individuals. The strategy assumes, first, that it will be possible to identify an individual to hold to account. In many cases, however, the actions, decisions, and bodies of knowledge that relate to liability may be scattered across a firm rather than held by one individual. The history of corporate manslaughter laws suggests that, all too often, mischiefs arise because there is no clear allocation of responsibility or decision trail that makes attributing responsibility to an individual possible. The very cause of the problems at issue may hinder the holding of individuals to account.

Even when a law is passed to overcome this problem—by ensuring that there is a designated individual to be held responsible for fulfilling a role or complying with a defined set of rules—there is a potential issue of under-deterrence. The ability of the corporation to do damage may vastly exceed any potential cost to be imposed on the designated individual and, as a result, the efficient level of deterrence is unattainable. This problem is exacerbated when steps are taken to mitigate the impact of a penalty on the individual, as, for instance when insurance or company-instigated compensation systems are operated.

The idea of individual deterrence also assumes that those persons who are potentially liable will be aware of their liabilities and will react rationally to the threats involved. The evidence, however, is that very many company managers are unaware of their potential liabilities and, in any event, will be driven to take actions and to make decisions by a host of factors other than their legal liabilities. Short-term financial, reputational, or employment incentives may loom much larger in their decisions and may favour non-compliant actions. Behavioural science also indicates that individuals will tend to suffer from biases that reduce deterrence effects. Thus, their optimism or their attractions to anticipated gains are factors that lead individuals to underestimate the risks involved in non-compliance. (They will tend to underestimate both the probability of being found liable and the consequences of liability.) A perverse effect of individual criminal liability, moreover, may be that it discourages conscientious individuals from taking up difficult positions in a firm, but it does not stop cavalier operators.

As for the effectiveness of personal sanctions in producing serviceable controls over risks or problems, it can be argued that holding the company to account offers a better way to incentivize the company as a whole to establish acceptable risk management systems. Similarly, it can be argued that when problems and breaches are encountered, remedial steps are better encouraged by incentivizing the company to change its systems and its cultures than by scapegoating individuals. Proponents of collaborative regulation would add that taking steps to encourage healthy cultures and ethical corporate systems will very often produce far better results than regimes that blame individuals—which bring dangers of concealment, unethical cultures, and organizational secrecy, all of which are practices that stand in the way of compliant and desirable behaviour.

Case in point: Senior managers' liability in banking

In 2013 the Financial Conduct Authority (FCA) supported an approach in which increased emphasis was placed on holding individual managers personally to account. The Financial Services (Banking Reform) Act 2013 section 36 introduced a new criminal offence of reckless misconduct in the management of a financial institution.

The Act imposes liability where the conduct of a senior manager is reckless, it falls far below what could reasonably be expected of a person in their position, and the implementation of their decision causes the failure of the financial institution. Conduct Rules also apply to senior managers and demand, inter alia, that they act with integrity, due skill, care, and diligence.

Identifying responsible individuals is facilitated by the Senior Managers and Certification Regime (SM&CR) which has applied to banks since March 2016. Under the regime, every senior manager needs to have a 'statement of responsibilities' that clearly says what they are responsible and accountable for. A senior manager also bears 'overall responsibilities' for each of the firm's business functions and activities.

Some critics have contended that applying individual criminal liability to senior managers will do little to address the sector's core problem of adverse industry culture. Hodges and Steinholtz argued: 'This approach is simply not going to work. It is not credible and scandals will continue. [It will be] ineffective in achieving behavioural change.'[22]

The FCA's SM&CR Stocktake Report of 2019[23] found that 'senior managers across all firms were clear on what accountability meant in the context of their jobs'—though many 'expressed concern' about the meaning of the 'reasonable steps' that they were obliged to take to avoid a contravention. Many firms 'were often unable to explain what a conduct breach looked like' but they reported a change in the 'quality of conversations on culture and expected behaviours'.

---

[22] Hodges and Steinholtz, *Ethical Business Practice and Regulation*, p. 184.
[23] FCA, *Senior Managers and Certification Regime Banking Stocktake Report* (FCA, 2019). https://www.fca.org.uk/publications/multi-firm-reviews/senior-managers-and-certification-regime-banking-stocktake-report.

Blame-shifting may be a further negative consequence of individual liability—as when managers avoid potential liabilities by delegating legally awkward tasks to subordinates or subcontractors (who may be less well-placed to manage the risks at issue).

Conclusions: Strategies for Positive Regulation

Arrayed above are a number of broad regulatory strategies that can be employed in various forms to control behaviour. Command approaches have been much attacked but all of the above strategies have strengths and weaknesses and many of the criticisms of 'command and control' are over-stated. As seen above, not all commands are inflexible and highly prescriptive. Many of the 'alternatives to commands' bring with them similar needs to build on rules and to rely on enforcement processes, and many have to be held in place and backed up with commands.

Positive regulation involves awareness that, in most regulatory contexts, there will be an optimal mixture of regulatory strategies and intervention styles. Controls that are based on state interventions are not, moreover, the only options. An important message from 'smart regulation' theory as developed by Gunningham, Grabosky, and Sinclair is that controls can be exerted by the state but also by professional or industry bodies (such as the General Medical Council) and by corporations themselves. The lesson is that it is often sensible to rely not simply on state control strategies but on the combination of state, quasi-regulator, and self-regulatory controls that will best achieve desired outcomes.

A 'positive regulation' strategy would endorse this last point and would stress the need to incorporate high levels of awareness, intelligence, and dynamism into the choice of strategic options. The aware and intelligent regulator will develop an appreciation of the different characteristics of the firms being controlled and will analyse the degree to which those of different profiles will respond to different regulatory strategies—whether those be state commands or taxes, intra-firm controls, or collaborative interactions.

In seeking to deliver outcomes efficiently the positive regulator would, as noted, be aware of the costs of achieving such outcomes under different strategic options. It would take on board its legal, financial, and political settings. Thus, it would appreciate the qualities of control that can be effected in the context of its legal powers, its governmental and account-ability framework, and the expectations that are made of it by various actors and institutions. It would be aware of those respects in which there will be interactions between different control strategies (such as commands and self-regulatory requirements) and it would have an intelligence system that constantly feeds back information on whether current strategies are working or need to be adjusted.[24]

The positive regulator's feedback system, it should be repeated, would relate not merely to the cost-effective production of mandated outcomes (such as cleaner rivers) but to the acceptability of the processes being used in the regulatory regime (such as the quality of transparency that is being offered by the mix of strategies being used). As for dynamism, this involves coming to grips constantly with the issue of change—by, for example, reacting swiftly to any indication of a need to adjust strategy, or responding without delay to changes of public or governmental expectation.

Finally, it has been emphasized that positive regulation is predisposed to operate by harnessing self-regulatory capacities. Controls within firms, meta-regulatory systems, and schemes of industry self-regulation all provide means of passing the task of front-line control to firms or their associations. These approaches, like collaborative processes, bring a variety of advantages, as discussed, but there are challenges in deploying such arrangements so as to produce desired results at lowest cost and in a manner that sustains public confidence. Central in judgements about the potential of self-regulatory or collaborative systems will be such issues as: the nature and number of the firms involved in the regulated sector; the profile, culture, and level of organization of the industry involved; the degree of heterogeneity, level and complexity of risks; the rate of change in the sector; and the extent of connected public sensitivities. The relative expertise and resourcing of the state regulators and the industry will be a further factor as will the availability of external pressures to make self-regulation succeed. It remains the case, though, that, whether full-scale self-regulation is feasible or not, all opportunities to work with the grain of self-regulatory capacities should be taken.

---

[24] See R. Baldwin and J. Black, 'Really Responsive Regulation', *Modern Law Review* 71(1) (2008): 59–94.

4

Impacts on the Ground

Enforcement

Enforcement lies at the heart of the process for delivering outcomes. Once a regulator has identified its objectives it has to carry out a number of sub-tasks in order to deliver desired outcomes. These can be set out as in Table 4.1.[1]

Table 4.1 The DREAM framework

Detection	• The gaining of information on non-compliant and undesirable behaviour.
Response development	• The developing of policies, rules, and tools to deal with the problems discovered.
Enforcement	• The application of policies, rules, and tools on the ground.
Assessment	• The measuring of success or failure in response development and enforcement activities.
Modification	• Adjusting strategies and tools in order to improve compliance and address problematic behaviour.

What these tasks involve can be seen in a simple example. Let us consider a hypothetical regulator, the Cod Protection Authority (CPA) that is responsible for ensuring that cod stocks in the North Sea remain at levels that will sustain UK fisheries. The first task the CPA needs to discharge is *detection*. It needs to gain information on behaviour that impacts on its aim of protecting cod stocks. This might be non-compliant behaviour—such as trawler operators breaking the rules on net sizes—but it might also be behaviour that does not breach the CPA's rules. Thus, newly efficient long-lining systems may be destroying cod stocks but these might be legal because all of the relevant laws relate to nets (their allowable length, mesh sizes, etc.). If the long-lining methods are used in order to escape the net regulations, they are examples of 'creative compliance'—processes in which

---

[1] See R. Baldwin and J. Black, *Defra: A Review of Enforcement Measures and an Assessment of their Effectiveness in Terms of Risk and Outcome* (London: Defra, 2005).

regulated concerns defy the purposes of rules by side-stepping those rules. This is usually done by reorganizing operations so that these are not covered by the rules. The CPA needs to know how much of this 'undesirable' behaviour is going on because it affects the achieving of CPA objectives. Only such knowledge will tell the CPA how much its efforts to secure compliance (with the netting rules) will actually achieve its desired outcomes.

Response development involves generating those rules and tools that are fit for purpose in detecting and dealing with activities that impact on realizing CPA objectives. Thus the CPA may need powers to search fishing vessels, to prosecute non-compliers, and to take a host of other actions. In the light of its detection work, moreover, the CPA may need to make the case to government for rules that allow it to control not merely the use of nets but other technologies, such as long-lines. For many regulators the challenge here is to persuade ministers to make time to revise regulatory powers so as to respond to changes in the regulatory environment.

Enforcement is the key process of applying policies, rules, and intervention tools on the ground. We return, below, to the challenges of enforcement and to choices of enforcement strategy.

Assessment involves measuring the performance of regulatory actions—as these relate to any of the five DREAM sub-tasks. The positive regulator's awareness, intelligence, and dynamism will be reflected in its being able to assess, for instance, whether its current rules allow it to deal with all forms of existing and emergent problematic behaviour, and whether there are high levels of creative compliance that hinder the achieving of desired outcomes. Poor regulators will enforce their rules and *hope* that this will achieve their objectives. Positive, high quality, regulators will know the extent to which the current rules and enforcement strategies are working and the degree to which these need to be revised.

Modification is the process of adjusting tools and strategies so as to improve the cost-effective securing of objectives. The positive regulator will act on the messages delivered by its assessment procedures—this is the mark of its dynamism.

Enforcement Strategies

When to Intervene

Regulating positively demands that interventions are made at the optimal stage in the emergence of a risk and its movement to a harm. Here we can think of a choice between three stages of action. Thus, controls can be used to prevent a dangerous act or situation arising (e.g. hotels can be inspected for fire safety before guests are allowed to be admitted). Interventions, however, can also be made in response to dangerous situations that may have developed (e.g. a fully operating hotel is inspected to see if there are adequate fire doors, escapes, and sprinklers). Finally, a regulator may be prompted to intervene by the realization of a harm (e.g. to investigate and potentially prosecute following the injury of a hotel guest in a fire). Steven Shavell has distinguished between controls that target these three stages, calling them, respectively: preventative, act-based, and harm-based interventions.[2]

How should a regulator decide how to balance interventions at the three stages? Let us consider the three different risks in Table 4.2. The first is that poorly constructed scaffolding may collapse and cause injuries or deaths, the second is that some drivers on country roads will not dip their headlights and oncoming drivers may crash when dazzled, the third is that avalanches will hit ski resorts and injure or kill people.

Table 4.2 Progressions across three stages of risk development

	PREVENTION	ACT	HARM
SCAFFOLDING		→	➡
DIPPED HEADLIGHTS		➡	→
AVALANCHE		➡	➡

[2] See S. Shavell, 'The Optimal Structure of Law Enforcement', *Journal of Law and Economics* 36 (1993): 255–87.

Shavell suggests that, when thinking about the optimal stage of intervention a first consideration is the benefit of preventing a progression from 'prevention' to 'act' or from 'act' to 'harm'. The benefit thus turns on what would happen in the absence of intervention. This is signified in Table 4.2 by the small and large arrows. Small arrows indicate that not intervening would lead to a low incidence of progression; large arrows suggest a high level of progression.

Thus, we might find (for the sake of argument) that, with scaffolding, non-intervention at the prevention stage would not result in the development of many dangerous situations because scaffolding is erected by specialists, it is not complex engineering, and scaffolders are strongly incentivized to do the job properly (they stand on it during construction). On those assumptions, the return from prevention is unimpressive since the progression that is prevented is small. Rather than seek to apply preventative measures to a large number of (generally satisfactory) operators it might be better to focus on 'act' stage interventions that home in on the much smaller number of poor performers.

With dipped headlights we might find the opposite—without a public education programme very many instances of dazzling might be anticipated. Again, with avalanches, allowing freedom to build resorts in the snowfields might be expected to result in a high incidence of dangerous situations. Other things being equal we would, therefore, incline to a greater spend on prevention in the case of headlights and avalanches than with scaffolding.

Turning to the progression from 'act' to 'harm', there is a large progression in the case of scaffolding (assuming that dangerously erected scaffolding produces a high incidence of collapses). With dipped headlights, in contrast, there is a low 'act' to 'harm' progression if it is the case that cases of dazzling very rarely cause oncomers to crash. With avalanches there is a high 'act' to 'harm' progression because mass injuries will frequently result when there are failures to act (e.g. by dynamiting) when dangerous situations have arisen (e.g. resorts have been built in the hills and dangerous slabs and cornices have developed).

The three examples offer different 'progression profiles' (on the factual assumptions made) from low/high to high/low to high/high. This suggests that: with scaffolding, the emphasis should be predominantly on act-stage interventions; with headlights, special attention should be paid to prevention; and with avalanches there should be more even distribution of intervention effort.

A further consideration, however, should be taken into account: the cost-effectiveness of the steps that can be taken at each of the three stages.

Where the intervention actions available at any particular stage are cheap and effective this would favour their use at that stage. Where such actions are cost-ineffective that would militate against such timing. In Table 4.2 there are perhaps some clear instances where cost-effectiveness (or lack of it) might be a strong indicator of optimal intervention stage. Thus, if it is the case that 'act' based interventions are very cost-ineffective in the dipped headlights case (because police would have to wait for hours on country roads hoping to catch a non-dipper), this would strengthen the case for preventative, rather than act-based intervention. With avalanches, it might be that banning the building of ski resorts in the hills (a preventative action) would be hugely costly, but, in contrast, periodic dynamiting of potentially dangerous slopes (an act-based intervention) would be relatively cheap and effective. This favours an emphasis on 'act' based controls.

The gravity of the harm at issue is a further relevant factor. Where lives are at stake, or the costs of rectifying a harm are very high, this favours interventions at the earliest stages in a progression from prevention to harm. It is also the case that most regulators will need to devote material resources to harm-based interventions where harms are grave—thus, political and ethical considerations call for accident investigations after fatal incidents.

Without further elaboration it can be argued that Shavell offers a useful framework for considering the stage at which the most positive interventions can be made by regulators. It is arguably an approach that can be applied right across sectors and risks—be these safety, environmental, financial, or any other. It assists with the pursuit of positive regulation because it directs attention at those intervention stages that will maximize the excess of all-round benefits over costs.

Understanding Motivations to Comply

Positive regulation calls for awareness and intelligence on the reasons why firms and individuals will comply voluntarily with rules and regulations. Such understandings will point the way to the least intrusive ways to influence behaviour and the more that firms' propensities to self-motivate can be harnessed, the more cost-effectively regulatory resources can be deployed.

Studies around the world indicate that three main factors impact significantly on propensities to comply.[3] The first of these is the *capacity* of the firm or individual: whether it knows what the rules and regulations

---

[3] See Dutch Ministry of Justice, *The Table of Eleven* (The Hague, 2004); OECD, *Reducing the Risk of Policy Failure: Challenges for Regulatory Compliance* (Paris: OECD, 2000).

require and whether it has the expertise, resources, and managerial skill to take the required actions. A second is *attitude or intention*. Key issues here are whether the firm is well-disposed towards the rules and the regulator. Does it accept the value and sense, authority and legitimacy of the rules or does it see them as unjustifiable impediments to economic activity? Does it respect the regulator, and the broader legal regime, as fair, open, and efficient? Are there, moreover, external pressures and attitudes that will encourage compliance? These might include those attitudes or preferences of peer organizations, industry bodies, or the public that will either favour or discount the importance of compliance.

The third major factor influencing motivations to comply is the relevant set of *incentives and risks*. The balance between the costs and benefits of coming into compliance is important. If compliance is costly and there are large market advantages to be gained by non-compliance, this does not favour voluntary compliance. In contrast are situations where compliance is cheap and the market/consumers will reward ethical/compliant producers generously.

The risks that are directly associated with regulation will, of course, also influence compliance and these will relate to such matters as the probabilities of being sanctioned (turning on the chances of being reported, inspected, detected, and acted against) and the expected severity/quantum of the sanctions. Where firms have a positive view of regulatory compliance and see this as a route into markets, or a method to stabilize or enable markets they will be inclined to comply—as when they see regulation as protecting their own investments (e.g. in research) or as underpinning consumer confidence (e.g. in the security of financial products). Similarly, firms will tend to embrace regulation and compliance when they see this as encouraging inward investors and lowering their costs of securing funds (see Table 4.3).

Table 4.3 Factors influencing a firm's compliance motivation

Capacity	• Knowledge of the rules
	• Level of expertise, resources, and managerial skill
	• Compliance assistance available
Attitude/intention	• Disposition, acceptance, and respect for rules and regulator
	• External influences on attitude/intention
Incentives and risks	• Perceived difficulty and costs of compliance
	• Perceived benefits of compliance (as offered by markets, consumers, investors, etc.)
	• Anticipated probability and severity of sanctioning for non-compliances

Positive regulators will be aware of the above points and will seek to maximize all opportunities for encouraging voluntary compliance. They are likely to pay attention to the potential of compliance-fostering measures as exemplified in Table 4.4.

Table 4.4 Measures likely to enhance compliance

- Rules that offer lowest-cost routes to regulatory objectives and are simple, short, and as easy to comply with as is feasible.
- Assistance in making clear what compliance involves and how this is best achieved.
- Enabling measures (e.g. guidance) to increase firms' capacities and skill levels.
- Efforts to: 'sell the regulatory mission'; to convince firms of the value and sense of the rules and the fairness, openness, and efficiency of the regulator; and to foster compliance-friendly cultures in firms.
- Working with relevant groups (e.g. industry associations) to garner 'buy-in' for the regulatory regime and to promote information on compliance.
- Steps to persuade consumers to demand compliant products and modes of production.
- Operating lowest-cost methods of regulation and that offer lowest-cost routes to compliance.
- Increasing the perceived probabilities of sanctioning for non-compliance.
- Increasing the perceived severities of sanctions for non-compliance.
- Steps to persuade firms of the market-related benefits of regulation and compliance.

Targeting Enforcement: Risk-Based and other Approaches

Regulators have to take actions on the ground in order to influence behaviour and deliver desired objectives. Some strategies focus on identifying the firms and activities that are to be prioritized for attention, others deal with ways in which to change the behaviour of those who are selected for such attention.

On the former matter, risk-based regulation is the dominant strategy on the global stage.[4]

Risk-based frameworks generally prioritize matters for attention with reference to analyses of the operators and activities that pose the most

---

[4] See generally J. Black, *Risk-Based Regulation: Choices, Practices and Lessons Being Learned* (Paris: OECD, 2008).

severe risks to the regulators achieving their mandated objectives. Such analyses can be used to determine priorities between regulated areas or within those areas, to select firms to be investigated or activities to be controlled. The UK's Environment Agency (EA) typifies the risk-based regulator. The Operational Risk Appraisal (Opra) system (recently withdrawn) was used for a number of years to target efforts at the greatest risks to the environment. The Opra system analysed risks with reference to five matters, as (paraphrased) in Table 4.5.

Table 4.5 The Operational Risk Appraisal (Opra) system

Complexity	• Of the activities undertaken, potential releases from the site, the regulatory effort to secure compliance.
Emissions and inputs	• Releases to air, water, and land; the waste coming on to the site.
Location	• The sensitivity of the location (e.g. proximity to sensitive areas).
Operator performance	• Operator performance, management systems, competence and training, and enforcement history.
Compliance rating	• How well the operator has complied, any enforcement activity.

The effect of such risk evaluation systems is to assess risks with reference to the severity of a potential harm and the probability of that harm occurring (as affected by such matters as the quality of the operator's risk management system). Operators are generally given risk scores but there is considerable variation across regimes and jurisdictions in the approaches that are taken to risk scoring. Some systems are highly quantitative and some are heavily qualitative.

These scores may rank firms or activities according to broad categories—such as 'traffic light' regimes that divide into 'high', 'medium', or 'low' risks—or they may use more fine-grained divisions. An important qualitative element is often the field inspector's estimation of a regulated firm's management and its capacity and commitment to control the given risk.

It is usual for the scoring system to guide the regulator in prioritizing operators for attention. High-risk firms will generally be accorded priority for intervention. It is less usual for there to be a direct linkage between the risk score given to a firm and the nature of the intervention tool that is deployed with respect to that firm (whether, for instance, the regulator will use an educative, persuasive, or sanctioning tool to influence the firm).

Risk-based regulation was originally promoted as a means of justifying regulatory efforts with reference to a systematic and transparent analysis. Experience, however, has revealed the extent to which risk-based frameworks are not neutral, technical instruments. Each aspect of a risk-based framework involves a complex set of choices and evaluations. Risk-based regulation, as a result, involves a number of challenges.

A first issue is the set of risks to be analysed and scored. The difficulty is that a 'risk' is a construct and different approaches to construction can be taken. Different 'drivers' of risk identification produce different sets of key risks. A first such driver is the legal mandate. Lawyers will tend to select key risks by looking at legally mandated objectives and focusing on the most severe threats to achieving these. Key risks are thus identified with reference to the legal mission. Regulatory managers, however, may define and select key risks in ways that make them most easily inspected and managed, or which reflect the organization of teams within the agency (e.g. where each team within the agency is given a priority risk to attend to). Staff from different disciplines, or doing different jobs, moreover, will tend to see key risks differently—the lawyers, engineers, and policy teams will diverge in their approaches.

Yet another driver of risk identification is the information-gathering system of the regulatory body. Just as 'what can be measured gets done', the way the data system is set up will tend to determine the selection of the important risks.

A further driver of risk priorities is often the regime of accountability that a regulator works within. If a central department of government, or a supra-national body, demands to know what a regulator is doing about risks X, Y, and Z, those risks become priorities.

Case in point: Risk priorities and Irish septic tanks

In 2012 the Irish Government was held to account by the European Court of Justice for its failure to introduce an adequate and timely regime of septic tank inspections. It was fined €2 million.

Suddenly septic tanks leapt up the agenda and became high-risk priorities for the Irish Environmental Protection Agency.

Finally, politics and public sensitivities often impact on risk identifications. All regulators need a certain level of political and public support to get their jobs done. That means that if politicians or the public care strongly about certain risks or related harms (such as odours in the air) the regulators would be foolish to ignore those sentiments even if they do not reflect the regulator's own priorities as constructed with reference to mandates or needs to account or other factors (see Table 4.6).

Table 4.6 Factors driving risk identifications

Legal mandate	• 'Risks' are threats to achieving statutory objectives.
Functional considerations	• 'Risks' are identified in a way that reflects bureaucratic structures or allows efficient use of resources.
Information regime	• 'Risks' are those that are identified by the information-gathering system.
Accountability	• 'Risks' are selected in the light of matters that have to be accounted for.
Politics/public sensitivities	• 'Risks' are those that the politicians or public care about.

The challenge, we see, is that a number of drivers compete to suggest how risks are to be identified and prioritized. Choosing key risks thus involves a good deal of art and measures have to be taken within regulatory bodies to ensure that there is consistency of approach in risk identifications. A lack of such consistency will lead to confusion, uncertainty, and ineffective regulation.

Another, often-cited, difficulty with risk-based regulation is that risk-based regulators tend to focus on firms rather than on industry-wide activities. They are inclined to attend to single-site, and highly visible risks rather than to systemic or cumulative risks, which require more resources and analysis to come to grips with. One of the causes of the 2007–8 financial crisis was a failure to deal with the systemic and cumulative risks that resulted from the extensive marketing of securitized products founded on subprime mortgages.

Nor is keeping an eye on the highest risk firms as easy as it might appear. If regulators pay the closest attention to those firms that present the greatest risks, some firms will 'fly under the radar' because they are only medium level risks and not, therefore, priorities for attention. If such firms are aware of this situation, there is a danger that they become slack managers of their own risks because they are not contacted by the regulator with any frequency or because they know or suspect that they are 'immune' from regulation. As a result, such firms may become high-risk operators who are liable to escape regulatory attention until the regulator re-evaluates their risk score—which may be some years away.

There are even problems with the assumption that it is efficient to prioritize for attention those sites or activities that present the greatest risks. The difficulty here is that the costs of influencing firm behaviours may vary according to their attitudes and capacities. (The regulator may have to spend far more resources to induce a given change of behaviour at one site than at another.) The dilemma then is whether to target the biggest risks or the firms/activities that offer the best opportunities for reductions in risks. If attention is paid to those firms that best respond to regulatory interventions, the effect is to establish perverse incentives—by interfering with well-intentioned firms and giving greater freedom from control to those businesses that are not cooperative. If, on the other hand, priority is given to the recalcitrant firms, regulatory resources will be directed away from the locations where they would produce the greatest positive effects. There is no easy answer to this dilemma.

Risk-based regimes make it clear which risks will be prioritized—but also which risks will not be prioritized. The regulator's risk tolerance is thus exposed to public glare, and this can lead to difficult political challenges. These are likely to occur where the public see that the regulator is not attending to certain risks that it sees as serious, or where an accident or harm occurs at a site that the regulator has not prioritized. The result is that, in practice, a regulator's risk tolerance (like its risk identification) is often strongly influenced by political considerations and that using the risk-based framework becomes more of a political art than a technical operation.

An implementation challenge is that risk assessments call for regulatory officials to make discretionary judgements on such matters as managerial quality. Regulators have to control these discretionary judgements and make them consistent, but avoid instituting processes that render the regime expensive and unresponsive. Cultural changes may also have to be made within regulatory bodies so that a focus on rules and compliance-seeking gives way to a concern with risks and their assessment.

Positive regulation demands high responsiveness to change but a danger in a risk-based regime is that the regulators become excessively attached to a certain basket of risks and that these become out-dated. The regulators may accordingly fail to detect and deal with new risks. They may also become slow to explore their risk model's inherent weaknesses. The Hampton Review of 2005 was well aware of such dangers and argued that regulation 'should always include a small element of random inspection' in order to uncover new risks and risk-creators, to check on the validity of the risk assessment system, and to counter the 'under the radar' problem.[5]

Using a particular framework for risk analysis tends, furthermore, to bring another danger: it gives no indication of the extent to which undesirable risk creation is escaping the regulatory net. There is liable to be no measure, for instance, of the prevalence of creative compliance or new types of risky operations or risk-creators that are not covered by the current rules. As a result, analyses of relative risk scores will not indicate whether the regulatory regime is addressing a major portion of threats to regulatory objectives or only a small percentage of these.

Risk-based regimes always have to contend with possible disjunctures between the regulator's perceptions of risk and those of the public (or certain groups of interests), but the additional problem is that those divergences are not static. Preferences concerning regulation often change—as seen in the post-credit crisis period in the UK when sections of the public, the government, the regulators, and the media lost a good deal of faith in 'light-touch' regulation. The public may want different things of regulators at different times, and so may governments, legislators, extra-jurisdictional bodies, and particular groups of interests. The problem is that if regulators are committed to the given risk framework, they may be slow to respond to changes—especially when the processes of constructing and developing that framework are positioned deep within the bureaucratic process and are, as a result, insulated from the public pressures that might be expected to galvanize change.

Contemplating radical changes in regulatory strategy may also be difficult from 'within' a risk-based regulatory regime. The problem here is that a mind-set that centres on analysing and reacting to risks will not be readily attuned to the consideration of ways in which risks can be 'designed out' of economic or social processes by moving towards pre-emptive managerial strategies or innovative production methods.

Performance sensitivity is an important aspect of positive regulation but risk-based regulators may find this challenging. First, because risk-based regulation is directed towards future events that may or may not happen. If a harm does not ensue from a risk, it can be difficult, if not impossible, to show that this outcome was the result of the regulator's actions. A further difficulty may be that risk-based regulation involves

[5] P. Hampton, *Reducing Administrative Burdens: Effective Inspection and Enforcement* (London: HMSO, 2005).

substantial delegation of control functions down to the risk management systems of the firms being regulated. This delegation makes performance assessment particularly taxing, notably because different actors—be they corporations, regulators, credit ratings agencies, or other bodies—may use different models or 'codes' to evaluate risks and they may operate with different cultures. Regulators may think of risk control objectives with reference to statutory purposes, whereas firms may see internal risk management as properly directed at profits and market share. The risks that the regulator is concerned with will, indeed, not always be the same as the risks that the firms are focused on. Firms, moreover, may make risk judgements differently from the regulators and this renders risk evaluations all the more opaque to regulators, as well as to the broader community.

An additional problem relates to the manner in which regulatory performance is assessed. It might be thought that risk-based regulation offers a ready means of judging performance since the risk scores of regulated firms and individuals can be compared year on year and this will reveal whether overall levels of risk are increasing or decreasing. This approach, however, tends to focus on a given set of historically established risks and, if this is so, they will reveal little about the regulator's success or failure in coming to grips with new risks and new risk-creators.

Justifying risk-based systems may be challenging because it is difficult to deliver on the idea of a rational, transparent, and logical guide to regulatory decisions. There are serious issues of risk identification and alignments between the risk priorities of regulators and firms, consumers and the public. The transparency of risk-based regulation is a positive feature in some ways but, as noted, it does render the regulator vulnerable to attack for its perceived risk tolerances. It may also be a transparency that is more apparent than real since many of the key decisions within risk-based regimes will be woven deeply within the assumptions used to make risk evaluations and prioritizations. Risk-based regulation, moreover, offers some information on which operators to go after but it tells us less about how to change their behaviour. It is perhaps best seen as a way to construct the regulatory agenda rather than a mechanical solution to the familiar challenges of regulation.

Problem-centred regulation, as popularized by Malcolm Sparrow,[6] shares many of the challenges associated with risk-based regulation. The

---

[6] M. Sparrow, *The Regulatory Craft: Controlling Risks, Solving Problems, and Managing Compliance* (Harvard University Press, 2000); M. Sparrow, *The Character of Harms: Operational Challenges in Control* (Cambridge University Press, 2008).

concept of a problem here is broader than that of a risk—it may include risks of future events, but it also takes in existing situations that are undesirable (such as harms that have already arisen). Sparrow draws an important distinction between 'problem-based' and 'process-based' regulation. In the latter, the regulator focuses on enforcing the procedures and powers that it has responsibility for. The disadvantage of this is that the eye is not on the overall objectives that are sought to be realized. The advantage of problem-based regulation is that (echoing risk-based regulation) problems are identified with an eye to the regulator's objectives and the regulator pays constant attention to the pursuit of those objectives. As with risks, however, the identification of 'important problems' is not an unproblematic task and establishing problem rankings in the face of competing drivers of priority is not easy.

Non-random intervention priorities can be established by means other than risk or problem analyses. Thus, regulators may prioritize operators and activities that may cause the greatest harms (even though the probabilities of these occurring may be low); they may prioritize areas where they may make most difference (a 'biggest bang for regulatory buck' approach); or they may pay attention to those issues that are most politically salient, or which they feel most accountable for. In some cases, the law will stipulate priorities quite precisely and the regulator will be obliged to act accordingly. The case for such alternative ways to set priorities will often turn on arguments about cost-effectiveness, legal requirements, and the politics of the regulatory game.

An alternative way to select operators and activities for priority attention is *random* investigation. In a random system, interventions are made on a wholly chance basis—as where a computer produces random names and addresses and the regulator investigates those sites and the activities being carried out there. The advantage of randomness is that regulated firms never know if there will be a knock at the door. As noted above, this addresses the problem of 'under the radar' complacency that is associated with risk-based regulation. Such an approach also helps to uncover new risks and risk-creators since some of the random investigations will chance upon novel and risky operations. The downside is that this is not an efficient way to deploy resources (many sites visited may be unproblematic) and it does not target resources at the biggest problems and risks.

In a process of *reactive investigation*, interventions are prompted, and priorities significantly driven, by sources outside the regulator, such as members of the public, consumers, or whistle-blowers. Typical of such a system would be a telephone hotline regime for dealing with fly-tipping.

The advantage of such a regime is that it can be used where the regulator lacks the resources to engage in direct investigations—the public and others become the eyes and ears of the regulator. This may bring a presentational advantage for the regulator as it is seen to be being responsive to the concerns of the public. The use of untrained 'detectors', however, brings potential problems. Parties outside the regulatory agency may care about risks and problems that would not be priorities for the regulator and they may not have the skills to uncover serious risks or to set about prioritizing these. They may act in ways that the regulator would think irrational—such as reporting the behaviour of some parties for vindictive reasons. Where, moreover, it is necessary to act to prevent harms that are serious or catastrophic (e.g. nuclear incidents) a reactive approach would be inappropriate. This is, nevertheless, a useful device where resources are very sparse and where risks are not serious or contentious.

Changing Behaviour: Compliance and Deterrence Approaches

Whichever method is used to direct attention to particular sites and activities, regulators must decide how to change behaviour in order to further their objectives. In a command regime (or, indeed, an incentive regime, such as emissions taxing) a broad distinction can be drawn between 'compliance' and 'deterrence' approaches to enforcement. The former emphasize the use of measures falling short of prosecution in order to improve behaviour or seek compliance with laws. Thus the regulator will typically educate and persuade, negotiate and advise in an effort to exert influence. 'Deterrence' approaches, in contrast, are penal and use prosecutions in order to deter future infractions by non-compliers and to encourage firms more generally to behave acceptably.

A cited advantage of 'compliance' strategies is that they produce good relationships between regulators and firms, which conduces to good information flows and allows regulators and firms to work together in pursuit of possible win-win outcomes. Compliance strategies, moreover, are said to be far cheaper than seeking deterrence through expensive and legalistic prosecutions. Compliance approaches also allow regulators' messages to be tailored to different kinds of firms and individuals within these, so that firms can be taught to think 'beyond the rules, beyond compliance' and to behave in a manner consistent with purposes and values promoted by the relevant regulation.

If, however, we return to the breakdown of firm-types that was discussed in Chapter 3 we see that different effects may be anticipated when compliance approaches are deployed (see Table 4.7).

Table 4.7 Impact of compliance strategy on different types of firm

Type of firm		Likely impact of compliance strategy
1. Well-Intentioned	High Capacity	Significant success can be anticipated as these firms are able and willing to act on reminders and advice.
2. Well-Intentioned	Low Capacity	Some success if there are resources available to advise and educate so as to improve capacity. Much will depend on the level of expertise required to comply or to behave responsibly.
3. Ill-Intentioned	High Capacity	Unlikely to succeed as such firms are not likely to take advice seriously if it does not suit their own interests—they do not fear the regulator as no threats are applied.
4. Ill-Intentioned	Low Capacity	Very unlikely to succeed as such firms are not likely to take advice seriously if it does not suit their own interests—they do not fear the regulator as no threats are applied. Even if they are persuaded of the need or value of taking certain actions, their limited capacity stands in the way of such actions and they will respond poorly to advice and education.

Critics of compliance will argue that, in relation to firms of Types 3 and 4, the perceived weakness of compliance approaches will be exploited by errant firms and little impact will be achieved. Since firms are unafraid of regulators, it will be said, non-compliance will be unaddressed for lengthy periods as firms simply wait for regulators to advise them what to do.

Other charges may also be made. Thus, the customizing of messages, and discretionary modes of interacting with firms renders 'compliance' regulators vulnerable to accusations that they deal unfairly with some operators, or are captured by others. Defending against such accusations may prove expensive as considerable efforts may have to be made to ensure, and to demonstrate, consistency of treatment. Politically, the charge may be that regulators are 'soft' on non-compliance and un-protective of public interests.

The case for deterrence approaches is, in contrast, based on claims that they can prove highly effective in changing corporate cultures and in stimulating management systems so that risks of infringement are reduced.

Deterrence approaches treat infractions seriously by stamping errant conduct as unacceptable and they, accordingly, reinforce, and give effect to, social sentiments of disapproval—which, in turn, can enhance social pressures to comply. Thus, the reputational impacts of punishment can reinforce the deterrent impact of the sanction imposed and, when this occurs, this enhances deterrence.

Case in point: The Volkswagen scandal

The Volkswagen emissions scandal began in September 2015, when the United States Environmental Protection Agency (EPA) issued a notice of violation of the Clean Air Act to Volkswagen Group. The agency had found that Volkswagen had intentionally programmed turbocharged direct injection (TDI) diesel engines to activate their emissions controls only during laboratory emissions testing, which caused the vehicles' nitrogen oxide output to meet US standards during regulatory testing, but to emit up to 40 times more nitrogen oxide in real-world driving.

US authorities extracted over $25 billion in fines, penalties, and restitution from VW for the 580,000 tainted diesels it had sold in the United States.

In 2020 Brand Finance, a brand valuation consultancy argued that VW had put its $31 billion brand at risk and had lost $10 billion in brand value since the emissions scandal had arisen.

Deterrence approaches, it is urged, can induce political shifts so that firmer approaches to regulation can be taken. Tough stances on enforcement, say deterrence advocates, make it rational for firms to give a high priority to compliance. The alleged expensiveness of deterrence can, moreover, be countered with the claim that, provided sanctions are severe, an individual prosecution, though costly in itself, may produce a substantial ripple of deterrence which brings value for money.

There are, however, a number of reasons to question the effectiveness of deterrence approaches in controlling corporations. Deterrence strategy demands that sanctions are sufficiently severe to incentivize compliance beyond the immediate case. In many instances, however, the courts do not impose fines of sufficient gravity to produce this result. This may happen for a number of reasons—a large fine may be seen as threatening an errant company's solvency, for instance, or it may be viewed as depriving the rule breaker of the finances that are needed to remedy the mischief at issue. It is difficult, moreover, to impose fines on a firm if it can 'pass through' the pain: to consumers (by increasing charges); to suppliers (by decreasing payments); or to employees (by laying off workers). At times of economic hardship firms may argue to political allies that the last thing they need is intrusive and legalistic regulation that increases their costs and reduces viability or growth.

Effective deterrence also demands that firms perceive that the probability of a sanction's application is high. They may, however, have scant knowledge of the law and may anticipate that the chances of being detected, prosecuted, and convicted are low. Their 'optimism bias' may exacerbate this weakness in deterrence. Low regulatory resources may, additionally, mean that the chances of being caught and sanctioned are actually very low. As has been documented by Keith Hawkins and others, many regulators have to counter this problem by engaging in a game of bluff in which they exaggerate their detective capacities and abilities to trigger sanctions.[7]

The assumption that firms will react rationally to threatened sanctions can also be questioned. Instances of non-compliance may be the result of 'irrationalities' within companies that flow from such sources as poor training and bad management. Responding to such problems with the tool of rational deterrence may, accordingly, involve a mismatch of mischief and response. The non-compliers (especially the Type 4 firms) will be those who are least likely to respond rationally to threats of sanctions.

Many small and medium companies, indeed, will not know what it would cost to comply with the rules, and they may tend to assume that they are compliant until they are told otherwise. They may, moreover, see compliance not as observing the rules but as behaving in accordance with the last negotiation that they had with an inspector.

Even if it is assumed that some companies will react rationally to threatened sanctions, it cannot be taken for granted that this will lead them to respond with compliance. They may see compliance as just one way to reduce the probability of suffering a sanction for breaching the rules. Other ways to reduce that probability might include: creative compliance; bringing pressure to bear on the regulator (to discourage prosecution); shifting risk or blame on to the shoulders of individuals or outsourced business partners; or evasion, non-cooperation with regulators, and concealment.

The prospect of possible sanctions may also induce companies to respond by reducing the potential impact of any sanction. They may thus take out insurance, share risks, or act to increase corporate resilience. On

---

[7] See K. Hawkins, *Environment and Enforcement: Regulation and the Social Definition of Pollution* (Oxford University Press, 1984).

rational deterrence assumptions, companies will balance the costs and benefits of compliance with the expected costs and benefits of non-compliance,
and will choose the combinations of risk-reducing responses that maximize
benefits over costs. The predominant position, moreover, is that many companies operate largely unaware of their exposure to punitive regulatory risks,
and the overall evidence is not highly consistent with effective and rational
regimes in which anticipated penalties stimulate compliance.

Other posited difficulties with deterrence approaches are that they can
produce very negative relationships between regulators and firms.
Cooperative work towards possible win-win outcomes gives way to firms
thinking about how to use lawyers and subterfuges to keep the regulators
at bay. This is likely to reduce the effectiveness of enforcement, as well as to
increase overall costs to both firms and regulators. In turn this may make
the regulator more vulnerable to capture since opponents are able to point
to the high levels of unproductive costs generated by the regulatory process.
This is liable to reduce political support for the regulator and weaken their
hand in resisting pressures from powerful business interests.

As with compliance strategy, the impact of a deterrence strategy is likely
to vary across different types of firm—as indicated in Table 4.8.

Table 4.8 Impact of deterrence strategy on different types of firm

Type of firm		Likely impact of deterrence strategy
1. Well-Intentioned	High Capacity	Unnecessarily alienates a virtuous firm at unjustifiable expense and undermines a productive relationship that could work towards win-win.
2. Well-Intentioned	Low Capacity	Unnecessarily alienates a well-intentioned firm and undermines potential for using advice and education to foster compliance.
3. Ill-Intentioned	High Capacity	Produces adversarial relationship that increases the expense of regulating. Threats of sanctions, however, may re-orientate intentions and such firms have the capacity to comply if they are persuaded that they need to do so.
4. Ill-Intentioned	Low Capacity	Produces adversarial relationship that increases the expense of regulating and undermines the possibility of a productive relationship. Even if threats re-orientate intentions, such firms often lack the capacity to comply. The worst of these firms may need to be excluded from the activity/sector if risks are considerable.

Both compliance and 'deterrence' strategies thus have strengths and weaknesses. Is it possible to combine the elements of these so as to produce a superior enforcement approach? Ian Ayres and John Braithwaite addressed this issue in popularizing the concept of enforcement pyramids.[8] One of these pyramids involves a hierarchy of sanctions, the second, a hierarchy of regulatory strategies. The former is produced in Figure 4.1.

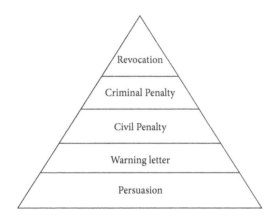

Figure 4.1 Responsive regulation: enforcement pyramid

The idea behind responsive regulation is that compliance is better induced when a regulatory agency operates with an explicit enforcement pyramid—a range of enforcement actions extending from 'compliance' methods such as persuasion up to highly punitive steps such as revocations and disqualifications. There would be a presumption that regulators should always start at the base of the pyramid with persuasive/negotiatory actions and would escalate with more punitive responses where prior control efforts had failed to secure compliance.

Such an escalating 'tit-for-tat' strategy has been highly influential around the globe but there are challenges to be faced. A first difficulty is that in some circumstances step by step escalation from the base of the pyramid may not be appropriate. For example, where potentially catastrophic risks are at issue it may not be wise to enforce by escalating up the layers of the pyramid. Immediate action at higher levels may be necessary (e.g. by taking the civil/administrative step of stopping the dangerous production line).

---

[8] I. Ayres and J. Braithwaite, *Responsive Regulation: Transcending the Deregulation Debate* (Oxford University Press, 1992).

Case in point: Tiered responses in food safety enforcement by the Dutch Food and Consumer Product Safety Authority (covering e.g. bakers, butchers, and fast food restaurants.)[9]

Business Closure
After serious non-compliance following several problematic visits.
Fine
For larger offences or failure to respond to prior warning.
Warning
For small offences (e.g. small temperature infractions).
Compliance Assistance
General first response.

Regulators may sometimes want to move the regulatory response down the pyramid and to decrease the punitiveness of the approach—as where the regulatee has become more inclined to offer greater levels of compliance than formerly. Moving down the pyramid, though, may not always be easy because the application of more punitive sanctions may have prejudiced the relationships between regulators and regulated firms that are the foundations for the less punitive strategies.

A related difficulty with responsive regulation is that escalating through the layers of the pyramid may simply not happen. Enforcers may prove excessively tied to compliance approaches for a number of reasons other than their desires to sustain good relationships with regulated firms. Resource constraints may impede escalation and the regulator may lack the legal powers to progress to more punitive strategies. It may fear the political consequences of progression and may not have the judicial, public, or political support for escalation. The regulator, moreover, may be reluctant to trigger an adverse business reaction to punitive interventions; it may find it difficult to assess the need for escalation because it lacks the necessary information on the firm's response to existing controls; and it may be disinclined to move up the pyramid unless it has sufficient evidence to make a case for the highest level of response (e.g. to prosecute or disqualify).

---

[9] See P. Mascini and E. Van Wijk, 'Responsive Regulation at the Dutch Food and Consumer Product Safety Authority: An Empirical Assessment of Assumptions Underlying the Theory', *Regulation & Governance* 3 (2009): 27–47.

It may also be wasteful to operate an escalating tit-for-tat strategy across the board. With ill-intentioned firms of Types 3 and 4 the regulator may be wasting effort when applying compliance strategies. Tailoring intervention responses to an analysis of firm-types may, in many contexts, result in more cost-effective enforcement than an across-the-board strategy of responsive escalation.

The responsive regulation approach looks most convincing when a binary and ongoing regulator-to-firm relationship is assumed. Such a scenario envisages the transmission of clear messages between these parties and a rational response to the threat of an escalation in punitiveness if there is non-compliance. There are, though, a number of difficulties here. Resource constraints may mean that regulators' contacts with firms are sporadic rather than ongoing. Regulatory regimes can also be highly complex, and inspection and enforcement activities can be spread across different regulators and layers of government. As a result, the messages flowing between regulators and firms may be confused or subject to interference. Firms may be uncertain about who is demanding what and which regulator needs to be listened to regarding a particular issue. Such regulatory 'white noise' may undermine the responsive regulation strategy. As for the assumption of a rational response to the threat of escalation, the familiar regulatory paradox applies—the firms likely to be the most troublesome tend to be those who are the least well-managed and least likely to exhibit a rational response to a threat.

There may also be legal problems in applying a responsive approach. In some areas, legislatures may have decreed that defaulters shall be met with, say, deterrence strategies and this may tie the hands of the enforcing agency.

A further concern relates to the fairness and democratic accountability of responsive regulatory strategies. A danger inherent in a system that tailors regulatory responses to the compliance practices of individual firms is that it involves high levels of discretion and may tend to operate in a non-transparent manner that makes the regulator vulnerable to accusations of capture or inconsistency of treatment across different firms. Such issues can be addressed by steps to confine, structure, and check discretions (e.g. with published guidelines), but there are dangers that such measures may straitjacket responsive regulation within costly bureaucratic controls.

Finally, there may be arguments for not confining the regulatory response to escalating punitive responses but for thinking laterally and breaking away from the punitive pyramid—for instance by placing more emphasis on *ex ante* controls such as screening, by moving to more collaborative strategies, by considering whether a restructuring of the industry will produce desired results better than regulation, or by exploring whether resort to non-state controls will be the best option.[10]

Changing Behaviour: Rules and Principles

Positive regulation demands awareness that the ways in which laws and rules are drafted can impact strongly on the success of enforcement actions. Let us suppose that a regulator needs to stop sick or frail airline pilots from endangering passengers by flying when there are risks of illness or collapse.

Three contrasting styles of prescription could be adopted as exemplified in Table 4.9.[11]

Table 4.9 Contrasting styles of prescription—pilot safety

A.	No one shall pilot a passenger aircraft if they are over 60 years old.
B.	No one shall pilot a passenger aircraft if they present an unreasonable risk to passenger safety.
C.	No one shall pilot a passenger aircraft if they have any of the following medical conditions: (There follows a hugely extensive list of medical conditions that might impact on fitness to fly.)

Formulation A is a precise and simple, bright-line, instruction in a rule. Formulation B offers a general principle incorporating the broad notion of an 'unreasonable risk'. Prescription C is a detailed rule containing a great deal of content.

Regulatory objectives are usually served by precepts that are: clear (so firms and individuals can self-regulate easily); simple and cheap to draft (to reduce costs); and easily enforceable. Regulators, moreover, will want their demands to be resistant to creative compliance (so they are not side-stepped) and productive of the desired outcomes.

The above three formulations can be expected to perform differently on a number of counts (see Table 4.10).

---

[10] See N. Gunningham and P. Grabosky, *Smart Regulation: Designing Environmental Policy* (Clerendon Press, 1998).

[11] See C. Diver, 'The Optimal Precision of Administrative Rules', *Yale Law Journal* 93(1) (1983): 65–109.

Table 4.10 Performance of different formulations of prescription

	Style A (Over 60 years old)	Style B (Unreasonable risk)	Style C (List of prohibited medical conditions)
Clarity	Good—a simple accessible rule that is easy for firms to deal with.	Poor—'unreasonable risk' is open to much interpretation. It is difficult for firms to deal with and creates uncertainty.	Medium—some easy answers may be given but there may be issues about which of a number of rules, governs a situation.
Rule-making cost	Good, costs are low but the regulator may need a cost–benefit calculation to fix the age.	Good, costs are low.	Poor, the regulator has to spend resources on medical drafting. Constant updating will be needed to cope with medical advances.
Enforceability	Good—regulators will have ready and reliable sources of evidence.	Poor—the vagueness of 'unreasonable risk' will make enforcement difficult and expensive and the regulator will lose control over rule content if the courts decide this issue.	Medium—not as good as 'A' but better than 'B'. An issue may be: 'Which rule applies?'
Resistant to creative compliance?	Good—it is difficult to redefine oneself as younger.	Good—it is difficult to know what will successfully avoid the principle.	Poor—these complex rules provide many opportunities for creative compliers.
Targets and produces desired outcomes?	Poor—the rule may be under and over inclusive as threats may be posed by sick 45-year-olds and there may be no good basis for stopping healthy 65-year-olds from piloting.	Questionable. The principle seems to encapsulate the policy objective but this is uncertain: the regulator may have limited ability to map out its meaning so that desired outcomes result.	Good. The regulator has control in putting flesh on the rule.

Table 4.10 suggests that positive regulators will deploy different formulations of rules according to their enforcement priorities. If low risks are involved together with a high number of potential cases and a need for cheap enforcement, formulation 'A' comes to the fore. If there are serious issues with creative compliers in a sector, formulation 'B' is useful (often as a back-up to more detailed rules) and if the regulator strongly needs to be well-positioned to define allowable behaviour (e.g. in a technical, fast-moving area) there is a case for formulation 'C'.

In deciding between rules and principles (formulations 'A' and 'C' versus 'B') a number of other considerations apply. A strength of principles-based regulation (PBR) is that it delegates the risk management function to the firm. The firm will be given no blueprint by the regulator but will be obliged to show the regulator that it satisfies the relevant principle—for example that it operates a control system ensuring that customers are not exposed to 'unreasonable risks'. This gives the managers of the regulated firm the freedom to design the control system that works best (that is most cost-effective) for them, and it harnesses the creativities, and specific pockets of expertise, of the firms, which may exceed those of the regulator. It is generally innovation-friendly as it does not tie firms to particular processes or technologies. Principles, moreover, can be useful in rapidly changing sectors since they will remain applicable across shifts in operations, markets, and products. They will not need to be changed constantly as detailed rules would, and they ensure continuing consistency of broad approach.

PBR brings challenges, however. Not all firms will respond well to PBR as Table 4.11 indicates.

PBR may also be opposed in some quarters on the grounds that it lacks the certainty, clarity, and predictability of precise rules. Principles, it can be said, are more vulnerable to political pressures and shifts (that may change interpretations of the flexible principles) and this creates further uncertainties. PBR may create uncertainties even for firms that are of high capacity since they may not be sure whether a new product or mode of production will be deemed compliant by the regulator. This may delay entries into new markets.

As for costs to the regulator, PBR may prove expensive as regulators will have to investigate the individual modes of compliance that all of its regulated firms bring forward—these may all be quite specific reflections of firm's particular conceptions of 'reasonable' compliance and detailed drilling-down into operations may be required if scrutiny is to be adequate.

Considerable time will have to be spent in communications with firms regarding their claims to be satisfying the principles.

Table 4.11 Types of firm and reactions to principles-based regulation

Type of firm		Likely reaction to principles-based regulation
1. Well-Intentioned	High Capacity	May work well as these firms have the competence and goodwill to develop acceptable risk control systems.
2. Well-Intentioned	Low Capacity	May not work well. These firms lack the skills and resources to devise their own control systems and will constantly ask the regulator to: 'Just tell us what to do.' Many just want bright-line rules.
3. Ill-Intentioned	High Capacity	These firms will use their skills to work principles to their own advantage and to convince the regulators that they are compliant. They will be expensive to control as many firm-specific, in-depth scrutinies will be required.
4. Ill-Intentioned	Low Capacity	May not work well. These firms lack the skills and resources to devise their own control systems and will prove unresponsive to regulatory demands. Enforcing against them will be difficult and expensive under PBR.

Regulatory dynamism may also be impacted by such communications. After a regulator has conducted a host of negotiations with firms on the suitability of their control systems, it may be difficult to institute changes as this will prompt a need to re-open numbers of negotiated settlements. The tendency of the regulator may, accordingly, be to revisit discussions only periodically and dynamism will diminish the more these periods lengthen (the duration of which will often be a function of negotiation costs and the regulatory resources that are available).

Principles-based regulators routinely have to make judgements on the degree to which they will supplement their published principles with explanatory guidance, policy statements, advice notes, and so on. Certain parties may push hard for these more precise prescriptions. Smaller and lower-capacity firms will do so because they want to be spared (or assisted with) the task of working out what they are called upon to do. Creative compliers (Type 3 firms) tend to press in this direction because they see the issuing of precise rules as opportunities to work around the requirements made. The 'pressures to explain' that result may be hard to resist. When regulators decline to state in detail what their principles require they will be vulnerable to protests that: 'They do not even know what their own rules mean!' If they do issue detailed rules they become more vulnerable not only to creative compliance but to charges that their rules and principles are inconsistent: that mixes of rules and principles lead to uncertainty; and that new guidelines are manifestations of 'regulatory creep' and increasing red tape. When explanatory rules proliferate there is potentially the further objection that PBR has given way to more restrictive rule-based regulation.

When regulators take enforcement actions against firms the latter will tend to respond by demanding more guidance on the meaning of principles and the more severe the sanctioning approach, the harder it will be to withstand the pressure to operate with precise rules. This may create tensions between the regulator's needs to enforce and its efforts to sustain a PBR regime.

Finally, operating PBR may render the assessment of the regulator's performance difficult. If, for instance, firms are required to act 'with integrity' or 'fairly', the degree to which these terms are subject to variations of interpretation means that any assessments are infused with contested qualitative judgements. A danger is that, because this impedes the clear establishing of outcome measures, the evaluation system focuses on compliance with processes rather than outcomes—a mode of assessment that, furthermore, may be at tension with the regulator's risk-based approach to assessment.

Changing Behaviour: GRID as a Positive Approach to Enforcement Tools

'Compliance', 'deterrence', and 'responsive regulation' approaches to enforcement tell regulators only a limited amount about the kinds of intervention tools to apply in order to change behaviour: whether inspections or self-monitoring processes should be used, for instance. They also provide limited help in matching intervention styles to the kinds of firms being regulated, or indeed to the kinds of risks involved. This is a gap in analysis because some intervention tools work well with some kinds of firm and not others. Some risks justify the use of expensive and intrusive intervention tools and others do not.

An alternative, more targeted approach to intervention comes to grips with these issues and customizes intervention methods according the types of firms dealt with and the kinds of risks at issue. This is the approach that Black and Baldwin have called the GRID (the Good Regulatory Intervention Design).[12] It not only offers a guide to the kinds of intervention tools that can be expected to produce most positive outcomes, it also offers a steer on the degree of intensity with which such tools should be applied.

Let us consider a sample of the kinds of intervention tools that, say, an environmental regulator might be expected to possess. These are set out in Table 4.12.

Table 4.12 Common intervention tools

Screening and rule-based strategies

1. Exemptions without notification or registration

2. Exemptions with notification or registration

3. Registration subject to conditions

4. Application of general binding rules without notification/registration

Inspection and monitoring strategies

5. Inspections on site

6. Audits of control systems

7. Proxy/themed/random monitoring

8. Advice and assistance visits to sites

9. Reactive investigations, responding to complaints, whistle-blowing or post-incident

investigations

10. Surveillance

11. Self-monitoring and self-certification by regulated firms

Engagement and incentive strategies

12. Information campaigns; generic advice, codes, and guidance

13. Dialogues with firms/other interested parties

14. Industry-led solutions

15. Incentive strategies

---

[12] This section is based on J. Black and R. Baldwin, 'When Risk-Based Regulation Aims Low: A Strategic Framework', *Regulation and Governance* 6 (2012): 131–48.

The resources required to use these tools on the ground will vary according to context but in a hypothetical application they might be coded, as in Table 4.12, where the symbols indicate the following:

LOW COST	MEDIUM COST	HIGH COST
●	■	▲

The positive regulator would avoid using expensive and intrusive intervention tools unless necessary and would be aware, as noted, that the effectiveness of any given kind of tool is likely to vary across firm-types as in Table 4.13.

Table 4.13 Firm-types and the effectiveness of intervention tools

	Tools of high potential (Some examples)	Tools of low potential (Some examples)
Well-Intentioned High Capacity	Screening tools (1–4) Audits of control systems (6) Self-monitoring (11) Information campaigns etc. (12)	Inspections on site (5) Surveillance (10)
Well-Intentioned Low Capacity	Inspections on site (5) Advice and assistance (8) Information campaigns etc. (12)	Screening tools (1–4) Self-monitoring (11)
Ill-Intentioned High Capacity	Inspections on site (5) Audits of control systems (6) Surveillance (10) Incentive strategies (15)	Screening tools (1–4) Self-monitoring (11)
Ill-Intentioned Low Capacity	Inspections on site (5) Proxy/themed/random monitoring (7)	Screening tools (1–4) Audits of control systems (6) Self-monitoring (11)

Table 4.13 indicates not only that intervention tools tend to vary in effectiveness according to type of firm, but that positive regulators would feel more worried as they progress down the list of firm-types, and would be inclined to intervene more strongly. Nor would positive regulators be unaware that firms who currently fall into one of the above categories might change their natures (e.g. with managerial shifts). Where such a regulator anticipates a movement in the character of a firm it would take this into account—by, for instance, considering a movement in intervention tools to reflect such a change.

Turning to kinds of risks, the more worrying these are, the more justified a positive regulator will feel in deploying higher levels of enforcement
resources and in intervening more intrusively in business activity. The
positive regulator will be highly aware that risks may change over time
and, thus, risks will be a special concern not only if they are currently large
but also if they have the potential to develop into larger risks in the intervals between the regulator's re-appraisals of risks.

A breakdown of risks would look as indicated in Table 4.14. In the
table 'inherent' means that the activity is not capable of causing harms in
the stated category, 'net' means that (though such harms could be
caused) the risk is placed in this category because good risk management reduces the probability of a harm occurring. Changes to inherent
risks may occur when the nature of the activity shifts (e.g. new, more
dangerous chemicals are used in a process) and changes to net risks may
result when there is a shift in the quality of the risk management system
used by the regulated firm.

Table 4.14 Risk types

Low risks, stable	• Inherent low risks or net low risks, the levels of which are not likely to change in the periods between regulators' risk reviews.
Low risks, unstable	• Inherent low risks or net low risks the levels of which may change in the periods between regulators' risk reviews.
Medium risks, stable	• Inherent medium risks or net medium risks the levels of which are not likely to change in the periods between regulators' risk reviews.
Medium risks, unstable	• Inherent medium risks or net medium risks the levels of which may change in the periods between regulators' risk reviews.
High risks	• High risks that are likely to remain so.

If firm-types and risk types are plotted together this produces a framework for selecting intervention tools and a basis for reviewing the intensity with which tools are used—see Figure 4.2.

The large arrows on the axes indicate increasing regulatory concern,
and an inclination to use more expensive and intrusive intervention
tools where these would be effective. The light grey, medium grey, and
dark grey sub-squares indicate the degree of intensity with which tools
are used (the darker the grey the greater the intensity). Thus, tools such
as inspections or advice visits can be used intensively (every month) or
non-intensively (every year). Towards the bottom right of the GRID
more intensive tools (such as on-site inspections) would be used with
greater frequency.

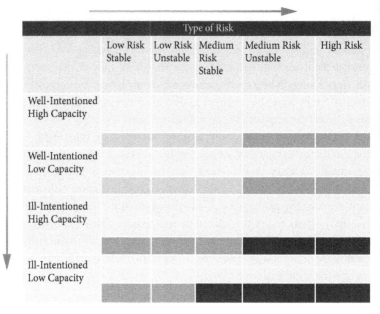

Figure 4.2 The GRID (Good Regulatory Intervention Design)

The GRID, moreover, offers some guidance on choosing modes of regulator to firm interaction. A given intervention tool, such as inspection, can be accompanied by a range of actions from negotiations or hard-line prosecutions.

The GRID suggests that, as with intensity of use, a movement towards the bottom right of the GRID will tend to justify the use of more urgent and insistent modes of interaction. Thus, 'compliance' modes, such as negotiations, may prove productive and appropriate with Well-Intentioned, High Capacity firms that present low risks, but a move to much tougher approaches, such as prosecutions and licence suspensions, may be called for when Ill-Intentioned, Low Capacity firms present medium or high, risks.

The GRID does not rule out there being contexts in which expensive and intrusive tools (such as on-site inspections) may have to be used occasionally to keep contact with even the best operators: the Well-Intentioned, High Capacity firms. On-site inspections and site visits may have to be used now and then to indicate to firms and the public that the regulator is not complacent. This may especially be the case where there are dangers that low or medium risk operations will become high risks with a decline in operator performance. If this is not done, political problems may arise—as was seen with Ofsted in 2019.

Case in point: Ofsted

From 2012 onwards, English schools that were rated 'outstanding' by Ofsted were exempted from routine inspections in order to free them from external intervention. (This exemption came from the Government, not Ofsted.)

A press outcry followed revelations in 2019 that:

- One in 20 children in England was in a school that had not been inspected for more than 10 years.
- There were 1,010 'outstanding' schools that had not had a visit from Ofsted in a decade.
- From September 2018 to the end of March 2019, only 16 per cent of formerly 'outstanding' schools kept their top grade on re-inspection. Twenty-five per cent dropped to 'requires improvement' and 5 per cent were 'inadequate'. Fifty-four per cent fell to 'good'.

In September 2019, the Secretary of State for Education announced that outstanding schools in England would no longer be exempt from routine Ofsted inspections.

The advantage of the GRID approach is that it provides a systematic rationale and a strategists' check list. It is alive to the reality that intervention tools vary in effectiveness across different kinds of firm and it takes on board the relevance of risk levels, and risk dynamics, to both choices of intervention tool and the intensity with which these are used. It thus takes on board two key dimensions of firms: their abilities to manage risks (which are incorporated in GRID categorizations of risks) and their likely responsiveness to different intervention tools (which GRID reflects in categorizing their intentions and capacities). By attending to these matters it directs attention to the lowest-cost methods that are likely to prove effective in given contexts and it offers a strategic performance measure.

In order to implement a GRID approach, a positive regulator must generate the data that allows it to characterize firms and risks according to the breakdowns used above. In practice the past compliance records of firms, together with field inspectors' feedback reports will provide evidence for characterizing firms' intentions and capacities. The use of other proxy measures, such as firms' performances in responding to regulators' requests for information or risk mitigation actions, can be developed. With risks, the modes of analysis currently used for risk-based regulation will be relevant but the GRID suggests that special attention should be paid to the volatility of risks. It is not enough, for example, to know if a risk lies in the 'medium' category, there is a need to assess whether it is liable to remain 'medium' or to escalate during the periods between risk evaluations.

Where, of course, potential risks arise from the actions of start-ups or new market entrants, the regulator will not have any past compliance records or other historical data that can be used to apply the GRID approach. In such cases, entry screening may have to be used in the case of significant levels of potential risk, and the onus may have to be placed on the firm to demonstrate its good intentions and high capacities to the regulator. In the period before the regulator is able to characterize the firm and categorize the relevant risks it will feel justified in using more inter-ventionist methods of control and in engaging with the firm relatively intensively.

Conclusions

Positive regulatory enforcement demands attention to the stage at which interventions are made and to any opportunities to encourage and harness firms' inclinations and capacities to comply voluntarily with rules and regulations. Enforcement actions revolve around two key issues—which firms to go after and what to do in order to change behaviour. Risk-based regulation offers a way of prioritizing targets for attention but, as seen above, it is more infused with qualitative judgements than might at first have appeared to those who saw it as a mathematical and certain guide to regulatory decisions. Nor does risk-based regulation assist a great deal on choices of intervention strategy. Selecting the important risks and the important problems is, furthermore, a considerable challenge for both risk-based regulation and problem-centred regulation.

In looking at different ways of changing behaviour, 'compliance', 'deter-rence', and 'responsive' approaches all brought strengths and weaknesses (as did rule-based and principle-based regulation). Collectively, though, they did not go so far as the GRID approach in combining attention to two needs: matching intervention tools to firm-types and taking on board both the levels of risks and their volatility.

The discussion of GRID emphasizes, again, the need for the positive regulator's awareness, intelligence, and dynamism. If a targeted system of enforcement is to be furthered it has to build on high awareness and intelligence regarding the different kinds of firms and risks within its domain, but also on dynamism and an ability to come to grips with changes in firms' intentions and capacities, and with risk volatilities.

5

Positive Regulation in a Changing World

All regulators deal with sets of issues that are constantly changing. Economic circumstances and technologies develop, and market structures alter as new products are launched, providers come and go, consumer preferences shift and so on. Positive regulators will be aware of such changes (anticipating them when feasible), they will have information on the nature of such changes, and they will respond dynamically to any such shifts. In doing so, central strategic issues will be: how best to respond to those new activities, technologies, and operators that do not sit easily within current regulatory frameworks; how to encourage healthy innovations by businesses; and how regulatory regimes can be adjusted in ways that impose least costs on firms, consumers, and others. These three issues are the focus of this chapter.

Responding to New Challenges and Risks

If a new technology or product is possibly harmful, regulators face a number of challenges in detecting and evaluating the new risk so that a response can be developed. A difficulty for risk-based regulators is, as already noted, their tendency to focus on the current basket of risks and to be slow to recognize and come to grips with new risks, especially if these are systemic or diffused rather than attached to a single site. That is why there is value in carrying out a percentage of random investigations within a risk-based regime.

With new activities, the evidence on the existence or extent of an alleged risk will often be limited and, here, the precautionary principle comes into play. This principle suggests that in those cases in which there is a suspected risk of harm to the public or the environment, there should be a willingness to take action in advance of conclusive scientific proof of the need for action. The principle was recognized in EU law and Principle 15 of the 1992 Rio Declaration, which stated that: 'Where there are threats of serious or irreversible damage, lack of full scientific certainty shall not be used as a reason for postponing cost-effective measures to prevent environmental degradation.'

Case in point: Icelandic volcanic dust and air safety

The 2010 eruption of Eyjafjallajökull in Iceland was followed by concerns that the emitted volcanic dust would damage aircraft engines. This resulted in the largest air-traffic shut-down since the Second World War. Airspace was closed over much of northern Europe from 15 to 23 April, and airspace was closed intermittently in different parts of Europe in the following weeks, as the path of the ash cloud was tracked. The International Air Transport Association (IATA) estimated daily losses to the airline industry worldwide to be £130 million a day.

Airlines were highly critical of what they saw as unnecessary closures based on fears rather than hard evidence.

In May 2010, the UK Civil Aviation Authority (CAA) issued new rules that would allow planes to fly at higher ash densities than formerly permitted, but, after further airport closures, airlines criticized the amended regulations. British Airways chief executive Willie Walsh said: 'I am very concerned that we have decisions on opening and closing of airports based on a theoretical model. There was no evidence of ash in the skies over London today, yet Heathrow was closed.'

He said that airlines flew safely in other parts of the world where there was volcanic activity.

General arguments in favour of precautionary action can be seen in Table 5.1.

Table 5.1 General arguments in favour of precaution

- By the time that 'full' evidence arrives it may be too late to take effective or affordable action.
- The costs of dealing with a possible harm may rise rapidly before 'full' evidence arrives.
- Serious or irreversible damage may occur before full evidence is available.
- In some cases no amount of research will produce 'full' evidence.
- Precautionary action avoids the regulatory paralysis that would result from an endless search for strong evidence.

In the consumer context, proponents of precaution argue that where evidence is uncertain, it is better to act to protect consumers (e.g. by restricting the sale of a product) than to come down on the side of producers by allowing products to enter markets freely and then acting later if this is seen to be necessary (see the points made in Table 5.2).

Table 5.2 When the evidence is uncertain: arguments for consumer rather than producer protection

- It is more important to protect consumers from harm than to enhance producer welfare.
- Producers reap most of the benefits of new technologies; they should, accordingly, bear most of the risks and costs.
- Consumers merit greater protection than industry, since they have less information on, and fewer resources to deal with, hazards introduced by producers.
- Lay persons should be accorded legal rights to bodily security. Minimizing industry risks on efficiency grounds offends notions of such security and would be morally offensive.
- Producers may not always be able to compensate persons harmed by their products; it is better, accordingly, to come down on the side of eliminating harms at source.
- If there is uncertainty about the level of harm, it is difficult to justify imposing an unknown risk on consumers.
- On democratic grounds there ought to be no imposition of risks without the informed consent of those who are to bear the risks.
- If consumers have not given informed consent, industry ought to bear the burden of proving that imposing a consumer risk is justified.
- Minimizing consumer risk is less likely to threaten social and political stability than minimizing producer risk.

Source: Adapted from K. S. Shrader-Frechette, *Risk and Rationality Philosophical Foundations for Populist Reforms* (University of California Press, 1991).

Many critics of precaution allege that the precautionary principle is so vague and given so many different meanings that it invites arbitrary and often speculative action by regulators. The effect of this, they say, is to impede or paralyse technological and economic progress without real justification or evidence of any serious risk or harm. They may add that the principle is open to exploitation by politically powerful groups that are able to build on evidential uncertainties to press for regulation by capitalizing on popular fears, phobias, and anxieties (resulting in what Cass Sunstein has called 'laws of fear'[1]). A counter-argument, of course, is that the producers of new risks may themselves be politically powerful and inclined to exploit the general public's ignorance of risks and their multiple limitations of reason and volition—as documented by behavioural science.

On some views, the precautionary principle produces unjustifiably protectionist or aggressive regulation and the principle, moreover, is said to be far from risk-free because stopping progress by banning particular practices or products may unjustifiably accept existing levels of risk, or may encourage the acceptance of greater risks by increasing the consumption of products or substances that were adopted before the passing of precautionary rules. Applying the principle, moreover, is said by some to draw attention away from real issues of risk trade-offs in favour of a search for some utopian life free of risks.

Case in point: The approval of new drugs for cancer and AIDS

In 1990 the US National Committee to Review Current Procedures for Approval of New Drugs for Cancer and AIDS said that the Government should speed up approval of experimental AIDS and cancer drugs by requiring less evidence of the drugs' effectiveness before they are put on the market.

The panel said that desperately ill patients were prepared to accept the greater risks inherent in the use of such medications. It added: 'Faced with the consequences of a lack of therapy for AIDS and cancer, an expanded mechanism for early access to investigational drugs is morally, ethically and scientifically justified . . . for cancer and AIDS patients time is running out.'

The panel advocated that for these life-threatening diseases the Government should approve new drugs 'at the earliest possible point in their development' and, in any event, 'earlier than has been true in the past'.

Committee Chair, Dr Louis Lasagna, said thousands of lives were lost each year because of delays in approval and marketing of AIDS and cancer drugs.

The panel reasoned that: 'Some of the drugs may eventually be found either to be ineffective or to present an unacceptable benefit-risk ratio, but patients with life-threatening diseases who have no alternative therapy are entitled to make this choice.'

---

[1] C. Sunstein, *Laws of Fear: Beyond the Precautionary Principle* (Cambridge University Press, 2005).

A further argument against precaution is made by those who attack regulators for their supposed tendencies to intervene excessively—namely that such inclinations should be countered by policies that consciously favour non-intervention when the evidence supporting regulating is uncertain.

On consumer safety in particular, the critics of precaution are liable to argue that, even if one accepts the value of consumer protection, there are a number of reasons for favouring producer rather than consumer protection and, accordingly, inclining towards permissive rather than precautionary stances. Thus, where there is strong evidence that the costs of prevention and compliance are liable to be extremely high and there is weak evidence of any risk of serious or irremediable harm, it may be contended that precaution is unduly restrictive and that it is preferable to counter any problems at the act or harm stage. Thus, precaution sceptics are likely to emphasize the case for using resilience strategies that are designed to limit harms and for 'non-regulatory' responses to possible risks, such as disclosures and insurance responses. They might also propose 'piloting' approaches in which potentially risky activities are allowed subject to periodic reviews and re-assessments of the need for any response. A strategy of precautionary regulation, they might emphasize, involves high opportunity costs since the search for solutions to all risks is extremely expensive.

How then is the positive regulator to tread a path through these conflicting arguments? The answer lies through an awareness that the precautionary principle is just that—a principle to be weighed against others and applied with judgement rather than treated as a precise and binding rule. In exercising such judgement, the positive regulator will look for important (non-binding) steers towards or against precaution. These may include the following.

- Where there is plausible evidence to raise the issue of a possible harm that is catastrophic in magnitude or irremediable (or both), this favours precaution.
- Where potential business/producer benefits are modest and there is a significant possible harm, this favours precaution.
- If the costs of dealing with a risk are rising rapidly this favours precaution.
- The availability of low-cost, effective controls favours precaution.
- Where the public have a high dread of the possible risk this favours precaution.
- If those creating the potential risk are far better placed to evaluate risks and harms than the state or consumers, this favours precautionary

action until those creating the risk demonstrate credibly that risks are acceptable.

- If the evidential basis for action is likely to improve in advance of substantial harm this favours an adaptive or incremental approach rather than strict precaution.
- If expected compliance and other costs of regulation are high, and the risk/harm is low, this does not favour precaution.
- If the anticipated cost-effectiveness of potential actions at the act or harm stage is high (e.g. where cost-effective steps could be taken to deal with a dangerous situation that has emerged, or to limit the impact of any harms) this does not favour precaution.
- When precautionary action to reduce one risk involves a material increase in (or reduction in control of) another risk, that trade-off should not be forgotten.

Positive regulation demands that, even if there is a case for regulating on a precautionary basis, the modes of control used should be as enabling as is feasible. Precaution is not an excuse per se for highly restrictive interventions such as prohibitions. In some circumstances, the appropriate precautionary measures may involve such steps as granting permissions to producers subject to limitations, periodic reviews, or obligations to supply evidence on impacts. Precaution in such cases can be a seen as an ongoing process of learning, feedback, and continuous assessment of evidence and response.

The positive regulator will pay special attention to intelligence and data issues when new risks and evidential uncertainties are at issue. It will keep informed about researches that potentially provide evidence relating to the risks and harms at issue. It will modify its approach according to the emerging information on these matters.

Encouraging Innovation

Business innovations can be valuable in generating new solutions to problems. They may introduce, for instance, fresh technologies that offer cleaner, more efficient, more sustainable and superior services to consumers. When new products and services are launched into markets, this may stimulate competition by laying down a challenge to existing businesses.

Whether desirable innovations will be produced by large or smaller firms will depend on a series of factors. In some sectors the scale and financial advantages of larger firms may facilitate research and development, though large firms with secure positions may focus on improving established products and technologies rather than changing paradigms. In certain sectors, smaller firms and new entrants may be more likely to produce radical changes to products and technologies.

Case in point: Uber

The ride-sharing service, Uber, has its origins in 2009 after the company's two co-founders could not find a taxi in Paris during a snowstorm. The basis of the original company, UberCab, was a simple idea: What if you could request a ride right from your mobile phone? With UberCab, this became possible: all a rider had to do was open their mobile phone, tap a button, and they could find an affordable ride in minutes.

In 2010 UberCab was renamed Uber, and the company raised $1.25 million in capital funding to expand. Ten years later, with 75 million global customers and three million dedicated drivers in 83 countries, Uber had radically changed the ride-sharing services market.

Where innovations are likely to spring from new entrants to markets, there is a case for positive regulation to encourage the introduction of new approaches by these operators, as well as from existing operators who possess imagination and creativity.

As noted when discussing 'win-win' in Chapter 2, certain formulations of laws incorporate flexibilities and are much more friendly to business-devised innovations than others and it is arguable that, in some circumstances, regulation can act as a stimulus for innovation.

Regulation can, however, discourage innovation for a number of reasons that are worth recapping. Delays caused by regulatory uncertainties (regarding, for example, potential compliance with new obligations) can discourage new entrants and innovators; and finance may be more difficult to obtain (or to source at competitive rates) because of regulatory unknowns. Investors may prefer the safe bet of established technologies that are controlled with familiar regulations. Smaller entrants to markets will also find that regulatory costs impact more severely on them (as a proportion of turnover) than on larger, established operators, and they will, accordingly, be placed at a disadvantage in competing with incumbents. This disadvantage is exacerbated when fresh entrants to markets face new controls that have immediate effect—in comparison to the rules applied to established operators which are phased-in.

Regulation, moreover, can tend to drive incremental technological improvements rather than true innovations. When, for instance, regulatory regimes demand the adoption of 'best available technology', this encourages the use of best versions of existing systems. In addition, the tendency to apply stricter standards to new technologies creates incentives to prolong the use of old technologies and to seek to modify these if necessary.

Positive regulators can, however, adopt strategies that are designed to encourage innovators. They can counter the above incentives to favour old technologies by ensuring, for instance, that the regulations covering new technologies will be no more onerous that those applicable to existing operations. On the collaborative model, procedures can be used to give innovative firms a voice in the design or mode of introduction of regulations governing new operations or products. Regulators and firms can even collaborate on projects to develop new technological or other solutions to problems and responses to risks. Where laws allow, regulators can ease the path of new entrants by granting 'innovation waivers' that give exemptions from regulations, or extended compliance schedules (under certain conditions) to firms that work with new technologies or products. Alternatively, they can permit companies that intend to conduct new business activities to apply for special regulatory treatment on a firm-specific basis (as in Japan). When enforcing, regulators can reduce innovation risks by undertaking to deal leniently with firms that engage in new activities, fail to satisfy the rules but make good faith attempts to comply (a 'fail-soft' approach). More radically, the regulators can act to institute changes directly—for example by banning a product or chemical. Often this will galvanize adaptive business innovation, as when superior substitutes emerged to replace polychlorinated biphenyls (PCBs), phosphate detergents, asbestos and chlorofluorocarbons (CFCs).

Enabling regulatory strategies are, as argued above, generally preferable to restrictive approaches but more specific programmes for encouraging innovation can also be adopted. Thus, the Financial Conduct Authority launched its Project Innovate in 2014 with the precise aim of fostering the development of new products and services that could enhance consumers' experiences and outcomes. The FCA's various Project Innovate initiatives demonstrate a range of innovation nurturing steps (see Table 5.3).

Table 5.3 FCA Project Innovate: six initiatives

Initiative	Description
Request Direct Support	• Gives tailored regulatory support for innovative firms.
Advice Unit	• Provides feedback to firms, automated advice and guidance.
Regulatory Sandbox	• Provides a 'safe place' in which firms can test innovative products without immediately incurring the normal regulatory constraints.*
Global Financial Innovation Network (GFIN)	• A network of fifty organizations committed to supporting financial innovation in the interests of consumers.
RegTech	• A project to explore how new technologies can be used to improve firms' experiences with regulation—e.g. to streamline regulatory compliance.
Engagement	• Proactive engagement with firms to make sure their potential for consumer-friendly innovation is not being held back by regulatory considerations.

*See FCA, *Regulatory Sandbox* (FCA, November, 2015).

Direct support and advice units help firms, especially smaller ones, to cope with the regulatory uncertainties involved in launching innovations and they lower the costs that firms incur in devising compliant risk control systems. As will be returned to below, they help firms cope with the regulatory changes that government agencies make in response to innovations. The downside of support and advice systems is that they can make it more difficult for regulators to take subsequent enforcement actions as firms may claim that they have obtained assurances on compliance from the regulator that estop such steps.

Sandboxing allows the testing of innovative products without subjection to the regulations that would otherwise apply. The model developed by the FCA and launched in 2016 provides a ready example. In that instance, the sandbox was introduced in order to encourage 'disruptive innovation' as a spur to competition. The procedure was designed to reduce delays in entering markets; to improve access to funding for new projects; and to improve the range of products available to consumers. It was planned as a process that would lower costs and regulatory risks to firms and allow the regulator to work with the innovators to design appropriate safeguards for consumers.

Procedurally, firms apply to the FCA for entry to the sandbox. Authorization to enter will be subject to restrictions that allow testing (but not 'full' restrictions). The FCA agrees on a case-to-case basis the disclosure, protection, and compensation provisions appropriate to testing together with measures for outcome reporting. Safety is offered to firms within the sandbox by a number of devices: 'no enforcement letters' that rule out enforcement provided that the firm adheres to the requirements agreed with the sandbox unit and does not harm FCA objectives; individual guidance that protects the firm from FCA action if followed; and waivers or modifications of rules for sandbox firms. After testing, the firm submits a report on outcomes and the FCA reviews this. The firm then decides whether to offer the new product outside the sandbox. If such a move is made to full commercial activity, the full range of relevant regulatory controls will replace the entry restrictions.

A cited benefit of sandboxing is that it can level the playing field between start-ups and incumbents by helping small firms to come up to speed with the regulatory system. It may also bring a worthwhile 'badge of honour' to firms that are admitted to the sandbox—though this will disadvantage firms who are not accepted.[2] A 2018 study by Deloitte suggested that a majority of firms found the authorization process 'daunting' and the challenges of testing considerable. Nevertheless, useful levels of assistance were reported to have been received from the regulator, the overall experiences of firms were said to be very positive, and working within the sandbox generally helped firms to refine products and to work positively with the regulatory system. Here there is a contrast with the US experience with innovation waivers, which have been said not to have produced their intended effects to any impressive degree. The cause of this in some cases, however, may have been poor implementation of the device.[3]

The range of innovation oriented mechanisms used in the financial sector demonstrates that positive regulators can do much to foster new products and services as well as to encourage new entries to business sectors. As ever, the impact of such strategies depends to a considerable degree on the level of resourcing enjoyed by the regulator. In relation to sandboxing, the above discussion indicates that the regulator has to devote a considerable level of resources to each sandboxed firm and this may rule out the processing of large numbers of firms (the FCA has sandboxed between forty and fifty firms per year since 2016). That said, the impact of a small number of innovations may be extremely valuable in driving a sector forward.

---

[2] Deloitte, *A Journey through the FCA Regulatory Sandbox* (London: Deloitte, 2018).
[3] See N. Ashford, C. Ayers, and R. Stone, 'Using Regulation to Change the Market for Innovation', *Harvard Environmental Law Review* 9(2) (1985): 419–66.

Firms with dissimilar profiles, moreover, may respond in different ways to the various strategies that are used to encourage innovation. Table 5.4 suggests some broad divergences.

Table 5.4 Innovation-enhancing strategies and different types of firm

Type of firm	Strategies with high potential to encourage innovation
1. Well-Intentioned High Capacity	• Principles based regulation/meta-regulation • Incentive based regulation • Trading mechanisms • Engagement • RegTech
2. Well-Intentioned Low Capacity	• Request direct support • Advice unit • Regulatory sandbox • RegTech • Regulator-mandated initiatives
3. Ill-Intentioned High Capacity	• Incentive based regulation • Trading mechanisms • RegTech
4. Ill-Intentioned Low Capacity	• RegTech • Regulator-mandated initiatives

The positive regulator will be aware of these variations in responsiveness. To take one example, where firms have lower levels of expertise than the regulator (e.g. in an industry marked by large numbers of small traditionalist 'low capacity' operators) innovation may best be driven by the regulator mandating an initiative such as a move to a new process or technology. The converse will be likely where the operators in a sector are large and fewer in number, 'high capacity' and closer to the technological cutting-edge than the regulator. As ever, the regulator that is aware, intelligent, and dynamic will be best placed to customize the approach according to such variations.

Changing Regulatory Regimes at Lowest Cost

Regulators often face competing demands when considering adjustments to their systems. On the one hand, they will be aware that regulated firms value the regulatory stability that will allow them to plan activities and investments. On the other hand, firms will want the regulatory changes that will allow them to adapt to new market conditions, launch new types of product, and that will provide regulatory improvements and adjustments to address any imperfections in the current regime.

Positive regulation demands that changes be made at minimal cost. It is important, therefore, to be clear about the kinds of changes that can impact on the scale of firms' costs and on how they can be passed on to others.

Major such changes can be set out as in Table 5.5. It should be noted that the emphasis here is on potential cost increases but regulators may institute changes that will reduce costs (e.g. by extending the periods for filing returns).

Table 5.5 Changes that may impact on business costs

Change	Example
Legal obligations/ standards	• More stringent environmental requirements are imposed and this calls for more spending on abatement.
Organizational structures, institutions	• The regulator closes down its compliance advisory team, which increases uncertainties and the time taken to launch products on the market.
Regulatory objectives	• The regulator changes its interpretation of the statutory mandate and demands stricter controls.
Regulatory procedures	• Figures have to be filed every six months instead of annually.
Intervention styles/ types of sanctions	• The regulator shifts from a 'compliance' to a 'deterrence' strategy and increases prosecutions.
Accounting/financial methodologies	• The regulator changes the accounting assumptions that are used to calculate costs of capital when setting price controls.
Regulatory charges	• Firms have to pay more for inspections.

Such changes may be driven by new primary or secondary legislation, or they may result from a court decision. They may be the product of funding decisions by central government or may stem from new requirements imposed by domestic or supra-national governmental bodies. Many of the above changes may also be made by the regulator on its own account. Thus, it might issue and follow a new policy, interpretation, or guidance note; it might reallocate resources; or it could change its own procedures and structures.

What is clear is that a variety of costs can be impacted by such changes. These include the costs of obtaining capital (e.g. where new uncertainties worry potential investors); planning costs (where funds are spent on adjusting strategies to cope with revisions in regimes); and implementing/

adaptive costs (e.g. of re-training staff and investing in new control mechanisms). Delays in launching products or entering markets may be caused by regulatory shifts and may involve new costs as may the sanctions that regulators apply when firms are found not to be compliant with new regulatory systems. Finally, the process costs of doing business may increase when, for example, firms are asked to collect more information for supply to the regulator.

How, then, can the positive regulator make regime changes at lowest cost to firms? Studies of global practice highlight the use of seven processes[4] (see Table 5.6).

Table 5.6 Processes for managing regulatory changes

- Term assurance
- Notice and information
- Negotiations
- Transition programmes, timescales, and reviews
- Oversight systems
- Flexibilities, parallel concessions, and compensation
- Advice, guidance, and assurance

Most of these processes are designed to make regulatory changes more manageable. Businesses commonly do no not object so much to regulatory changes per se as to changes that they have difficulty in managing—because their systems and plans are subject to shocks and sudden disruptions or uncertainties that prove costly. The processes work as follows.

Term Assurance

Term assurance typically involves regulators or governments undertaking not to change certain aspects of their regimes (e.g. regulators' objectives, or statutory obligations, or modes of intervention) within a specified period of time. Examples can range from a commitment to a price path in a price control to a more general commitment on regulatory principles.

A noteworthy example of term assurance is encountered in the New Zealand regulation of network industries. In the new millennium, the New Zealand Government was drawn by 'the allure of certainty' in the regulation of network industries. (Utility companies were worried that

---

[4] See R. Baldwin and M. Cave, *Regulatory Stability and the Challenges of Re-regulating* (Brussels: CERRE, 2013).

when regulators changed their methods of calculating such matters as costs of capital this impacted on utility profitability by feeding through to price controls.) The Commerce Amendment Act 2008 was passed and required the Commerce Commission (the regulator, as well as the competition authority) to publish the 'input methodologies' or regulatory approaches, which it would use for periods of up to seven years. This meant that, unless changes were made through a complex notice and comment procedure, the utilities would enjoy 'stable state' regulation for the stated period.

Inevitably, this regime demanded a high degree of specificity. The statement of input methodology for airport services of 2010 ran to forty-three pages and the Reasons Paper explaining it was 375 pages long. As for the effect of term assurance, the New Zealand experience makes it clear that the process of giving greater certainty by this means can be legally fraught as well as drawn-out and exacting. The level of detail of the New Zealand methodologies made them highly vulnerable to legal challenge on a wide variety of 'on the merits' grounds and it became clear that the legal contestability of such term assurance devices is a key factor that impacts on their capacity to deliver greater certainty.

The optimal durations of terms of assurance are, moreover, difficult to assess. In New Zealand, an initial preparation period of nearly two years and a litigation period of more than two years raised issues about the 'shelf life' of the input methodologies.

Notice and Information

In this approach, the regulators undertake to give notice to firms when they are contemplating changes. A central aim is to render changes more tractable and to avoid the costs associated with shock or surprise changes that firms find expensive to adjust to at short notice. Portugal, for instance, imposes a general obligation of consultation regarding changes in the electricity code and, in the UK, regulators commonly give notice and information. An example of a complex, multi-stage, notice and information process was the consultation that Ofcom undertook following the expiry, on 31 March 2011, of the UK Mobile Call Termination Rules (MTRs).

Some regulators will consult stakeholders on changes in regulatory objectives. Thus, in November 2011, the UK's Ofwat carried out a consultation on charges for new connections. At issue here was a modification of Ofwat's regulatory principles. The regulator adopted a procedure that was designed to reset its regulatory objectives by agreeing them with the stakeholders. In the UK electricity sector, Ofgem has a record of consulting on such matters as proposed changes in modes of assessing the depreciation of assets.

Negotiations

Regulators may address the tractability issue by going beyond the giving of notice. They can offer firms the opportunity to suggest ways in which changes can be effected so as to reduce adjustment costs or increase consumer benefits. Such a process occurred in 2010–12 in the UK, when Ofgem carried out a two-tier consultation process regarding all the ring fence conditions of the Network Operator Licences. Regulators may also assist the firms to plan for change so as to reduce adjustment costs.

Under such arrangements, the potentially negative impacts of regulatory changes are considerably diminished because operators have to be alerted in advance about changes and because they have a chance to give indications to the regulator about the challenges they face in adapting to the new requirements. The aim is to manage changes in a non-punitive way.

Transition Programmes, Timescales, and Reviews

In these processes the regulators implement changes by stages and indicate the timescales by which compliance has to be achieved incrementally. They may also undertake to review regulatory approaches periodically so as to reduce the costs of over-inclusiveness (e.g. the costs created by regulatory constraints that involve undue compliance costs or unnecessarily prevent the exploitation of markets).

Periods of grace can also be used to temper the effects of change. The Portuguese financial services regulator, for instance, has sought to manage regulatory transitions by providing certain operators with such periods during which they have time to adjust to new regulatory rules. Also in Portugal, the change from analogical to digital terrestrial television was staged through a three-year transition interval to allow operators to create all the necessary conditions for the move. In the Italian energy sector, also, the implementation of regulatory changes in some areas has been made conditional on the achieving of relevant technical preconditions. In the UK, Ofcom has used periods of grace to facilitate change and phased changes have been used in Portugal to ease regulatory transitions in the energy sector.

Reviews of regulatory systems and the monitoring of changes constitute another form of change management strategy—one seen in the Italian energy sector. In the French postal and telecommunications sector, the regulator has, on certain issues, promised to engage in reviews of its decisions, taking on board the evolving technological and market conditions.

Oversight Systems

A rather different way to limit the pain caused by regulatory changes is to take steps to ensure that regulators make change-related decisions on the basis of proper evaluations of the relevant evidence. This can be encouraged by use of a variety of devices that will limit regulators' abilities to make unjustified or excessive changes. Thus, decisions and policies can be made subject to review by institutions that will hold regulators to account for their use of discretion and render decisions more transparent, rational, and predictable. Laws, courts, systems of judicial review, and administrative checks and balances can accordingly be used to avoid arbitrary and capricious changes and to foster 'regulatory credibility'.[5]

Flexibilities, Parallel Concessions, and Compensation

Regulators sometimes manage changes by allowing businesses some freedom of scope regarding the means chosen to deliver desired outcomes. In the Italian energy sector, the implementation of regulatory changes in some areas has provided for considerable flexibility on the timing and technologies that can be used to comply with new regulations. This approach was prompted in 2009–11 when the regulator found that, because of competitive pressures and lack of technological capability, not all firms were able to comply with their new duty to replace meter readers within a stipulated time limit.

More radically, regulators can reduce the unwanted impacts of regime shift by allowing changes to be compensated for by balancing concessions. For example, in July 2012, the European Commissioner for the Information Society announced a regulatory change which disappointed operators'

---

[5] See generally B. Levy and P. Spiller, *Regulations, Institutions and Commitment* (Cambridge University Press, 1996).

hopes with respect to one matter, but offered a concession in relation to another. This strategy can be used to reduce overall costs by lowering the frictions involved in a move to a new scenario. Concessions have also been seen in the Spanish, Italian, and UK energy sectors.

Incentives have also been used in the Italian energy sector in order to encourage the embracing of new rules. Monetary awards of up to 5000 euros have been made available to firms who have successfully complied with new regulations and guidance within the stipulated timeframe.

Advice, Guidance, and Assurance

The final commonly used strategy for managing regulatory change is one that seeks to ease transitional difficulties and uncertainties by offering advice or guidelines on new compliance requirements or other regulatory changes. A central aim here is to limit regulatory risks by ensuring a high level of knowledge regarding the behaviour that the regulator will deem to be compliant.

In the Portuguese water sector the regulator has, for instance, given technical feedback to operators and deployed its own laboratories and consultants in order to clarify means of complying with new requirements. The requested opinion is another device that has been used in Portugal— this allows a regulated electricity concern to ask the regulator for a non-binding opinion on a regulation.

In the Portuguese financial services sector, the regulator has been prepared to disclose the market practices that will be accepted or not in the wake of a regulatory change. In the UK, financial regulators have used workshops to inform regulated firms about current and coming enforcement strategies.

A challenge that many regulators around the world have encountered is that offering advice on compliance can make it more difficult to take subsequent enforcement actions against errant firms. As already noted, the latter are liable to contend that what they have done is consistent with the assurances given by the regulator and that the regulator is accordingly estopped from proceeding against them. This will often prompt fraught discussions between a regulator's advisory and prosecution teams regarding the nature of any advice given and whether this has been followed. For this reason, numbers of regulators around the world have either stopped offering prospective compliance advice or have ruled that such advice can only be issued by their enforcing divisions.

Case in point: EPA compliance assistance

The US Environmental Protection Agency (EPA) provides 'compliance assistance' to help regulated entities understand and meet their environmental compliance obligations but it does so in an integrated strategy alongside enforcement and through a single Office of Enforcement and Compliance Assurance.

Choosing Change Management Strategies

As seen above, the challenges presented by different types of regulatory change can potentially be addressed by the use of an array of strategies. In choosing the combination of strategies that will ensure lowest-cost change, the positive regulator will be aware that different categories of costs may be best controlled by different strategies. Thus, in a given context, *term assurance* might be identified as capable of reducing capital and planning costs especially well; *notice and information, negotiations and compliance discussions* and *transition programmes, timescales and reviews* might be expected to have special value in relation to implementation/transition and adaptive costs. Effects on competition might be seen as best dealt with by *parallel concessions and compensation*, and sanctioning costs could be best reduced with strategies of *flexibilities, and advice, guidance, and assurance*. Awareness and information on the above matters offers an organized way of designing a change strategy.

Studies of regulatory change management emphasize a number of messages that positive regulators will heed. A first is that regulatory change is often not a problem, per se, but changes that are low in tractability tend to be problematic. Even changes that are positive in substance may be effected by re-regulation strategies that are unduly wasteful of resources.

A second message is that many regulators have experience of using change management strategies, but very few regulators approach the issue of regulatory change management in an organized way. It is, however, possible to deal with such strategic choices in a conceptually coherent manner.

Finally, there is a point to be drawn about expectations: regulated firms can argue with some force that regulators should refrain from introducing regulatory changes without first considering, not merely the case for change, but also the relative potential of different change management strategies. Positive regulators will be aware of and heed those expectations.

Conclusions: Positive Regulation and Change

Positive regulators have to embrace change and this involves: coping with the new regulatory challenges that innovations throw up; encouraging businesses to engage in innovative practices; and adapting regulatory systems to new circumstances in the most responsive and lowest-cost ways that can feasibly be implemented. The awareness and intelligence of the regulator will be reflected, first, in its ability to anticipate, recognize, and gather information on such new challenges and, second, in its acuity in designing responses to these. Its dynamism will be seen in the energy with which it both encourages business innovations and adapts its own systems accordingly.

PART II
SPECIAL CHALLENGES

6
Can Regulators Ensure Environmental Sustainability?

Sustainability is an urgent concern that grows in importance as the earth's fragility becomes increasingly apparent. Regulating in order to promote sustainability, however, brings a number of challenges. The first section of this chapter discusses those general challenges and the second part deals with a specific issue of central importance to sustainability—the control of carbon emissions.

The Challenges of Regulating for Sustainability

The difficulties associated with regulating for sustainability stem not least from what might be called the 'indeterminacies of sustainability'— the lack of precise and agreed understandings on not merely the *content* of the principle of sustainable development, but on the *force and reach* of the principle.

Content

The *content* of the principles of sustainability and sustainable development is viewed in ways that are peculiarly plentiful and disparate. Sustainability is of concern to a wide variety of interests and communities, it covers a broad policy agenda that transcends portfolios and levels of government, and it commonly prompts political contention. The pursuit of sustainable environmental outcomes, moreover, is very often undertaken in a transnational context and, as has been noted, there are substantial barriers to cooperating to develop policies and laws to achieve such outcomes. These include divergent interests, and cross-jurisdictional differences in conceptions of, and political attitudes to, sustainability. In addition, many entities beyond governments may interact on sustainability issues, from non-governmental bodies and groups of experts to sub-national and supra-national bodies that may be either public or private in constitution and operation. (On transnational issues see Chapter 10.)

Sustainability, moreover, covers the preservation of numbers of resources or values over various periods of time that may extend far into the future. In many formulations it seeks to further a number of priorities and factors that interact in ways that are evidentially uncertain, that are not easily measured, predicted, or quantified and which are often in tension with each other.

Numbers of different disciplines and theories, furthermore, offer their own approaches to sustainability. Familiar in the literature are divergences between environmental, economic, and social conceptions of sustainability and between weak and strong notions. Well-known formulations include: the systematic long-term use of natural resources so that these are available for future generations;[1] development that allows countries to progress economically and socially, without destroying their environmental resources; development that meets global challenges related to poverty, inequality, climate change, environmental degradation, peace and justice;[2] and development in which environmental indicators are as important as economic indicators. Even within a given culture or discourse, different conceptions of content may be applied in different contexts and there may be variations of conception from domain to domain (e.g. environment to health) or across topics covered within one domain.

Sustainable development is thus a malleable and dynamic concept that evolves in response to changes in social, environmental, economic, technological, and other settings. It cannot be assumed that today's conception of sustainable development will hold tomorrow.

A compounding difficulty is uncertainty—as when there is a lack of clarity on the meaning of sustainability that applies in a given context or at a stated time. Many institutions and parties, furthermore, may see 'sustainability' as a concept that neither provides nor demands precise meaning—either because it is an aspirational or theoretical concern or because it is not so much a freestanding objective as a set of considerations to be borne in mind in pursuing other objectives.

---

[1] See *Report of the World Commission on Environment and Development: Our Common Future* (the Brundtland Report) (Oxford University Press, 1987).
[2] See the United Nations Sustainable Development Goals (2015).

Force and Reach

Sustainable development is treated within many settings as a principle of legal relevance. It is found, for instance, in a number of international and national treaties and other legal instruments. In other contexts, however, sustainable development is seen as a political or philosophical, rather than a legal principle. For their part, regulators will see the principle sometimes as a legally binding constraint and, at other times, as a mere policy objective. There is also historical evidence that sustainability appraisals have often been seen as mere paper obligations and exercises.

Some lawyers see the principle as binding law in so far as it forms a basis for enforceable rights and obligations. Others view it as having only indirect force—as a guide to interpretation or a set of values that decision-makers are invited to further. Even where sustainability objectives are contained in legislation, they may be seen by regulators and other parties as secondary rather than primary objectives, or as too broad in nature to demand implementation through policies or programmes. In such cases, the principle may be seen, as noted, to be aspirational only.

Particular uncertainties of force arise in the increasingly common situation in which sustainability requirements flow from transnational regulatory regimes in which instruments range from 'laws' and 'soft-laws' to 'quasi-regulatory' 'governance' and myriad other types of prescription. When private and hybrid (public/private) actors are involved in the promulgation of a variety of sustainability requirements, and, in doing so, carry out the control functions of public bodies, questions arise as to the force of sustainability norms that may possess real but informal authority. The power of such controls may derive as much from membership of a private transnational organization as from formal, state-based laws. In this complex, hybridized world, assessments of force may be multi-dimensional and difficult to determine with precision.

The force of the requirement to further sustainability, moreover, may be seen in substantive or procedural terms: as the obligation to produce certain outcomes; or as a duty to take heed of certain values in decision-making or policy-making processes. In some procedurally oriented usages, the principle imposes an obligation to strive (often by best, or reasonable efforts) to foster sustainable development.

As for force in different contexts, an issue in some jurisdictions has been a lack of clarity on the priority that is given to sustainability objectives that are set out in different statutes. Positions on force can also change over time. Thus, in the 1990s, Ofwat was induced over a period, and through legal argument, to accept that it had a legal duty to recognize sustainability obligations that was not secondary to its duty to ensure affordability of water services.

Even when there is agreement on what 'sustainability' means, there may be different opinions on the *reach* of the principle—the range of environmental or other factors to which the principle applies. Thus, sustainability principles have been seen, in some contexts, as generally observable and, in others, they have been linked to particular projects or sectors. Sometimes it will be uncertain whether the principle is to impact on particular activities or on the complete array of regulatory operations. When sustainability issues straddle the portfolios of various regulatory agencies and government departments, there can also be questions whether the principle of sustainability reaches to the activities of different institutions and who bears responsibility for furthering sustainability. In Australia, for instance, it has been found that uncertainties on these matters have tended to undermine the successful forwarding of sustainability.

As noted in Chapter 2, all regulators need to discharge three essential tasks if they are to succeed. They need to set objectives, deliver substantive outcomes, and meet procedural expectations. When regulators seek to further sustainability they face considerable challenges on all these fronts.

Setting Objectives

Giving content to sustainability objectives is more difficult than in most policy domains for reasons already noted. Economic, environmental, and social perspectives offer their own separate approaches to the formulation of sustainability objectives and the relative priorities of economic, environmental, and social considerations are often unclear. Multiple objectives and values stand potentially to be furthered and trade-offs between present and future gains and losses are involved. There is no readily available, uncontentious way to deal with such matters as the balance between the needs of today's less affluent consumers and the environmental interests of future generations.

Opinions on the content of the principle of sustainability can, furthermore, be strong as well as widely divergent. Sustainability objectives, perhaps more than most regulatory aims, involve a level of contestability that presents powerful regulated concerns with considerable opportunities to grasp the initiative in defining the objectives of a given regime.

A further regulatory challenge is to ensure that consistent approaches to sustainability are adopted throughout relevant regulatory regimes. Even if precise understandings of sustainable development objectives are encountered at the highest policy levels, challenges are likely to be encountered in attempting to apply these conceptions consistently throughout organizations—not least because sustainable development involves very different and complex trade-offs in different sub-sectors or activities, be these fisheries, land contamination, waste management, industrial pollution, or other domains.

When, moreover, numbers of regulators are involved in an area, it may be extremely difficult to ensure that all of these subscribe to a common conception of the content of sustainability objectives. Nor can regulators assume that they will enjoy complete control in giving content to principles of sustainability. Governments may issue guidelines on these matters and both domestic and supra-national courts will have an impact on this front when they make rulings on sustainability issues. In addition, the positions of supra-national bodies can impact on national regulators. The conceptions of sustainable development that regulators operationalize can be expected to reflect the institutional and accountability settings in which they find themselves.

In regulating for sustainability yet another difficulty stems from the tendency of sustainability priorities to change over time. Political shifts present a special challenge for regulators. A regulatory body may use its best endeavours to generate a degree of common understanding on the content, force, and range of sustainability objectives for the purposes of its regime but spanners may be thrown in such works when conceptual shifts occur at the governmental level. Thus, under the Conservative Government of 1990–7, sustainability was seen in economic terms (as the relationship between economic growth and environmental protection) whereas New Labour promulgated a social welfare approach to sustainability after 1997.

A final regulatory challenge arises because the very idea that objectives can be established with some precision may be especially misplaced when dealing with sustainability. As indicated above, some observers argue that the principle of sustainability offers not so much a precise set of aims as a cluster of criteria or values to be taken into account in making decisions on other matters.

All of the above difficulties are compounded by data challenges and evidential uncertainties. Sustainability regulators have to collect and analyse data in order to set objectives and operationalize these but they face the special difficulties of valuing future social and environmental effects—such as intra-generational equity and conservation of biodiversity. Even the levels of currently available data are often insufficient to support the setting of sustainability objectives. These kinds of informational difficulty are added to where the numbers of governmental departments and agencies that are involved in a regulated activity collect data by different methods and according to different framing values and assumptions.

Moving to questions regarding the *force and reach* of sustainability objectives, these pose challenges because of the indeterminacies already described. Regulators need to be clear whether the objectives being set are legally binding or not, whether they are intended to have a degree of precision that underpins implementation or whether they merely set out values or aspirations to be accorded respect in decisions and policies. It must also be understood whether sustainability is a principal or a secondary objective. The role of the objectives within the regulatory regime must also be clear—do they apply generally or to specific projects, institutions, and policy areas only? Do they relate to environmental concerns alone or also to economic and social issues?

Positive regulators can respond to these challenges with awareness, intelligence, and dynamism. In establishing clear objectives, being aware demands advertence to the variety of conceptions of sustainability objectives that have to be accommodated. How can this be done so that legitimate conceptions of sustainability objectives are developed and maintained by regulators? A deliberative approach offers one route. Numbers of commentators have suggested that the way forward lies in developing procedures for consultation and policy development that allow, so far as possible, agreed conceptions of sustainability to be generated in the face of divergences of discourse, interest, and so on.

It is especially important in the sustainability field to identify the array of regulatory stakeholders in the relevant area and to engage them in the processes of policy and decision-making. This is likely to involve discussions on preferred modes (and aims) of participation as well as the tailoring of engagement methods to different stakeholder types. It will demand ongoing dialogues, information exchanges on regulatory proposals and feedback mechanisms together with follow-up processes of monitoring, reporting, and engagement.

Deliberations provide mechanisms for negotiating positions on such matters as the *content*, and the *force and reach* of sustainability principles. They also allow the regulator to attune its own position to the approaches being adopted by other parties and to changes in such approaches. A central challenge is to bring such deliberations into a focus that allows actions to be taken. Positive regulators must, accordingly, develop leadership skills and managerial qualities as well as procedures, cultures, and strategies for ensuring that there is consistent buy-in to the given sustainability mission across and within organizations as well as across regulatory tasks and issues.

Delivering Substantive Outcomes

In seeking to deliver appropriate substantive outcomes, the successful regulator will build on clearly identified and legitimated objectives before gathering information about problems, issues, and challenges that need to be overcome to further those objectives. It will then be necessary to devise positive strategies for dealing with identified problems, to make interventions to modify parties' behaviour when necessary to produce desired outcomes at lowest feasible cost, and to assess performance and adapt approaches where necessary.

When gathering information on issues and problems, sustainability regulators are very often confronted by institutional structures and constraints that hinder detection and information collection and which add to the difficulties of collecting data—especially in relation to issues as that are intrinsically complex and contestable (such as matters of equity between generations or classes of consumer). As noted, responsibility for regulating for sustainability is very often shared across agencies and levels of government as well as industrial and community locations. Disparate modes of data collection will be involved and, when different institutions have different ideas about the relative importance of economic, environmental, and social considerations in the pursuit of sustainability, this can lead to a lack of direction in informational work. In addition, different cultures and disciplines, as noted, will tend to see the requirements of sustainability divergently and this will impact on information gathering. If there is to be a coordinated and effective approach, all involved parties have to be engaged in deliberations regarding the content, and the force and reach of sustainability and the route to common data analysis.

Effective institutional coordination will be needed not merely for informational reasons but in order to discharge other key regulatory tasks such as the devising of strategies and the application of these on the ground. Parties who see the force of sustainability in political terms will not see potential intervention strategies in the same way as those who see the principle as legally binding. The measurement difficulties associated with certain social and environmental impacts may impede the fully-informed consideration of regulatory strategies and, more particularly, impact assessments do not lend themselves readily to the integration of economic, social, and environmental issues. This, again, may stand in the way of intelligent strategy development.

When sustainability regulators act in a transnational context there are additional challenges to be faced when devising and applying strategies.[3] Issues often cross borders and have to be addressed with actions taken transnationally at various levels of government by bodies occupying different positions on the scale from public to private. Such governmental diversities, together with variations in firms' characteristics, routinely combine with resource limitations to obstruct the production of technical standards and specifications that are appropriate across the board. Regulatory authority is less secure in such contexts and the sanctions necessary to underpin commands and secure compliance may be lacking. The argument can be made that this demands an escape from old models of law and regulation (which focus on state-centred legal authority and precise prescriptions) and an acceptance that modern transnational law and regulation is, and has to be, a much more messy and 'decentred' mixture of institutional types, kinds of normativity, modes of influence, and governance structures.[4] In Chapter 10 we discuss the special challenges of furthering positive regulation in this transnational context.

Many of the challenges that sustainability regulators encounter in developing strategies will also be faced when interventions are made on the ground in order to modify behaviour. Thus, the methods used to apply any given intervention tool may be subject to contest and it is difficult to ensure that common conceptions of risks, problems, and approaches can be fostered across organizational levels (or across horizontal divisions of departments). When regulatory objectives are highly prone to contest and competing conceptions, the challenges just noted will be all the more severe.

Performance assessment is a special challenge in the field of sustainability. All of the problems of identifying objectives authoritatively will make it difficult to produce performance indicators with secure foundations. Data will also be intrinsically difficult and expensive to gather and analyse in this field because many impacts will lag interventions considerably and

---

[3] See V. Heyvaert, *Transnational Environmental Regulation and Governance: Purpose, Strategies and Principles* (Cambridge University Press, 2019), Ch. 4.

[4] See Heyvaert, *Transnational Environmental Regulation and Governance*.

long timeframes of analysis have to be committed to. In addition, the measurement of non-pecuniary benefits such as environmental and social impacts is intrinsically problematic and expensive. The absence of comprehensive datasets, and fragmentations of these will stand in the way of accurate performance assessments as will the multi-agency nature of sustainability—which will often involve numerous disparities in the data systems.

Similar points can be made regarding regulatory efforts to respond to changes in a dynamic fashion. The various indeterminacies of sustainability principles and objectives will play their own roles in impeding the ability of a regulatory regime to adapt to change. Thus, separation of sustainability concerns into the economic, social, and environmental has been said to underplay the extent to which there is change in each of these conceptions and the interplay between these—it accordingly fosters a static view of the world.

Galvanizing changes of regulatory direction can also be difficult when shifts mean that numbers of regulators and stakeholders have to be coordinated afresh. Where objectives are contested, regulators often have to negotiate numbers of settlements between many parties and the need to engage in complex renegotiations on objectives is a constraint on dynamism.

Sustainability also throws up special impediments to regulatory dynamism for another reason. Regulatory responsiveness has to build on good intelligence and, as just noted, performance assessments involve a host of challenges. These difficulties are frequently compounded because scientific knowledge on natural resource impacts is often limited, uncertain, and expanding so that the regulatory evidence base shifts. If, moreover, strategic and policy modifications are to be driven by performance assessments, feedback systems have to be operated. In the multi-agency world of sustainability, however, numbers of policy processes have to be impacted upon and there may be resistance to adjustments. Agencies will often be attached to their own methods (some systematic, some ad hoc) and considerable efforts may be required to renegotiate collaborative relationships when numbers of institutions are involved in the control regime. Even in the absence of resistance, different agencies will often operate to different timescales and use their own policy learning approaches, both of which factors conduce to systemic inertia.

How can positive regulators address the above delivery challenges? A first task that underpins the successful delivery of outcomes is the collection of relevant data. In discharging this task an aware sustainability regulator will, accordingly, devote much energy to ensuring consistency of approach in data collection and to devising systems that will cope with any mismatches between its breakdown of sustainability issues and the categorizations used by other governmental and regulatory institutions. Here again, deliberative processes have an important role.

The intelligent and dynamic sustainability regulator will, in addition, operate data systems that allow it to assess its performance and which enable it to cope with changes by adjusting its informational approach. Such a regulator will position itself to see the need for any new vision of sustainability that is appropriate and to adjust its information system to reflect that new vision. Feedback systems may be an especially effective way for the intelligent and dynamic regulator to address the indeterminacies of sustainability related policies.

With respect to response development, the aware regulator will be conscious of its institutional context. It will be conscious that, where numbers of agencies and departments, and levels of government are involved in an area, individual institutions may be wedded to particular intervention strategies and this may stand in the way of coherent and coordinated approaches to strategic design. It will also be aware of the effect on strategic choices of varying conceptions regarding the *content* and the *force and reach* of sustainability. Different conceptions favour different regulatory approaches and these may not always cohabit harmoniously. In responding to such disparities the aware regulator will engage in deliberations with the aim of developing a holistic view that overcomes the barriers between disciplines and produces a more integrated conceptual framework—one in which economic, social, and environmental conceptions of sustainability are seen as connected and mutually constitutive.

In regulating for sustainability, moreover, there may be a special need to facilitate discussions on strategy with stakeholders so that disputes about choices of intervention strategy are kept to a minimum.

When interventions are made in order to modify behaviour, the aware regulator will be heedful of special sensitivities regarding particular intervention methods and will seek to manage stakeholder responses to choices of intervention methods. The potential offered by alternative intervention tools in relation to different parties will be taken on board as will potential interactions between tools.

Positive regulators will seek to harness the potential of businesses to develop innovative modes of production and delivery that are more sustainable than current processes and technologies. As noted in Chapter 5, they can adopt a number of approaches to the fostering of innovation, such as using enabling rather than restrictive controls, and processes, such as sandboxing, that facilitate the entry into markets of new operators, technologies, and production processes. At times the regulator may have to institute radical changes in production methods by banning existing processes or substances. Fostering innovation through such strategies may advance sustainability in a way that risk-based regulation finds more difficult. Risk-based regulation tends to focus on controlling the risks that current operations and technologies present, and, as noted in Chapter 3, it may be slow to stimulate a movement to 'change the paradigm' and introduce radical changes to produce operations that are far more sustainable than anything achievable with existing systems.

Under different conditions sustainability objectives may best be served by three distinct responses: (a) policies of diffusion that extend the use of existing, best practice/best available technology approaches to risk control; (b) developing improvements in current best practice methods of dealing with existing risks; (c) radical transformations that move the sector to wholly new production methods.

The appropriate response will turn on such factors as: the availability of opportunities to move to better best practices or radical new (more desirable) technologies; the breadth of current use of best practice methods; and the profile of the industry (whether there are a few highly competent operators or a large, mixed population of firm-types). The need to implement radical changes will depend on the realization and acceptance that current technologies and systems will not meet objectives and the identification of ways to meet objectives with new operational methods.

As for stimulating a movement to more sustainable systems, such shifts may, under different conditions, be driven more effectively either by firms themselves under various self-regulatory arrangements (including metaregulatory and collaborative systems) or by governments and regulators. Table 6.1 outlines some of the major considerations that steer towards either industry/self-regulatory or governmental/regulatory drivers.

Whatever strategy is used, a positive approach to sustainability regulation demands that the regulator be well-placed to assess the performance of the control regime across the core tasks of regulation: from setting objectives to delivering outcomes to meeting procedural expectations—not least because this paves the way for improvements in strategies and processes. Effective performance assessment also provides a basis for both rendering account and seeking continuing approval through processes of justification. Assessments also provide a basis for dealing with changes in conceptions and approaches relating to sustainability. Positive regulators will accordingly devote energy to the developing of commonly understood objectives and performance indicators for sustainability that can be applied consistently across a wide variety of projects.

Table 6.1 Driving change to improve sustainability

Type of response to sustainability challenges	Factors favouring industry or self-regulatory drivers	Factors favouring governmental/regulatory drivers
Diffusing use of current best available technology/control method (BAT).	Slack in sector uptake and usage of BAT. Market incentives (e.g. consumer preferences) that will lead firms to adopt BAT. High numbers of firms with the will and capacity to improve.	Slack in sector uptake and usage of BAT. Absence of factors favouring self-regulation. Regulatory expertise to identify BAT. Regulatory ability to change behaviour through commands, incentives, or other devices.
Improving best available technology/control method (incremental improvement)	Technological opportunities to improve BAT. A sector marked by numbers of firms with the willingness and capacity to improve performance. Market incentives (e.g. consumer preferences) or industry associations that will lead firms to improve BAT.	Technological opportunities to improve BAT. Regulatory expertise to identify ways to improve on BAT. A sector marked by powerful traditionalist incumbents or numbers of firms that are unwilling or unable to improve performance. Absence of market incentives (e.g. consumer preferences or industry associations) that will lead firms to improve BAT. Regulatory ability to change behaviour through commands, incentives, or other devices.
Radical transformations	A sector with a small number of high capacity firms that are willing to innovate radically. Incentives to transform, such as a market that will reward radical innovations that are consistent with socially desired objectives.	Inability to meet objectives with currently used technologies. Absence of market incentives to transform or a lack of the level of industry willingness or expertise that will foster radical changes. Regulatory expertise to identify the need to transform the sector and to calculate how best to do this.

Type of response to sustainability challenges	Factors favouring industry or self-regulatory drivers	Factors favouring governmental/ regulatory drivers
		Regulatory ability to change behaviour through commands, incentives, or other devices.
		Availability of regulatory processes designed to stimulate radical transformations (e.g. sandboxes or innovation waivers).

The ability to modify its approaches responsively is the mark of the dynamic regulator. Such a need for responsiveness applies across all the tasks of regulation, from setting objectives, through all aspects of outcome delivery, to the meeting of procedural expectations. Sustainability is arguably an area whose pervasive indeterminacies, complexities, and shifts mean that adaptive regulation and constant improvement is the only feasible route to satisfactory performance. The dynamic sustainability regulator will place the need to respond to changes at the heart of its deliberations and policy processes.

Meeting Procedural Expectations

The indeterminacies surrounding sustainability make it especially difficult for a regulator to convince parties of its fairness. As noted, complexities in, and contests regarding, sustainability mandates provide myriad opportunities for powerful parties to influence regulatory approaches and actions in a self-serving manner. Accusations of substantive bias and capture are liable, accordingly, to be difficult to defend against.

As for procedural fairness, a special difficulty that many sustainability regulators face is that they operate within decentred, fragmented regulatory regimes in which interests and claims are made by a very wide range of methods and processes.[5] This makes it very difficult to provide

---

[5] J. Black, 'Constructing and Contesting Legitimacy and Accountability in Polycentric Regulatory Regimes', *Regulation & Governance* 2 (2008): 137–64.

assurances of procedural fairness because comparisons cannot readily be made with respect to a single scale—there is little obvious procedural equivalence. Similar issues arise in relation to fairness of access and participation. A message that is open and transparent to one kind of stakeholder may be opaque to another with a different profile. Again, the need to render account and justify regulatory actions involves mirroring challenges since account is often rendered through a host of different types of conversation or claim.

All such challenges are the more severe in the transnational, multi-level governance context in which communications will often flow not from one regulator to a receiving audience but will be the product of a series of decisions by a network of regulatory authorities. When there are multiple such mediations, the messaging that is needed to offer reassurances of fairness and due process becomes especially difficult to deliver.

As for responding to the above challenges, the positive sustainability regulator will operate with processes that meet expectations. Thus, procedures have to be fair, open, and transparent and the regulator has to be able to secure support and legitimation from a wide range of stakeholders. The aware regulator will, accordingly, devote special attention to operating ongoing deliberative processes that are designed to convince parties of its fairness and it will be mindful that the high contestability of the content, and the force and reach of sustainability will perpetually render it very vulnerable to accusations of bias and capture. In seeking to demonstrate procedural fairness, the aware regulator will be conscious that the field of sustainability involves widely varying procedural expectations.

Demonstrating appropriate openness and transparency in the sustainability field gives rise to the same challenges as just mentioned in dealing with fairness of access and participation. A message that is open and transparent to one kind of stakeholder may be opaque to another. The aware regulator, accordingly, will be prepared not only to ensure that interested parties are identified comprehensively but to develop and apply processes that facilitate understandings by the full range of stakeholders. This may require a good deal of bespoke interactions and the resource implications of this will be borne in mind.

The intelligent sustainability regulator will collect such information as allows it to make convincing justificatory claims and it will operate information systems that will take on board the above variations in regulatory actors and expectations. It will also take steps to ensure informational fairness and will be prepared to act in a facilitative role so that it assists and enables participation where this is necessary for the required equivalence (where necessary by packaging information in the form most digestible for the party at issue).

The dynamic regulator will be able to adjust processes quickly to ensure fairness of participation, transparency of processes, and the proper rendering of account. Fresh routes to transparency, for example, will have to be developed as new kinds of issue come on to sustainability agendas and the dynamic regulator will be quick to ensure that parties are not excluded from the relevant processes. Responsiveness to the advent of new regulated concerns and to changes in the receptivity of regulated parties will also be a feature of the dynamic regulator.

Is the routine testing of regulatory proposals through impact assessments likely to contribute positively to meeting the challenges of sustainability regulation? The hope, as expressed by the OECD, is that using impact assessments will ensure that sustainability policies are more evidence-based; that the expected contributions of policies to sustainability will be better revealed; and that participation in decision-making processes will thereby be increased.[6] It can be argued, furthermore, that impact assessments can valuably counteract a number of cognitive weaknesses such as tendencies to exaggerate immediate or publicized effects and to under-value future harms.

Potential problems, however, are not hard to identify. Sustainability issues are notably difficult to feed into impact assessments. Environmental and social considerations, in general, do not lend themselves to ready quantification and, in some contexts, this will lead to their being trumped by economic factors in impact assessments. Methodologically it is difficult to estimate long-term sustainability effects and trade-offs (especially where these occur at different times). Special problems arise with inter- and intra-generational equity considerations and effects concerning which there is scientific uncertainty. Similarly, it can be argued that the predictive nature of *ex ante* impact assessment often demands that heroic assumptions are made about future preferences and innovations (either policy, societal, or technological) which may affect benefits and costs. It is also the case that adequate databases are needed to calculate costs and benefits, yet resources are scarce in most jurisdictions and data on sustainability is often unavailable and expensive to obtain.

---

[6] OECD, *Sustainability in Impact Assessments* (Paris: OECD, 2012), http://www.oecd.org/gov/regulatory-policy/Sustainability%20in%20impact%20assessment%20SG-SD(2011)6-FINAL.pdf.
 See more generally: OECD, *Regulatory Impact Assessment: OECD Best Practice Principles for Regulatory Policy* (Paris: OECD, 2020), https://doi.org/10.1787/7a9638cb-en.

Trade-offs are another assessment difficulty. How can one weigh potential environmental impacts against the number of jobs being affected by a policy? Or economic prosperity against social risks? There is no single currency which allows aggregation of different impacts on sustainable development and comparison of different options on a purely scientific basis. The challenge, in impact assessments, is to take account of economic, social, and environmental considerations in an integrated and transparent manner and to produce reliable quantifications of relevant matters so as to provide clear underpinnings to objectives, strategies and justificatory arguments. This will demand clarity on potential trade-offs between numbers of issues, notably: social, environmental, and economic objectives; global, regional, national, sub-national, and local matters; and short-, medium', and long-term effects on respective groupings and interests. It calls for quantitative evaluations to be used to supplement rather than displace qualitative descriptions of relevant effects.

On participation, it is often difficult to provide fair inclusion to all relevant parties (organized and non-organized) within impact assessment processes. Deliberative procedures will often have a role in resolving differences regarding sustainability issues but the processes of impact assessment may impede deliberations in favour of more politically driven outcomes.

Impact assessment, it can be concluded, provides no easy answers on delivering aware, intelligent, and dynamic regulation for sustainability. As with other forms of policy analysis it must build on deliberative procedures to identify and evaluate such matters as relevant impacts, stakeholders, and trade-offs. Whether it increases transparency or conceals difficult decisions will turn on the levels of skill, resource, and even-handedness with which it is deployed.

Summary

Positive regulators face a number of special difficulties when they seek to further the principles of sustainability. Many of these difficulties flow from the indeterminacies associated with the notion of sustainable development.

Should it be concluded that regulating for sustainability is not a feasible or coherent project? The answer is that the challenges of regulating for sustainability vary greatly across sectors and issues, and some are much harder to deal with than others, notably those that contain inherent contradictions in content or indeterminacies of force, or reach, that cannot be resolved in a broadly accepted manner.

In most cases, it is clear that positive 'sustainability regulators' need, in the first instance, to render their projects feasible and coherent—often by taking steps to translate their mandates into understood and realizable missions. In doing so they must establish clear conceptions of the content, and the force and reach of sustainability objectives. They must also ensure that these conceptions are endorsed within the regulatory body and across organizations within the relevant regime. Substantive outcomes must be delivered and procedural expectations satisfied by negotiating a path through complex institutional and informational landscapes as well as changing expectations and regulatory environments.

The challenges of sustainability regulation are high on the scale of regulatory difficulty but there are means to address them. Sustainability regulators need to be aware, intelligent, and dynamic in the manner described above so that they recognize and deal with the numerous and often acute problems that they face. It is by displaying such qualities that positive sustainability regulators can act with vision, discharge the array of tasks on their agenda, and position themselves to justify their regulatory performances to parties within and beyond their regimes.

Regulating to Meet the Climate Emergency

We now turn from general issues to a particular aspect of the search for sustainability: the need for a regulatory response to climate change. Adverse side effects on the environment from human production and consumption take many forms: noise pollution, water pollution, the emission by vehicles of carbon monoxide which risks the health of those living nearby, and so on. Currently, though, the most conspicuous and controversial emission into the atmosphere is that of gases (particularly carbon dioxide, methane, and nitrous oxide) which have the greenhouse effect: their presence in the atmosphere deflects energy back to the planet's surface, with the consequence that climate change occurs: temperature and humidity increase, the oceans rise and acidify, and snow and ice decline. The long-term disastrous consequences of the resulting disruption and change of our climate system are well known.

We will discuss this effect largely with reference to the single greenhouse gas which is most important—carbon dioxide. Carbon dioxide is mainly emitted in producing energy and in various chemical reactions used to make goods such as steel and cement, and this means that a vast range of production activities undertaken by humankind involve carbon emissions, often at numerous points within their value chain.

These circumstances make decarbonization a particularly urgent requirement. It is the case, moreover, that the emission of greenhouse gases in any country has an impact anywhere in the world. This means that an agreed international programme of collective action is required to accomplish the goal of preventing climate warming. How this issue is resolved goes way beyond the reach of regulation—although regulation may be required to support any solution.

Equally, decarbonization at the national level requires substantial strategic policy decisions which fall within the domain of parliaments and government. These include the major decisions about fair ways of distributing the costs of decarbonization, including particularly the degree to which tax revenues rather than service prices are used to finance it.

The UK has been successful in reducing its carbon emissions considerably, as Figure 6.1 shows.[7] The figure also highlights the important role played by three particular sectors: electricity, transport, and the heating of buildings, in respect of each of which energy regulation plays a considerable role.

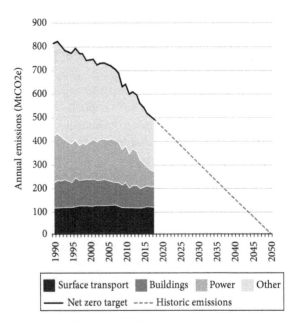

Figure 6.1 The net zero challenge

---

[7] Note that these are emissions within the territory of the UK. Emissions associated with UK consumption, which include those associated with imports and exclude those associated with exports, are significantly higher and have fallen more slowly.

Setting Objectives

At the macro level, objectives on decarbonization are established internationally via a series of agreements reached at international conferences, notably the Kyoto Protocol adopted in 1997 and the Paris Accord agreed in 2015. The interests of the countries represented vary, as does the degree of industrialization which they have achieved—which also reflects their historic responsibility for current problems. Their disparities of per capita income levels also determine the degrees to which different countries can afford action to staunch emissions. As a result, the Paris Agreement established an overall target (of holding global average temperatures to 'well below two degrees C above pre-industrial levels' with 'efforts to limit...to 1.5 degrees C'—Article 2(A)) but it leaves member countries to determine their own contributions to the global effort and to devise and implement regulatory actions at national level.

In this regime, accordingly, much weight has been placed on the setting (and implementation) of objectives at the national level—initially through negotiated targets for the developed nations, and now through presentation of self-identified nationally determined contributions to the overall global target.

These have emerged from a political process in more or less complex ways. In the UK, 2008 legislation set up an independent Climate Change Committee, to advise United Kingdom and devolved governments and parliaments on tackling and preparing for climate change. In 2019 the Committee recommended net zero greenhouse gas emissions[8] in the UK by 2050, and the British Parliament amended the 2008 Act to adopt such a commitment. Other countries have since followed suit, as may the European Union as a whole.

More focused government interventions also occur. For example, these may involve the phasing out by law of carbon-intensive coal-based electricity generation by a specified date (as in the UK), or (for reasons unrelated to decarbonization) of low-carbon nuclear power (as in Germany). This is only the start, however. A decarbonization programme will have an impact on all producing sectors and all consumption activities. For one thing, they all involve consumption of energy, and as shown below, decarbonization may alter the level and structure of energy prices. This will

---

[8] A net zero target does not require zero emissions, but only that any emissions be counterbalanced by an equivalent reduction in greenhouse gases, accomplished for example by forestation or removal of carbon from the atmosphere.

mean changes in the costs and prices of all goods and services. Such changes in prices as well as concurrent changes in consumer tastes will alter the structure of demand.

This means that, at the policy level, once an overall target has been set, pathways towards decarbonization will have to be devised for each major sector. This may involve the specification of additional quantitative targets.

It will then fall to the relevant government body or independent regulator to implement measures which are designed to meet the targets adopted. For example, to electrify road transport, an end date may have to be set for the sale of new cars and vans with internal combustion engines (as illustrated by the 2035 target announced by the UK Government in February 2020). Subsidies may be introduced to promote the sales of electric vehicles. The energy sector and its regulator will have to cooperate with the relevant organizations in transport to ensure that generation and network capacity is expanded to provide recharging facilities throughout the country.

Even at the national level, setting coordinated objectives for decarbonization is an activity rendered complex by the number of sectors, activities, and kinds of bodies (central government, regulatory, self-regulatory, and private sector) that are involved. Positive regulation requires, at its heart, an awareness of the coordination challenges to be faced. It demands intelligence on the extent to which objectives are being served by different control initiatives, and it calls for dynamism in adapting both objectives and implementing strategies in response to an evolving complex of controls over carbonizing activities.

Delivering Substantive Outcomes

Positive regulation involves using available evidence to choose the lowest cost, most effective combination of regulatory controls that can be devised. In fostering decarbonization, therefore, it is necessary to take on board the variety of control methods that can be used. The first of these, which has had considerable effect, is command and control, exemplified by simple prohibitions of, or conditions for, certain activities which emit carbon; for example a prohibition of the use of coal to generate electricity; emission controls on vehicles; or insulation standards for new houses. These can be supported by mandatory information disclosure, for example by compulsory publication of the energy ratings of domestic electrical equipment.

The price mechanism can also be deployed to counter adverse spillovers. When one activity (heating a home, making a car journey, making steel) imposes costs on wider society as well as on the supplier, the standard remedy for such spillovers is to require the provider (of energy, fuel etc.) to pay a tax or equivalent to the state which reflects the cost of the adverse side effect. These additional costs of supply are then reflected downstream in higher prices paid by customers, which reduce demand. The tax rate established by the government thus strikes a balance between the incentive to reduce carbon emissions and the impact of such a tax on the cost of living.

Decarbonization, accordingly, may very well be promoted by the setting of a carbon tax. If the money raised is then recycled back to those whose purchases of goods and services entail payment of the tax, the process can also be represented as a 'carbon dividend'. The basis for this characterization is that while the tax increases the cost of living, if the revenue from it is then distributed generally across a population, the price rise is largely compensated. Depending on how the revenue is allocated, this can have a variety of effects on the distribution of income.

Thus, suppose the manufacture of ton of steel involves emission of a ton of carbon, and that the tax on carbon amounts to £50 per ton. That tax will first encourage enhanced energy efficiency and then, probably, raise the price that a car manufacturer, for example, pays for a ton of steel, and thus indirectly the price of cars.[9] As a result of such a process, steel manufacturers in the country where the tax is imposed will now have an incentive to reduce their carbon emissions.

This raises an immediate difficulty in the case of internationally traded goods. Suppose country A imposes a carbon tax, which is reflected in prices which its steel manufacturers charge. Country B does not, and its exporters will both be able to undercut their competitors in country A and have no incentive to reduce carbon emissions. As a result, global emissions will be maintained or even worsened, while A's manufacturers will have lost out. The only effect of country A's tax will have been to 'offshore' supply to its home market.

To deal with this problem the best way so far devised is to allow country A to impose a tariff on steel imports from country B which is set equal to the tax which would have been paid by the exporter if it had been subject

---

[9] Note that the price of steel will not necessarily rise by £50 per ton, as the steel manufacturer may carry some of the burden itself.

to A's tax. Steel manufacturers in A and B are thus put on an equal competitive footing in A's market. There are, however, significant legal and practical problems in devising and setting such tariffs.

Taxation is not the only way to make emitters pay for the carbon they generate. An alternative is to issue and possibly auction tradable emissions permits.[10] The government first decides how many tons of carbon emissions it will permit. In the auction variant, qualified bidders then make offers to buy permits to emit via some kind of auction process. A market clearing price is found, at which the permits are purchased. The permits can be traded at any time. The detail of such schemes is important; they may involve the distribution of permits free of charge to firms which are historic emitters of carbon.[11]

Which of these two methods should be used? The choice of either a tax rate or use of tradable permits is made under uncertainty. In the case of a tax, the quantity of carbon which will be subsequently emitted will be uncertain, and in an auction of a limited quantum of permits, it will be the price of a permit (and hence the impact on the cost of living) that will be unpredictable. If certainty over the level of emissions is crucial, it will be advisable to sell permits; if certainty regarding the cost of living effect is essential, a tax will be preferable. Carbon taxes or tradable emissions permits have been in use for several decades, and their impact has been studied in a number of industries. Their impact on electricity generation is described below.

It would be a mistake to suppose that a carbon tax or emissions trading can by itself solve the problem of decarbonization. As the account below shows, in relation to three key sectors requiring decarbonization, that process requires close coordination over strategic actions to be taken between governments and other public bodies, firms, regulators, and household and business consumers, and probably the development of pathways towards decarbonization for the various activities which may be required, including (for example) nuclear generation, air travel, and home heating.

Accordingly we now turn to the question of how combinations of energy policy, regulation, and energy supplier and customer behaviour can promote decarbonization in the three key sectors illustrated in Figure 6.1—electricity generation, transport, and heating. Inspection of

---

[10]   See further the discussion of tradable permits in Chapter 3.

[11]   See R. Tol, *Climate Economics: Economic Analysis of Climate, Climate Change and Climate Policy* (Edward Elgar, 2019) and A. D, Ellerman, F. J. Convery, and C. de Perthuis, *Pricing Carbon: The European Emissions Trading Scheme* (Cambridge University Press, 2010).

Figure 6.1 may suggest that good progress is being made to achieve the UK's net zero target. This may be misleading though. Inevitably the easiest and least painful means are exploited first, and the task will become progressively more difficult as net zero approaches.

Power Generation

Decarbonization of power generation can be accomplished by command and control methods—as when the use of particular carbon-emitting technologies is prohibited. Alternatively, price incentives can be applied by such mechanisms as carbon taxes, emissions permits, and direct subsidies to renewable operators. All three incentive methods have been used in Great Britain. In the last case, renewable operators have competed over the minimum subsidy for which they are willing to supply electricity, on top of whatever price emerges in the wholesale electricity market. Over the period 2015–19, the subsidy required per unit of output fell by about two thirds, reflecting a rapid decrease in the costs of generating renewable energy, especially in offshore wind farms.

The British energy regulator estimates that from 2010 to 2018, carbon taxes and permits reduced carbon emissions by about 40 million tons, and large renewable subsidies by about 30 million tons; in 2018 this represents more than half the 2010 level of emissions.[12]

Transport

Figure 6.1 shows that there was no significant reduction in carbon emissions in Great Britain in the surface transport network in the period illustrated. Here we focus on road transport of all types, where the possibility of replacing the internal combustion engine in cars, buses, and trucks with electric power or hydrogen offers considerable opportunities, which can be supported by energy regulation.

A ban on the sales of petrol, diesel, and hybrid cars and vans is likely to take the share of EVs (or hydrogen-powered) new vehicles from about 2 per cent in 2019 to 100 per cent in 2035, and will entail an increase in the quantity of electricity generated, transmitted, and distributed. But there is also a potential 'chicken and egg' problem here: customers need to be confident of recharging their cars before they will buy an EV, while investment to provide the power for recharging may not be forthcoming until the extra demand is guaranteed. The difficulties associated with such a

---

[12] Ofgem, State of the Energy Market 2019, pp. 126–31, https://www.ofgem.gov.uk/system/files/docs/2019/11/20191030_state_of_energy_market_revised.pdf.

necessary expansion may, however, be mitigated by the potential to recharge EVs at night when other demands for electricity are low. This would allow a great saving to be made in both generating and network capacity.

Several regulatory initiatives, indeed, offer opportunities to reduce the cost of transport decarbonization:

- Completion of 'smart meter' programmes, which allow more accurate measurement and control of customer consumption and the adoption of cost-saving measures.
- Encouraging the offer of 'time of day' electricity tariffs by energy retailers, which offer savings for recharging at non-peak times, such as between the hours of 2 and 4 a.m.; households can also be 'nudged' to act in this way.
- Enabling new technologies and new business models to use vehicle batteries as a form of distributed energy storage ('vehicles to grid' technologies); this will help meet the needs of a system powered by renewables and nuclear power, neither of which can respond to user demand.
- Allowing anticipatory investment by monopoly network operators, which allows them to come together to ensure that network capacity is always kept ahead of demand, both at the driver's home and away from home. The second part of this provision is designed to allay 'range anxiety'—the fear of not being able to get safely home in an EV. This could be accomplished by making changes in the manner in which investment by the energy network to expand capacity is regulated.[13]
- Ensuring that network companies offer timely and affordable connections to new users, and that their systems can be inter-operable.

This looks like a complex but quite feasible outline structure of how regulation can be brought into play to decarbonize road transport. What makes it more practicable is that there are grounds for believing that EVs will ultimately provide a means of transport which is both cheaper and cleaner than the systems they replace.

Heating

The third area in which we consider how energy regulation can promote decarbonization is the least developed and most problematic. In temperate

---

[13] See Chapter 7 for an account of how the revenues of and investments made by a monopoly network company can be regulated.

or colder countries where gas is available, it is widely chosen for space heating since it is often substantially cheaper than electricity or other alternatives. As a result, gas heating is responsible in the UK for around a third of carbon emissions.

There are many possible alternatives to gas heating, including:[14]

- Replacement of gas boilers by electric heat pumps.
- Development of heat networks, in which water is heated centrally (often by electricity, or possibly by hydrogen), piped to homes in a district and sent through (larger than current) internal radiators.
- Repurposing the existing gas distribution network for use in circulating hydrogen, which can be carbon-free when used for heating.

Each of these approaches entails replacement of the gas boiler within given premises, and some entail replacement of the system of radiators that is used for heat conveyance. This can often be done in the normal cycle for replacing such equipment.

The feasibility and costs of the hydrogen option have not been tested at scale in a commercial environment. But it is a feature of the use of both heat and hydrogen networks that they involve a single collective choice in any given area. Thus the single system of pipes available in any area cannot deliver both gas and hydrogen. Equally, a district heating system requires very high take up rates to be financially viable. The outcome may well be the use of different heating methods in different areas.

Policy-makers and regulators are still in the foothills of the process of decarbonizing heat. More research and experimentation are required—and quickly. The solution may prove quite different from area to area. Unlike the EV case considered above, there appears at present to be a lack of solutions that would allow decarbonization to occur without significant increases in the short term in the prices paid by downstream heat consumers.

Meeting Procedural Expectations

If decarbonization is to be delivered in a manner that meets the procedural expectations of affected parties, regulators must be aware that

---

[14] Note that each of these alternatives requires some use of electricity, which must accordingly be generated in a way which does not emit carbon.

different stakeholders will have different expectations about the kinds of processes and communications that are appropriate for making decisions and policies and for offering explanations. They will have to be prepared to use an array of processes to explain and justify their actions. Not only that, they will have to adopt a facilitative role and act to enable various groupings to participate in discussions about decarbonizing proposals.

As the account above suggests, decarbonization is a regulatory problem of unprecedented complexity because of its pervasive impact on all sectors of the economy and society. Some decarbonization measures will bring cost increases for a substantial number of actors, and maintaining popular approval for the procedures used to make difficult decisions may accordingly prove challenging, particularly given the pronounced (often contentious) distributional consequences of the various measures described above.

This is exemplified by the transport decarbonization issue discussed above. A switch to EVs is likely to be led by the more affluent members of society. Any government subsidy of new EV purchases will benefit them. This will also be the case if the costs of network expansion to meet their recharging needs are socialized across all energy users. The decarbonization of private vehicles—as well as of public transport—is, nevertheless, an essential means of achieving the net zero objective.

With such distributional impacts at issue, allegations of unfairness and failures to make decisions sufficiently accessible and transparent may be difficult to defend against. The aware and intelligent regulator will anticipate such challenges, first, by amassing information on the parties and interests that are impacted by its decisions and policies, and, second, by taking care to gather together all the available evidence that it needs to justify its actions to the various parties. In doing so it will be prepared to discuss openly the trade-offs being made between various stakeholder interests and between economic, social, environmental, and other objectives, and to devise mitigation where it is needed on distributional grounds.

The positive regulator will also display dynamism in picking up and dealing with changes in the domain that it regulates. It is not a matter of moving from the current situation to a new steady state. Innovation is likely to be a constant feature. Thus the regulator must adjust its systems to react to changes in such matters as the technologies used to decarbonize, the interests affected by decarbonization steps, and the trade-offs being made among different social or business groups.

In the face of such challenges how can the regulator's obligations be squared so as to achieve a so-called 'just transition' to net zero? The enabling requirement to do so is to have access to a set of data which shows the impact on different groups of society, both of significant decarbonization interventions—particularly in the power generation, transport, and heating activities picked out above—and (ideally) of other regulatory interventions, such as price controls.

If the relevant individual household income and expenditure datasets are available, it is possible to assess the likely impact of individual regulatory changes on households at different places in the relevant income distribution curve—for example on the group with the lowest 10 per cent of incomes. The impact on these households can be compared with the impact on those with average levels of income or with the highest incomes. If data exists at a more granular level—for example covering pensioners, households already relying on (more expensive) electricity to heat their homes, and so on—the same calculation can be made.

When a string of decarbonization initiatives is undertaken, the effects of individual measures can be cumulated to show the impact of the programme as a whole. Armed with access to these calculations, the regulator (and the government) can seek to craft its decarbonization and other interventions in a fashion which prevents disadvantaged households from bearing an unfair burden in decarbonization processes.

In this way the regulator can ensure a level of transparency which should help well-informed discussions about fairness to take place. What constitutes fairness in this context will depend upon the objectives the regulator is set in its governing legislation. It might be possible to bolster this by introducing additional more democratic consultation processes such as citizens' assemblies.

This is a possible way of dealing with equity issues within a given generation of households. But there is also an intergenerational issue: how much should the current generation of consumers be expected to pay for investments which primarily protect its successors?

Answering this question requires the choice of a discount rate by which benefits to future generations are made commensurate with benefits here and now. This question has engaged and even perplexed many analysts of climate change regulation.[15] In practice, however, this issue is largely resolved, in the area under discussion, by the nature of the decarbonization targets set by governments and legislatures: the tighter they are, the greater and more immediate is the sacrifice required of the current generation.

---

[15] N. Stern, *Why Are We Waiting? The Logic, Urgency, and Promise of Tackling Climate Change* (MIT Press, 2015), part 2 ; W. Nordhaus, *The Climate Casino: Risk, Uncertainty, and Economics for a Warming World* (Yale University Press, 2013), Ch. 16.

Conclusions

The broad challenges of regulating for sustainability are very considerable and have been summarized above. In looking at the specific difficulties involved in decarbonization it has been clear that regulation needs to be at its most positive. Governments and agencies need to set objectives, deliver outcomes, and meet procedural expectations under stressful conditions. They, accordingly, need to be highly aware of the complex sets of expectations and institutional frameworks within which they find themselves. They need to operate with systems of intelligence that provide the evidence with which they can deliver decarbonization effectively, assess their performance, and meet the procedural expectations of a host of affected parties. They need to operate dynamically so that they can react to changes in such matters as: markets, costs, technologies, emissions types, stakeholder expectations, and political constraints. These are, in all senses, non-trivial challenges. In favour of the regulators, however, is the increasingly broad acceptance that urgent regulatory action is necessary.

7
Controlling Traditional Network Monopolies

Introduction

This is the first of two chapters about the particular challenges of delivering desired outcomes when regulating operational networks. Chapter 8 focuses upon the problems presented to regulation by the development of networks based on digital platforms as operated by firms such as Amazon, Facebook, or Google. These providers have quickly gained strong market positions, in part by acting as an intermediary between customers and other groups of providers.

This chapter focuses upon the century-old regulatory challenge that is posed by a key feature of traditional utility sectors such as energy, fixed telephony, and water: their reliance on a physical (not a digital) local distribution network for delivering the relevant service to millions of dwellings and business premises, and the incorporation of bottlenecks within such networks.

The original businesses providing these services typically were started on a private enterprise basis in richer communities, and spread out from there. As demand grew, it became obvious that the local distribution network was a 'natural monopoly', in the sense that having two networks serving the same locality would—other things equal—cost more than having just one.[1] In these areas initial rivalry among providers gradually turned into actual monopoly supply, which was augmented by further monopolies in other related activities, often including a retail monopoly.

The development of policy towards the regulation of utilities was further complicated because the services provided—energy and water initially, telephony later—were increasingly viewed as essential for all households, and pressure grew for them to be made universally available.

---

[1] This arises because, while the costs of connecting each house from a 'mains' connection in the street is the same with either one or two networks, a second network requires a significant extra cost in having two rival 'mains' connections.

Two objectives of simultaneously (i) controlling monopoly and (ii) promoting universal availability emerged. In the United States, the network firms in energy and telephony largely remained in private ownership,[2] and markets were often shared among different monopolies, with the tacit or explicit agreement of the US Government's competition body.[3] Progressively the task of controlling the prices charged by these monopolies was undertaken by regulatory bodies expressly created for this purpose by the US Congress and state legislatures, which had powers to set customer prices.[4]

The 'European solution' was broadly to take the network companies into public ownership. Services were either provided by a government department, or later by a state-owned or public enterprise expressly set up for this purpose, and supposed to be guided by government-determined commercial or financial objectives.

In the UK, much of this nationalization process took place after the Second World War. Previous owners were compensated for the acquisition of their assets, and Boards of Directors were appointed by the Government to control the companies. The duties placed upon these boards were somewhat vague, and governments were often suspected of intervening in such matters as pricing decisions.[5]

Subsequently it became not uncommon for some form of external or independent regulation of utilities in public ownership to be set up. This was the case for the then publicly owned UK Royal Mail, which had its own regulator ('Postcomm') established in 2000. As the box below shows, a somewhat similar situation has recently emerged in the Australian fixed telecommunications sector. The implication of this is that, even though the manner in which pricing decisions are made may change, public ownership may still entail the presence of a fairly busy independent regulator.

The main direction of change in the ownership of utilities in the last four decades has, however, been towards privatization, not nationalization. This has been the case in all continents where networks were not already in private hands.

The general consequences of privatization were summarized in a number of research reports prepared about twenty years ago. A typical set of

---

[2] Many water companies remain in local public ownership.

[3] Thus in 1913, the telephone market was divided between long distance service provided as a monopoly by AT&T, and local service provided by many monopoly operators, either affiliated with or independent of AT&T. This structure persisted for more than forty years.

[4] See Chapter 9 for a discussion of the alleged capture of these bodies by their regulatees.

[5] See T. Tutton, "Political Control of State-Owned Utilities in the UK" (CCP UEA, December 2019) available at http://competitionpolicy.ac.uk/documents/8158338/28809492/CCP+WP+19-8+Complete.pdf/a31e5951-48f4-4a26-7255-6259ace48624.

conclusions is that newly privatized firms almost always become more efficient and profitable, and increase their investment spending. Employment may fall, but does not do so invariably. There is little empirical evidence on how consumers are affected.[9]

Case in point: Regulating the Australian National Broadband Network

In 2009 the Australian Government decided to place under public ownership and monopolize the provision of a fixed telecommunications fibre access network. This was intended to ensure the near-universal availability of such access to Australian homes. The network would be 'wholesale only', and a set of retailers would sell its services on to households and firms.[6] After several changes of plan, a substantial proportion of the roll-out was accomplished by 2019.

As the project progressed the question arose whether the National Broadband Network (NBN) could be relied on to provide an adequate quality of service to retailers and their end customers—for example with respect to arrangements for NBN employees to visit customers' homes to install the fibre connection. The relevant regulator (the Australian Competition and Consumer Commission, or ACCC) concluded that it needed to impose regulations.[7] Then in 2019 the ACCC opened an inquiry into whether it should intervene in NBN's wholesale prices as well, especially for fibre broadband speeds.[8]

In this instance, public ownership was found to be incapable in itself of offering necessary protection for consumers.

Several authors have remarked upon a potentially significant aspect of the 'political economy' of change of ownership: in a nationalized network

---

[6] R. Nicholls, 'The Australian Telecommunications Regulatory Environment: An Overview', *Australian Journal of Telecommunications and the Digital Economy* 4 (2017): 196–213.

[7] ACCC, *NBN Wholesale Service Standards Inquiry* (2017), https://www.accc.gov.au/regulated-infrastructure/communications/national-broadband-network-nbn/nbn-wholesale-service-standards-inquiry, accessed 29 December 2019.

[8] ACCC, *Inquiry into NBN Access Pricing* (2019), https://www.accc.gov.au/regulated-infrastructure/communications/national-broadband-network-nbn/inquiry-into-nbn-access-pricing, accessed 29 December 2019.

[9] W. Megginson and J. Netter, 'From State to Market: A Survey of Empirical Studies on Privatization', *Journal of Economic Literature* 39(2) (2001): 321–89.

sector, a unionized labour force may be able successfully to bargain for wage increases which might either impose losses on the relevant firm (ultimately financed by taxpayers), or provide a cost-based argument for raising service prices. In network industries in private ownership, on the other hand, investors—as residual legatees of any surpluses—will benefit from the kind of regulatory failures described in Chapter 9. Within any given sector this can have a significant impact on the relative scale of the rents accruing to labour and to capital, with both outcomes adversely affecting consumers.

The impact on efficiency has both a short-term aspect (are firms using existing technologies to good effect without waste of resources?) and a longer-term, dynamic aspect (are there continuing incentives to innovate in services and processes in ways which benefit consumers?). Unregulated investor-owned monopolies are not kindly judged in either of these respects: it has been observed that the true monopoly profit is the quiet life. We note below that attempts to impose innovation by regulation on an investor-owned firm often run up against lack of effective incentives on that firm to innovate. Similar difficulties arise in encouraging innovation by public firms, where any profit motive may be weaker or absent.

Ownership decisions are normally regarded as decisions that fall within the field of policy and hence the domain of parliaments or governments rather than of regulation or regulators. Indeed, EU regulatory Directives and other legislation in the network industry space usually apply to all firms in the relevant sector in the EU, irrespective of their form of ownership in any given Member State. Notwithstanding such matters, the discussion above suggests that ownership does profoundly influence the context in which regulators act.

The Scope of Regulation within a Network Utility

The local distribution network is only a part of a utility company's value chain. In the three sectors noted above, other activities take place which may account for a very large part—more than half—of the sector's value added. Some of these additional elements are shown in Table 7.1.

These other activities do not reproduce the natural monopoly property described above, which gives such advantage to a monopoly supplier of a dense local distribution network. But there are likely to be serious problems in replicating, for example, high voltage lines in electricity transmission, or long distance gas pipelines between two given points, or—to take an example from another sector—a set of train tracks between two cities. These activities will also require regulatory counter-measures to the abuse of market power.

Table 7.1 Utility value chains by sector

Electricity	Gas	Fixed telecommunications	Water
Generation	Extraction	Content	Extraction
Transmission	Pipelines	Core networks	Treatment
Access network	Access network	Access network	Access network
Retail	Retail	Retail	Retail

Many other activities in the value chains are potentially competitive; examples are:

- Electricity generation, based on different fuels—coal, gas, wind, solar, nuclear, etc.
- Wholesale gas supplies from various geographical areas, including LPG (liquid petroleum gas) and the output of fracking.
- Long distance and international fibre telecommunications networks, which are now widely replicated.
- Almost all retailing activities to households, firms, and other organizations.

The variation in the degree of market power exhibited across the value chain allows the regulator to adopt a 'pick and mix' approach in its treatment of them. Suppose that the structure the regulator inherits consists of a monopolist integrated across the whole value chain. The regulator can then open up some competition within the value chain by allowing competitive entry into those parts of it which might support competition, while requiring the historic monopolist to grant access by those competitors to its monopoly assets, at a cost-based price which it determines. This approach has been successfully implemented in fixed telecommunications in a fashion which has promoted competition on a substantial scale.

As this process worked through over the past twenty-five years, an issue arose with this mixed solution. There was concern that the former monopolist would use its control of the local access network to weaken or drive out its retail competitors by discrimination against them—for example, by delaying repairs to network connections of customers which had been signed up by a competing retailer. Once news of such 'sabotage' becomes public, customers may be reluctant to leave the former monopoly supplier for a competitor.

Case in point: The shrinking scope of regulation in fixed telecommunications

The starting point of fixed telecommunications policy within the EU was that many Member States were served by a vertically integrated monopoly. New firms were then allowed to enter retail and other markets by purchasing access to the former monopolist's local access network at cost-based prices. Competitors were encouraged by the structure of access prices to choose an access product which simply comprised the copper line from the telephone exchange to the customer's premises. The new entrant had to conjure up the rest of the value chain from elsewhere.

This chiselling away at the extent of 'natural monopoly' led to a substantial growth of competition in the markets for voice and broadband, all predicated on rivals being granted access at a fair price to the incumbent's irreducible bottleneck assets in the local access network. As a result, by 2007, 46 per cent of retail customers in long established EU Member States were being sold broadband by other firms than their historic monopolist.

When the time came to replace the copper line with a fibre connection, some countries in Europe increased competitors' reliance on the incumbent's network, while others doubled down on promoting competition by requiring the incumbent merely to make available its civil works infrastructure to competitors—essentially the ducts and poles which carried the newly installed fibre. Fibre roll-out, take-up, and competition fared much better in the second group of countries than in the first, suggesting the beneficial effects of a stronger pro-competitive regulatory policy.[10]

Regulators have responded by imposing further restrictions on an incumbent controlling a bottleneck, in the form of various separation requirements. These range from a requirement to provide separate accounts on the profitability of the different activities in the value chain in

---

[10] T. Shortall and M. Cave, 'Is Symmetric Access Regulation a Policy Choice? Evidence from the Deployment of NGA in Europe', *Communications & Strategies* 98 (2015): 17–42.

which the monopolist is engaged; through an obligation to re-engineer its business processes in a way which would make any discrimination of the kind described above more transparent; to the requirement to set up a legally separate company for the monopoly activity. In the UK, the owner of the local access network, BT, was progressively and cumulatively subjected to each of these steps in the twenty-five years leading up to 2017. The final and even more draconian step in this progression is to prohibit common ownership of competitive and monopolistic activities. This too has been proposed for BT but not adopted.

Similar 'line of business' restrictions are imposed in the energy sector but not in the water sector, where the impact of competition across the value chain remains negligible—except in certain water-poor areas of the world, such as Australia, Southern California, and the Middle East, where vigorous wholesale markets in extraction rights and raw water operate.

What have been described above are ways of injecting head-to-head competition *within a market*. Another route for augmenting competition operates by creating competition *for the market*, in this case the right to undertake a network-based project.

For example, suppose that increased demand for electric vehicles requires an increase in electricity transmission capacity on a particular stretch. This task could simply be entrusted to the existing transmission operator. Alternatively, the regulator or its agent could ask for competitive bids from a number of suppliers and choose the one which offered the best price for build and operation over, say, a twenty-year period. This process has been applied in several jurisdictions across the world in a number of sectors, especially energy, and especially in the case of new and high value projects which are largely separable from—i.e. independent of—the rest of the network. Significant savings have been claimed for this approach.

Some commentators have gone further and proposed that almost all network projects be made contestable in this way. Taken to the limit, this would replace the network operator with a series of temporally and geographically overlapping investment projects juggled by a public sector counterparty, rather than—as now—a complex operation with a supply chain managed by a single network. This would be at best a difficult and, at worst, an impossible task.

Finally, network natural monopolies are threatened increasingly by the consequences of digital transformation, which allows substitutes for network build to become available. One generic way of describing these changes is that they substitute 'software' (in the sense of adaptable and non-capital-intensive processes) for the traditional hardware.

To take an energy sector example, a case may arise for strengthening a network connection in response to increased peak demand. However, alternative methods may be available, including:[11]

- Inserting battery storage somewhere in the network, which can be used to supply peak needs there without network investment.
- Using the storage capacity of electric vehicles to transfer resources from vehicle to grid at moments of peak demand.
- Setting up a simple auction system to ration capacity on a link serving several renewable or other generators.
- Encouraging demand-side response, in the form of offers from some customers to abate their peak demand for a price if notified so to do.

In telecommunications, networks increasingly rely on software defined networking (SDN). This transfers the functionality needed in the network such as switching and handover from hardware to software, enabling variation in services and functionality to be made more readily.

Network function virtualization (NFV) involves implementing the functions of the communications infrastructure in software running on standard computing equipment, rather than traditional hardware—following the precedent of data centres, which have gone through a similar transformation. This reduces costs, and simplifies the addition of new services. The thrust of this development is to strengthen the trend towards the heterogeneity of network provision, for example to accommodate the higher immediacy of communications required to service automated vehicles.

The combination of these two advances allows network resources to be controlled decentrally by third parties who manage their own physical or virtual resources individually as needed to meet their own requirements. This is often described as 'network slicing'. The effect of this, in the right regulatory circumstances, is to allow users of network services to take control of what they receive. This change is particularly significant in mobile communications, where a relatively low-cost access network has permitted viable competition between a small number of spectrum-based local networks.

In summary, the scope of network regulation is a movable feast. Pro-competitive policies can be introduced to control the market power of

---

[11] See Centre on Regulation in Europe (CERRE), *Smart Consumers in the Internet of Energy* (Brussels: CERRE, 2019).

network incumbents. The outcome varies across sectors. In the water sector, regulation typically covers the whole value chain from water extraction from rivers and aquifers and the operation of desalinization plants through the treatment and delivery of clean water, and associated retail activities, to the complex removal and treatment of dirty water.

In the other two sectors discussed above—energy and fixed telecommunications—the opening to competition of upstream and downstream (i.e. retailing) activities to competition has focused residual network regulation in energy on transmission and distribution and in telecommunications on the local access network.

How Network Prices Are Regulated

We now examine how a regulator might set the wholesale prices that a network is allowed to charge its competitors for access to its network, taking as an example an investor-owned local distribution network for electricity. The regulator's assumed objective, which is normally set by law, is to ensure that the distribution network acts as a conduit for electric power (produced by upstream generators and transmitted by a high voltage transmission network) that is distributed or delivered locally to end users in a way which protects their interests. This will normally require high levels of safety and reliability, availability of service to (nearly) all potential customers of electricity in the service area, and provision of the services at a 'fair' cost-based price which recovers efficiently incurred—but not other—costs. This price is paid by a retailer of electricity, which then recovers it from end users in the retail prices they pay. The network should also continually bring its customers and end users the benefits of cost-saving and service-enhancing innovation.

Why require 'fair cost-based pricing'? In the case of an investor-owned network, the incentive, in the worst case, to carry on operating an existing network depends on whether its revenues at least cover its running costs. This would not include whatever (mostly capital) costs have been sunk historically and irretrievably in the business. If even those sunk costs are not covered, the investors will not necessarily walk away at once.

If further investment in the business is required, however, investors will also need to expect that they will make an adequate return on that investment. This is what will persuade them to invest their funds in that firm in that sector, rather than elsewhere.

This is often known as the 'financeability condition': Are expected returns in the firm large enough to ensure continuing investment in the business? If not, supply will dry up when current assets expire. On the other hand, offering a higher return than the one described above is unnecessary and adverse to customers' interests.

There are two distinct ways of finding regulated prices which are capable of ensuring financeability. These are shown in Table 7.2.

Clearly, the 'incentive regulation' method is much more complex to apply, since it involves forecasts of how demand, costs, and technological change in respect of the services in question will interact in the period to come. This creates scope for error—and that possibility places a practical limit on the prospective period over which prices can be set. The commonest range chosen is three to five years.

This limitation, however, creates the problem of renewal, and of how it is managed. It is probably inescapable that the task of making a further projection for a second five-year cost-and-price trajectory when the first

Table 7.2 Rate of return and incentive regulation: two approaches

---

First method: Ask the network firm what its actual costs are, and then set prices for customers which allow it to recover those costs, including an allowed rate of return on investments. This is often known as 'rate of return regulation' as it implicitly guarantees a return on any investment allowed by the regulator. Allowing for some caricature, it is a description of how regulation of investor-owned utilities developed in the last century in the United States.

This method suffers, however, from the obvious flaw of any 'cost-plus' pricing arrangement—the lack of any incentive for efficient production. If the customers pay all the firm's bills, why try to keep them down? And there is a further problem: if the regulator allows an excessive return on investment, it gives the firm an incentive to expand its investment programme almost without limit, as each new project yields an extra margin of net profit. Despite this drawback, this basic approach is quite widely used, though sometimes combined with specific measures to prevent the most flagrant inefficiencies or other abuses.

Second method: The alternative is to allow the recovery not of costs already incurred, but of *expected* costs. Under this scheme, the regulator identifies a trajectory of efficient unit costs, including capital costs, going forward for a period of, say, five years. Depending on circumstances, these costs might be constant over the period, or they might move up or down. That trajectory of costs is then translated into a trajectory of pre-ordained future prices over the period. The firm is then challenged to beat those assumed efficient costs. If it does so, it earns higher profits, but if it falls short, it will incur losses. For obvious reasons this is called 'incentive regulation'.

A form of this alternative approach has been in use in the UK and elsewhere since the first price control imposed on the newly privatized UK telecommunications monopoly in 1984. Both methods, hybrids of them, or other bespoke alternatives, are used in other jurisdictions.

---

one nears its end will start from the level of cost then observed. This is needed to avoid carrying over earlier forecasting errors into the next period. A regulated firm which knows this is happening, however, will adapt its behaviour accordingly—in particular by limiting its cost reduction towards the end of the price control.

An information or intelligence issue arises here, however, because the regulator knows a lot less about what the firm can really do than the firm itself. Nor does it help very much if the regulator is setting controls for multiple local network operators simultaneously, and so can compare their performances: it will find that all the observations will be confounded by the same problem of information asymmetry.

This is a familiar problem which arises in any context when targets for the next period depend on performance in the current one. Thus a sales director might be reluctant to exceed her targets in the current year, for fear of the impact of so doing on next year's targets. In the highly target-based former Soviet Union, the name 'planning from the achieved level' was given to the same phenomenon.[12]

This effect can be particularly insidious when all the levels of management in a regulated firm are separately withholding information from the regulator, or their superiors, about their true productive potential. An unusually tough price control may be needed to elicit this information.[13]

The product of such challenges is that most network regulation, in practice, is a hybrid of the two pure methods set out above. Thus firms submit investment plans, which are vetted by the regulator. Forward-looking allowable revenues and prices are computed on the basis of approved investment plans. This is beginning to look like the 'rate of return' approach—but greater than expected efficiency will still win the firm higher profits. An incentive, moreover, is often in place which allows a firm *not* to make an approved investment in instances where this turns out not to be required because a better and cheaper solution has appeared. In such a case, the firm will receive a proportion of the cost of the investment saved in the price control period. The same investment may then be approved for the next price control period.

---

[12] J. Berliner, *Factory and Manager in the USSR* (Harvard University Press, 1957).
[13] A natural experiment of this kind occurred in the UK water sector, where two lax price controls in the 1990s generated zero growth in total factor productivity. A much tougher price control covering 2001–6, initially greeted with horror by the companies, then provoked a substantial productivity improvement which confirmed the regulator's assumption that the price control was reasonable. See F. Erbetta and M. Cave, 'Regulation and Efficiency Incentives: Evidence from the England and Wales Water Industry', *Review of Network Economics* 6(4) (2007): 425–52.

From Minimizing Network Costs to Regulating Outputs More Broadly

The discussion so far has assumed that there is a single output in question, with defined quality and other attributes. The task is thus to produce that output at a minimum cost. But this is never the case in network regulation. The electricity that a distribution company conveys may be as close to homogeneous as can be imagined, but the reliability of the supply and the speed with which any outages are dealt with are also matters of great importance to end users.

Accordingly, regulators have developed output related incentives to shape firms' production decisions across a broader range of outputs. As Rious and Rossetto have written:

> Output regulation can apply to a variety of specific activities. Basically, any output can be identified, monitored, subjected to targets and rewarded or penalized. For instance, outputs can encompass environmental policy goals (minimizing power losses...) or social policy objectives (...rewarding actions by distribution licensees to help vulnerable customers on affordability).[14]

A regulated network, accordingly, can in principle be incentivized to perform in these dimensions by a system of sticks and carrots. But care must be taken to calibrate rewards properly: if the reward for a particular quality of service is set at a level that exceeds end users' valuations of the relevant improvement, it will very likely be over-provided—to the detriment of those customers. Regulated firms are adept at identifying and profiting from any regulatory error of this kind—and end users pay for the mistake. Experience suggests that, absent reliable cost and benefit information, the proliferation of such rewards carries significant dangers. It may be preferable to use separate network licence conditions to prevent quality degradation in aspects of greatest concern to consumers.

These embellishments have made price controls in some jurisdictions very complex and time consuming, at least in comparison with the earliest price controls of thirty years ago. It is not unusual for the construction of a five-year network or wider price control to take fully three years, with

---

[14] V. Rious and N. Rossetto, 'The British Reference Model', in L. Meeus and J.-M. Glachant (eds.), *Electricity Network Regulation in the EU: The Challenges Ahead for Transmission and Distribution* (Edward Elgar, 2018), p. 13.

numerous intermediate consultations and decisions. This long process does create the space which the regulator can use to mobilize consumer and customer groups to subject the plans, and implicitly the priorities, of the regulated firms to serious scrutiny, which expands the challenge capability of the regulator itself. Time must also be set aside to accommodate a process by which the regulated firm or others with an interest in the decision—notably end users themselves—can appeal against the regulator's decision.

How to Set the Rate of Return on Capital Allowed to the Network

This is the most vexed generic issue in network price controls. Networks, especially in energy, rail, and water, are highly capital intensive. An increase in the allowed rate of return of even 1 per cent over a five-year price control period will transfer hundreds of millions of euros from consumers to investors. If identical regulatory errors on the cost of capital are cumulated across many sectors, as may the case,[15] the transfer will run into billions.

The problem is greater than simply the earning of excess returns on a given volume of assets. As noted above, if firms expect to earn returns in excess of their cost of capital, they will have an incentive to aggrandize their investment allowance, generally preferring a capital investment or hardware solution to an operating cost or software solution. Consumers are then penalized first by paying investors a greater return than necessary and second by having too much investment inflicted on them.

It is thus vital in consumers' interests to avoid over-paying the investors. But with so much pure profit at stake, the amount of regulator, company, and consultancy effort directed at this discussion is enormous. What follows is necessarily a somewhat simplified account of the crucial debates surrounding this issue.

The starting point is the observation that investor-owned utility networks are financed by both debt and equity. Since demand for their services is not very volatile, they are relatively low risk, and hence contain a high proportion of debt finance.

---

[15] On the circumstances in which this possibility might arise, see Chapter 9.

The rate at which such utility companies can borrow in the debt market is likely to be pegged to the rate at which the government in the same jurisdiction can borrow, known as the risk-free rate. Typically, utility company borrowers will have a pay a premium of 1–2 per cent over that rate. Since we are making an allowed return decision for a future period in which we do not know the rate of general inflation, we seek a 'real' risk-free rate, which is equal to the nominal rate of return in the debt market adjusted by the rate of inflation.[16]

Before the global financial crisis of 2008, the real risk-free rate in the UK for several decades hovered around 2–3 per cent. Thereafter, it has fallen (by about 3 per cent) to around minus 1 per cent. This has placed UK regulators in the position of choosing whether to rely on long-term trends or upon more recent observations.

Assets that are not backed by debt are backed by investors' equity. Perhaps surprisingly, there is a high degree of unanimity among regulators and regulated firms in many countries about the approach that should be used to address the problem of estimating the forward-looking cost of equity, although this is combined with fierce argument about how the model should be populated with data to make the necessary numerical calculations.

This approach was invented in the early 1960s by economists who later received the 1990 Nobel Prize in economics for their efforts.[17] It is known as the capital asset price model, or CAPM. It is predicated upon the notion that share prices are fundamentally determined by real underlying economic forces, refracted by the opinions of millions of rational participants in equity markets. This so-called 'efficient market hypothesis' came under criticism in the events surrounding the 2008 global financial crisis, but that has not undermined confidence in the CAPM.

The essential idea is that investors require a higher rate of return to invest in the equity of firms that incur more risk. They can protect themselves from the specific risk of success or disaster associated with a particular firm by buying a portfolio of shares, but they cannot so easily avoid the risk associated with macro-economic movements in the economy affect all firms.

---

[16] Choosing a rate of return which ignores inflation is helpful because it makes it possible when implementing the price control to compensate for whatever inflation turns out to be simply by uprating the price by the annual rate of inflation, as measured by the consumer price index (CPI), diminished by whatever annual increase in productivity (known as X) the regulator deems possible. Prices thus change by CPI – X.

[17] The winners were William F. Sharpe, Harry Markowitz, and Merton Miller.

Some sectors are more insulated against such general movements than others. For example, a firm providing an essential service such as energy which households have no choice but to buy will be less risky than a firm making luxury goods. Accordingly, an energy firm can offer a lower return in excess of the risk-free rate than a firm making luxury goods. Some investors, for example pension funds, have liabilities that extend long into the future, and hence prefer investments that can offer secure long-term returns, even if those returns are quite low.

According to the CAPM, there is a precise and particular way of calculating the degree of risk in each share (known as its beta). This is based upon a comparison between its degree of variation and that of the equity market as a whole, which is, by assumption, set at one. Where returns to a company's share fluctuate more widely than those to the market as a whole, its beta exceeds one. Where they fluctuate less widely, its beta is less than one. For our three sectors of interest, typically internationally observed betas might be: energy—0.6; fixed telecommunications—1.0; water—0.5.

The final piece of the puzzle is the gap to be expected over the price control period between the risk-free rate and the expected return to the equity market as a whole. This is known as the 'equity premium'. Although a forecast of this premium is required, past observations of it may be relevant. They are available over periods as long as a century, but changes in economic circumstances may render older observations moot.

We can now put together the overall formula for the cost of capital to a firm, and hence the real rate of return (before inflation is added) which the regulator will be inclined to allow. The maths is extremely simple, and all the components required have been discussed above:

- The weighted average cost of capital, or WACC = (the share of debt in the firm's capital × the cost of debt) + (the share of equity × the cost of equity).
- The cost of debt = the risk-free rate + a small mark-up.
- The cost of equity = the risk-free rate + (the regulated firm's beta × the market average equity premium).

Table 7.3, which has been designed for illustrative purposes only, and not to reflect market conditions in any jurisdiction, shows how populating the formulae above can yield quite different estimates of the cost of capital—purely on the basis of the cumulation of alternative estimates of the various components. Thus the 'regulator's view' produces an allowed rate of return cost of capital which is less than a half that in the 'company's view'.

Table 7.3 How estimates of the allowed real rate of return (in % per year) in a network sector may diverge

	Regulator's view	Company's view
1. Real risk-free rate	−1	−0.5
2. Mark-up for private debt	1.5	2
3. *Real cost of debt (1+2)*	*0.5*	*1.5*
4. Real risk-free rate	−1	−0.5
5. Market equity premium	6	8
6. Company beta	0.6	0.8
7. *Real cost of equity (4+(5×6))*	*2.6*	*5.9*
(We now assume half debt and half equity finance)		
8. **WACC** *(3+7)/2*	1.5	3.7

It is thus not hard to see why debates about the cost of capital are extremely heated in network regulation. As noted in Chapter 9, this is an area where costly regulatory mistakes may be made. If the regulator persists in its view, ultimately the dispute may have to be resolved by an appeal body, which might be a court or a special administrative body or tribunal.

The Future of Network Regulation

In key network industries, network costs—of wires, pipes, and tracks—often make up about a third of the costs of supply of the end product: and spending on the relevant final services can amount to more than 10 per cent of total household expenditure. This makes network pricing very important, especially for poor households.

As a consequence, a lot of controversy surrounds how wholesale network prices in sectors such as energy, telecommunications, and water are set, and factored into retail prices—because, typically, the networks are monopolies. This applies whatever the system of ownership—public or private.

In the case of investor-owned assets, some progress has been made in improving the cost information used to generate future prices, but there are constant criticisms that regulated firms are able to use their access to better information than the regulator to earn excess returns. For the reasons given above, the prospect of finding a comprehensive solution to identifying efficient levels of costs within the present framework is limited—though greater determination by regulators to bear down on costs can make a big difference. Perhaps for too long, consumers have been overpaying for using the assets that they have financed, in the form of excess profits and the financing of excessive capital investment.

This is of particular importance in the decades ahead which will see two significant developments requiring major network investments. The first is digital transformation. So far, the communications sector is the most highly digitized, but all other sectors are likely to follow, including education, health, advanced manufacturing, and transport. The impact of the internet of things will be a major aspect of these developments. Regulators will have to ensure that the associated expansion of capacity of fibre to the home and of 5G networks does not create renewed opportunities for the abuse of market power.

As far as the energy sector is concerned, the challenge of climate change (outlined in Chapter 6) is likely to require a significant expansion of electricity transmission and distribution capacity—even allowing for the complementary software developments described above—and the decline or re-purposing of the gas networks. The challenge for regulators will be to elicit what additional network investments are necessary at the lowest cost to end users.

Digital transformation introduces new options and opens up more opportunities for both competition in the market and the greater use of competitive tendering. The focus of this book is the positive role that regulation can play to protect consumers and achieve other benefits. It is clear that the scope for innovation in the network space is very large. Despite some good work on the experimental relaxation of regulatory rules via sandboxes and 'tournaments' in which firms compete for subsidies to provide first commercial applications of new techniques, this is an area where regulators must continue to work hard.

8
Regulating Digital Platforms

Introduction

One of the most discussed and pressing regulatory challenges of recent years has been what to do about the hugely successful digital platform and related companies which now bestride the world. Their emergence provides a rather brutal and urgent test for positive regulation: Can legislators and regulators maintain the benefits generated by such influential new actors, but also control the adverse effects?

Towards the end of 2019, the world's eight most valuable companies comprised five US-based tech companies (Alphabet (Google), Amazon, Apple, Facebook, and Microsoft), two Chinese tech companies (Alibaba and Ten Cent), and Berkshire Hathaway (which owns several energy network companies, including one in the UK). Visa, the credit card company which intermediates between customers and merchants, was just below the above in the value table.

The ranking of the five US companies changes frequently, and each of the individual valuations moves around—up to and surpassing a trillion US dollars. All of them are worth more than the titans of old, such as the established automobile manufacturers, banks, chemical companies, oil companies etc., and they are worth far more than those traditional 'physical' network companies such as AT&T, Verizon, Deutsche Telekom, National Grid, British Gas, EDF, Eon, etc., that once dominated network valuations.

More traditional physical network companies in the telecommunications sector have now become somewhat resentful suppliers of transport services to the so-called 'over the top' digital platforms such as Facebook and Google, which rely on the physical networks for data transport but make no direct contribution to their costs, nor to the costs of the vital task of extending internet coverage to the second and poorer half of the human population. Other platforms such as Uber, in mobility markets, and Airbnb, in renting accommodation, have caused similar disruption and attract similar controversy.

The five US companies enumerated above do many different things. They are big players in the cloud; they offer e-commerce; they produce and sell very successful consumer devices such as the iPhone; they provide software for business processes. In this chapter, though, we focus chiefly on one aspect of their activities, their acting purely as platforms which intermediate commercial transactions between different sorts of economic agents such as suppliers and customers of goods and services, or advertisers and users of social media, or would-be passengers and vehicle drivers.

Alphabet's original and still major activity—Google search—and Facebook's primary social network activity are the outstanding examples of so-called two-sided platforms; their commercial rationale is to put in contact broadband users and advertisers. To do so, they operate in the 'market for attention'; they offer services to users, who reward them by being receptive to the accompanying ads. Advertisers pay the platform directly, and users contribute free of charge not only their immediate attention but also the data concerning their preferences, which the platforms further monetize by offering increasingly bespoke opportunities to advertisers.

As well as providing cloud computing services, Amazon runs an e-commerce platform which both offers goods for sale on its own account, and allows other suppliers to offer their own products. Only in the latter aspect is it a two-sided platform. Similarly, Microsoft's Windows platform attracts both computer users and applications developers to transact on it, but it also sells complementary Microsoft products such as Microsoft Office. Although it is not Apple's main business, the Apple store is effectively a walled garden in which users of Apple devices can trade with apps providers, including Apple itself.

The liberating and beneficial effect of digital platforms, or of tech companies more widely, has been generally recognized.[1] However, various less benign consequences are also observed. For example, it has been argued, with respect to the USA in particular, that the extraordinary profitability

---

[1] Several studies have asked Facebook users to specify what monetary compensation they would need to give up their use of the service for a month. In 2016–17, the monthly figure for US participants in a major survey was at the $35–50 level. The figure for access to search tools was even higher. See E. Brynjolfsson, A. Collis, and F. Eggers, 'Using Massive Online Choice Experiments to Measure Changes in Well-Being', https://doi.org/10.1073/pnas.1815663116. A later study found, however, that a four-week period without Facebook 'improves subjective well-being and substantially reduces post-experiment demand, suggesting that forces such as addiction and projection bias may cause people to use Facebook more than they otherwise would'. H. Allcott, L. Braghieri, S. Eichmeyer, and M. Gentzkow, 'The Welfare Effects of Social Media', *American Economic Review* 110(3) (2020): 629–76.

of tech companies is one of the reasons for the concentration of the benefits of economic growth on the super-rich, while incomes of the middle class have languished.

Some of the most prominent digital platforms have also appeared persistently to enjoy the benefits of market power. This tendency may be strengthened by a much-discussed feature of two-sided platforms, their propensity to tip into a monopoly. Some platforms have been accused of abetting this outcome by buying up, and sometimes suppressing, potential competitors. The regulators tasked with dealing with these issues are typically competition authorities, which have taken or are taking action in many jurisdictions. Governments and parliamentary groups are also considering whether legislative changes are required. The result so far is a few headline-grabbing completed cases and many proposals for new obligations on the companies concerned.

The almost endless US and EU Microsoft competition case of nearly twenty years ago did not revolve primarily around a two-sided digital platform; it rather involved the leveraging of Microsoft's market power in operating systems into related markets, such as that for browsers. In more recent years, the European Commission has fined Alphabet nearly €4 billion (under appeal) for biasing the order of its general search results to favour its affiliated shopping sites (the Google shopping case) and for abusive behaviour in the digital advertising market. Amazon is under investigation in several jurisdictions for using the data which it acquires about other vendors on its two-sided platform to compete with them as a vendor itself.[2] And while Apple has had its fair share of involvement in competition cases, it differs from Facebook and Google in being scornful of the manner in which they exploit their customers' data in the digital advertising market.

The discussion rages further, however, than just over competition law and economic regulation. Social media platforms are also charged with, amongst other things: spreading fake news; permitting covert or otherwise inappropriate interventions in elections and other political proceedings, often from outside the country concerned; being responsible for cybersecurity lapses which jeopardize customers' privacy; and avoiding tax payments. This has caused social media sites to take on thousands of employees to check and take down posts, led to calls for greater disclosure of advertisers' identities, and encouraged some nations to set up a special tax regime for platforms.

---

[2] https://ec.europa.eu/commission/presscorner/detail/en/IP_19_4291.

This represents a powerful challenge to regulation: is it possible to use it to retain the benefits of digital platforms but to eliminate their adverse effects. Can these new gigantic corporations be tamed?

Here we focus upon the challenges posed by the platforms' abuses of their market power—probably the most complex of the problems noted above. We start with an exposition of the special features of two-sided platforms which may create a heightened or special need for regulation.[3] The discussion then considers how these features might play out, and focuses on the risk of markets 'tipping' into monopolies. It then discusses how general competition law might be strengthened to keep up with the new dynamics of digital platforms. The final section contains conclusions and discusses prospects for positive regulation meeting these new challenges.

What Is So Special about Two-Sided Market Platforms?

Digital platforms exemplify the growing trend for profits to be made not from labour and tangible physical assets (as with utility networks) but out of intangible capital, often in the form of intellectual capital. This so-called 'capitalism without capital'[4] is exemplified by two sectors where significant digital transformation has occurred, in communicating content (such a search and social media) and in payment services (via traditional methods such as credit cards or new ones such as blockchain).

Digital transformation, moreover, is also affecting other sectors in which physical products or services rather than only information are transmitted between parties. Examples are utility services such as energy and water, social services such as education, health, and social care, and advanced manufacturing. It is thus reasonable to expect significant extensions of the role of digital platforms throughout the economy. While it is hard to avoid discussing the most prominent current examples of digital platforms, we should be looking to create a regulatory regime that takes on board scenarios in which individual platforms proliferate much more

---

[3] For a fuller and very readable account of such platforms, see D. Evans and R. Schmalensee, *Matchmakers: The New Economics of Multisided Platforms* (Harvard Business Review Press, 2016). Evans and Schmalensee are the two economists who developed much of the related analysis.

[4] J. Haskel and S. Westlake, *Capitalism without Capital: The Rise of the Intangible Economy* (Princeton University Press, 2018).

widely, but each platform has a lesser impact on consumers. In pursuit of this aim, what follows cites illustrations from more 'everyday' two-sided platforms.

Many commercial transactions involve a direct exchange between the provider of a service and the customer, who pays for it. In a two-sided market, however, an intermediary—the platform—interposes itself between supplier and user, and contrives the provision of an independent 'match-making' service of some kind to both sides, almost invariably in exchange for money or another consideration from at least one, or more normally both sides.

The existence of two sides opens the door to a special form of network effect. Network effects first entered the currency of economic analysis in connection with one-sided markets. They identify the phenomenon that consumers or producers of a good or service may have a positive or a negative effect on each other's welfare. Thus more traffic on a road may encourage the appearance of ancillary services such as petrol stations—a positive effect. But as the road gets busier, congestion may appear, which has a negative impact on road users.

In a two-sided market context, there is still scope for direct network effects. Thus, the value of Facebook to those who use it as a social network grows with the number of such users. But the presence on Facebook of a different group of agents—advertisers—opens the door to the existence of (positive or negative) *indirect* network effects, which make a platform more or less attractive to participants the more agents there are on the *other* side.

Thus, the more subscribers Facebook has, the more attractive it is to advertisers, the more advertising revenue there is available to it, and the more Facebook can improve its offering. Similarly, the more passengers a ride-hailing platform like Uber has, the more attractive it is for drivers to sign up to it, and the more drivers a service has, the more attractive it is to passengers. This is also the case with merchants and shoppers in relation to credit card providers, and with households and restaurants in the case of food-ordering platforms.

Positive network effects, whether direct or indirect, place a premium on size: the larger the platform the more attractive it is. If both types of positive outcomes are present, as seems quite frequently to be the case, this effect is super-charged and leads to a greater prospect of the market tipping into a monopoly. This can itself be detrimental to consumers, if it leads to excess profits. It also gives the monopolist an incentive to maintain its position by excluding new entrants.

We discuss below how this danger can be averted, or how one might deal with a market which has tipped by means of regulation. But it is useful first to point out some special features of pricing in two-sided markets, both from the standpoint of the platform itself and from that of the users of its services.

The first point is that the platform does not necessarily charge both sides of the market, or charge them in the same way. Facebook and Google are prominent examples. They receive monetary payment from digital advertisers, which may be based on the number of clicks-through to the advertiser's site received.[5] Users make no monetary payment but contribute their attention and their data, which the two companies can then use to offer better targeted (and more expensive) advertising, or to sell on to other companies.

Even when both sides pay, the logic of the platform may require different prices on each side. An often discussed illustrative example from the early days of two-sided markets analysis was provided by then common 'singles bars', in many of which introductions could be effected between men and women. For this platform to work commercially for the benefit of both sides, it was necessary to strike some sort of balance between men and women. This could be efficiently accomplished by differential pricing. This might include below marginal cost pricing for one side, such as the offer of free drinks for one gender. According to the earlier wisdom of competition law, below-cost pricing, at least by a dominant firm, raises the suspicion of unlawful behaviour. Yet in this case it looks to be in the overall interests of both sets of end users.

The wider point is that, in a two-sided world, familiar propositions in competition economics seem to falter—notably about how prices should be set to maximize firm's profits and (more importantly from a regulatory point of view) to promote consumer welfare or to identify a possible abuse of dominance. In the rather conservative and slow-moving world of competition law, this is a challenging and disruptive conclusion.

One important determinant of the operation and degree of competition of a platform market is the degree to which the agents on both sides of the market either sign up for and exclusively use a single platform ('single-home'), or alternatively choose on each occasion which of two or more rivals to use ('multi-home').

---

[5] Between them, Facebook and Google account for roughly 50 per cent of global digital advertising.

By way of a worked example, consider food-ordering platforms, which permit customers to order food deliveries from a set of subscribing restaurants—both purchasers and restaurants usually paying fees to the platform.[6] This is an activity where competition can be observed in varying degrees in different jurisdictions.

If every party on both sides is truly a multi-homer, then normal competition is feasible (subject to a variety of other problems, such as strong direct networks effects). If both sides single-home, then platforms compete to capture any buyer or seller on either side which can then be 'sold' to the other side.

The more interesting case arises when one side single-homes and the other does not—so becoming, in the jargon, a 'competitive bottleneck'.[7] The platform then tries to recruit as many single-homers as possible, which can then be sold on to the highest bidder on the other side. This puts a premium on converting a multi-homing agent, for example a restaurant, into a single-homer. In the case of retail customers this can be accomplished by loyalty rewards.

These possibilities are illustrated in Table 8.1.

Table 8.1 Single- and multi-homing in the food-ordering market and the resulting effect on platform competition

		Restaurants	
		Single-homing	Multi-homing
Consumers	*Single-homing*	Platforms compete on the consumer side and on the restaurant side	Platforms compete on the consumer side; platforms face little direct competition on the restaurant side, as they provide access to separate sets of consumers
	Multi-homing	Platforms compete on the restaurant side; platforms may face little direct competition on the consumer side, as they provide access to separate sets of restaurants	Platforms compete on both sides and may try to push restaurants (or consumers) towards single-homing, e.g. through exclusivity (on the restaurant side) or loyalty rewards (on the consumer side)

[6] See further M. Cave, 'Platform Software versus the Software of Competition Law', *Journal of European Competition Law & Practice* 10 (2019): 472–8.

[7] See M. Armstrong, 'Competition in Two-Sided Markets', *Rand Journal of Economics* 37(3) (2006): 668–91.

In the case of a merger inquiry dealing with the above scenario,[8] the UK competition authority concluded that the larger merging party had more single-homing restaurants than the smaller one, but a higher share of single-homing consumers than single-homing restaurants. On the basis of this and other nuanced evidence, the authority concluded that competition between the partners would mainly be focused on the consumer side.

The Strength of the Indirect Network Effects and the Risk of Tipping: What Can Be Done to Forestall it by Regulation?

In order to assess the strength of the indirect effects, it is a great help to have observations from a range of similar markets, or to track the data of a single market over time. Where tipping has occurred on a near global basis, the mere existence and continuation of a monopoly may lead us to suspect (but not to be sure of) the presence of powerful indirect network effects, but in such cases we get little insight into how the market has become increasingly concentrated.

To consider how to measure the strength of indirect network effects, we revert to the example of two-sided food-ordering platforms, which inevitably operate in multiple geographic markets, determined by distance over which meals can be delivered within a given time. In this instance, the relevant questions are: (i) Does the value which a restaurant derives from being on a platform increase with the number of customers on the other side of the platform? (ii) Does the value to customers of being on a platform grow with the number of restaurants on the platform?

In each case, there is a notional function connecting the number of customers or restaurants, and the resulting benefit accruing to the other side of the market. If the graph of this function is completely flat, there is no indirect network externality. If it rises constantly, there is a positive indirect network externality across the whole range. But it could take any shape, including rising up to a 'critical mass', flattening out, and then even falling. Thus, the benefit that a customer might derive from access to restaurants via a food-ordering platform might first rise with the number of restaurants, then remain constant when customers are broadly satisfied with the choice

---

[8] Competition and Markets Authority, *Just Eat and Hungryhouse* (CMA, 2017).

available, but then fall as the process of scrolling through a long list of restaurants becomes tedious.

To investigate the extent of indirect network effects, some empirical evidence was available in the merger inquiry discussed above. For example, a statistical study was made of how changes in the number of restaurants on platforms in different geographic areas affected market shares of the platforms. The results showed that increases in the number of restaurants available on one of the merger partner platforms had a negative impact on the value of orders placed on the other. But these effects diminish, in absolute terms, over time. This is consistent with the notion that, once each platform has 'enough' restaurants, customers are not attracted by a platform with a number in excess of this amount.

Collecting and extending the points above, three factors likely to affect the probability of tipping are: (i) the degree of platform differentiation (which is an outcome of strategic decision-making in the relevant market); (ii) the strength of the direct and indirect network effects (which depends upon the parties' utility and profit functions); and (iii) customers' homing practices (where the key point is that, if one side can multi-home at a comparatively modest cost, then a major force leading to tipping—the pressure on all agents to choose only the most advantageous platform—evaporates).

Now, suppose the regulator has a well-founded belief that market tipping is a likely outcome. What can be done about it? Again we illustrate this with a topical example—that of ride-hailing platforms which link passengers seeking rides with drivers owning vehicles willing to provide them.[9]

Ride-hailing markets in different cities exhibit different and changeable structures. In many US cities, a duopoly is often observed, between a larger firm (usually Uber) and a smaller one (Lyft). In the UK the limited evidence available suggests that Uber has a strong position in the narrow ride-hailing marketplace, with some entry occurring. Asian countries exhibit a variety of generally highly concentrated outcomes.

A key policy or regulatory problem is that, if a two-sided market with strong indirect network effects has tipped, it can then be very difficult then to correct the situation by entry. A correction may have to wait until the next disruptive new service comes along to undermine the current market leader, and in the meantime price controls or other interventionist measures may be needed in order to address customer detriment. So it is

---

[9] For further details see G. Barker and M. Cave, 'Predicting and Forestalling Market Tipping: The Case of Ride-Hailing Apps in the UK' (17 January 2020). Available at https://ssrn.com/abstract=3521477,

pertinent to ask what a regulator might additionally do on a precautionary basis to forestall such an outcome.

A possible list is given in Table 8.2, tailored to the ride-hailing example. Pursuing a policy along these or related lines requires considerable fore-sight, and it may not work if the tendency to tip is too strong.

Table 8.2 Potential corrections in the ride-hailing market

- Impose data reporting requirements to monitor market developments.
- Seek to establish the strength of the direct and indirect network effects.
- Prevent explicit exclusivity arrangements with drivers and riders; thus in Singapore, a ride-hailing platform may not offer drivers an exclusive contract. Outlaw incentive arrangements which have the same effect.
- Impose a special merger regime (there is a precedent in the UK for such a special regime—in the regulated water sector).
- Ensure that the competition authority's or equivalent agency's administrative priorities are configured in a way which ensures that potentially anti-competitive behaviour is carefully scrutinized.
- Prevent a large or prospectively dominant licensee from enhancing its attractions by showing rival or interconnecting transport services on its platform.
- Impose a data remedy, requiring the potential tipping firm to share certain data with its competitors, within the limits of customers' privacy; the extent of the obligation could be flexed in accordance with the scale or growth of the largest supplier.*

* For further discussion of this option, see J. Prufer and C. Schottmüller, 'Competing with Big Data' (16 February 2017). Available at https://ssrn.com/abstract=2918726.

Other Platform Regulatory Proposals

This section moves beyond description and analysis to consider what regulatory responses have been proposed and are appropriate to the emer-gence of very powerful digital platforms. There are literally hundreds of proposals for new arrangements, but so far relatively few enactments of new legislation. This section discusses certain proposals in five categories:

- Proposals to regulate large platforms relying on digital advertising.
- Proposals to change merger regimes.
- Broader changes to competition law.
- Radical proposals for the break-up of 'big tech' companies.
- Partnering competition law with a regulator.

Proposals to Regulate Large Platforms (Facebook and Google)

Governments and regulators have prepared many documents that outline potential changes in the regulation of digital platforms. Many of these focus on the problems in social media and search, where Facebook and Google are pre-eminent.[10] The two companies are extremely and persistently profitable—almost from the outset. (In contrast, two other firms which are the subject of much debate in this context—Amazon and Uber—took some years to show a profit.)

One way of interpreting what Facebook and Google are doing is that they are platforms operating in what are called attention markets. As Evans puts it, they 'solve a transaction cost problem. Marketers would like to deliver messages to consumers in order to increase sales of their products and would pay to do so. Consumers would be willing to receive advertising messages if they were paid enough, but it is hard for marketers and consumers to get together on their own to do this deal.'[11]

It has also been argued, however, that if an attention platform reduces the number of advertisements it sells, it will reduce the number of upstream firms that have access to consumers, thus increasing their market power. This bottleneck strategy can generate higher total profits for the upstream industry that are partly captured by the platform through higher total advertising revenue.[12]

Elements of analysis of attention markets can be found in an Interim Report into platforms funded by digital advertising paper published in December 2019 by the UK Competition and Market Authority (CMA). This followed and built upon an earlier report to the UK Government presided over by Jason Furman.[13]

---

[10] For penetrating insights into these companies, see K. Auletta, *Googled: The End of the World as We Know It* (Penguin, 2009) and S. Levy, *Facebook: The Inside Story* (Penguin, 2020).

[11] D. Evans, 'The Economics of Attention Markets', *Review of Industrial Organization* (February, 2019).

[12] A. Prat and T. Valletti, 'Attention Oligopoly', working paper, 19 June 2018, http://dx.doi.org/10.2139/ssrn.3197930.

[13] Competition and Markets Authority, *Online Platforms and Digital Advertising Market Study: Interim Report* (London: CMA, December 2019); *Unlocking Digital Competition*, Report of the Digital Competition Expert Panel (the Furman Report), March 2019. See also in this connection: Australian Competition and Consumer Commission, *Digital Platforms Inquiry—Final Report* (July 2019); J. Cremer et al., *Competition Policy in the Digital Age: Report to Commissioner Vestager* (Brussels: EC, April 2019); Chicago Booth Stigler Center, *Stigler Committee on Digital Platforms: Final Report* (September 2019).

The two activities discussed here—search and social media—are characterized by economies of scale and considerable direct and indirect network effects. Thus, a firm intending to provide answers to searches must first incur the large sunk cost of crawling over and indexing the internet. In addition, a firm responding on a daily basis to more searches is better placed to improve its algorithm and hence the quality of searches it offers.

The CMA report finds that in the UK Facebook and Google hold strong supply positions in the relevant advertising markets, which allow them to enhance their revenues by controlling supply, ultimately to the detriment of purchasers of goods and services.

In addition, the two firms are able to organize their relations with users in such a way that the latter, in order to save time, default into arrangements which are highly advantageous to the firms with respect to their willingness to share their data and accept personalized advertising. Taking these and other features of the relevant markets into account, the Interim Report concludes that they have allowed Facebook and Google in 2018 to make returns on capital of 50 per cent and 40 per cent respectively, when their cost of capital is about 9 per cent.

The CMA's Interim Report considered three potential responses:

- The imposition of an enforceable code of conduct on digital platforms satisfying certain conditions, as proposed by the Furman Report. This would require legislation to establish a form of *ex ante* intervention which would be complementary to competition law. That legislation would have to specify criteria for any platform's inclusion in the scheme, and the scope of the code of conduct.[14] It would be principles-based and would address concerns that speedy intervention may be required to avoid lasting competitive harm.
- Introducing rules to improve transparency and give users greater control over data. These might include arrangements which give consumers an easy option to use the platforms' services without requiring them to allow use of consumers' data for personalized advertising, for which changes to the default settings would expressly be required, to make this option a reality.
- Providing for specific interventions to address problems of market power and to promote competition. Possible examples include the sharing of Google's ability to be the default search engine on devices

---

[14] The notion of codes of practice can, of course, be applied to digital platforms more generally.

and browsers.[15] Equally Google could be placed under an obligation to provide certain data to its competitors.

The Furman Report also considered the institutional framework within which such changes would be implemented, proposing the creation of a digital unit within the UK competition authority. Other proposals also embody plans to establish a separate digital regulator—discussed further below.

Changes in the Merger Regime Covering Digital Platforms

A recent study examined 300 mergers carried out by Google, Amazon, and Facebook from 2008–18.[16] In most cases, the acquirers portrayed the targeted services to be largely unrelated to their own offerings, but—after the merger—the same services were shown increasingly to converge with, and to be integrated with, their own offerings. Target companies, moreover, seem to be particularly young, being four years old or younger in nearly 60 per cent of cases at the time of the acquisition.

This acquisition wave has attracted attention and criticism. It is asserted that large platform companies are constantly on the look-out for potential competitors, and when they find them they buy them up, in some cases to exploit the acquisition alongside their current portfolio, in other cases to stifle them.

Competition authorities have been criticized for approving mergers on the footing that they did not create competition concerns at the time of review, when the subsequent history of the combined entity did lead to some convergence of services produced. The 2014 merger between Facebook and WhatsApp was represented, at the time, as a merger of different services, one not involving horizontal integration. But subsequently they converged and their infrastructures are now being integrated.

In the European Union and elsewhere, mergers are only subject to scrutiny if they exceed certain turnover thresholds. Thus the purchase of a young company with negligible turnover, even at a very high price, avoids

---

[15] Google was alleged by a Goldman Sachs analyst to be about to pay Apple US$12 billion in 2019 to install its search engine on iPhones, iPads, and MACs.

[16] E. Argentesi, P. Buccirossi, E. Calvano, T. Duso, A. Marrazzo, and S. Nava, *Merger Policy in Digital Markets: An Ex-Post Assessment* (Munich: CESifo Working Paper, 2019).

regulatory scrutiny. A simple suggested response is to lower the sales threshold value, or to investigate mergers which satisfy a threshold value of the acquisition.

A more radical proposal for dealing with cases of so-called digital merger adopts a tougher criterion for the merger to proceed. Several authors have noted that in most jurisdictions, a merger inquiry hinges upon the difference in outcome with or without the merger. This requires two separate projections of future market developments, and an estimate of the difference between them, in order to answer a question such as: will the merger have an adverse effect on competition?

There is a risk in this process: both of mistaken prohibitions and of mistaken clearances. Where changes are occurring at speed and where tipping is a risk, the harm from the latter may be large. Competition authorities should be aware of it. The precise wording of the test is significant. The Furman report (page 13) notes that the current UK merger test depends on whether the smaller firm 'is more likely than not' to be able to survive. It suggests that this should be replaced by a test which assesses whether a merger is expected to be beneficial or harmful, taking into account both the likelihood and the scale of the effects.

Other Changes to Competition Law

Jean Tirole discusses the challenges that competition policy faces when confronting two-sided markets, and 'the review of the software of competition policy' which is required.[17] His phrase refers to the analytical procedures or 'operating system' which bridges the gap between the 'hardware' of the statutes and the 'apps', or individual case decisions.

As noted above, this 'software' needs to pay attention to special features of two-sided markets, such as homing practices and the risk of tipping, as well as finding new ways of addressing classic questions such as how to define markets and conduct a price-concentration analysis. A recent publication by the OECD discusses how this is being done on a piecemeal fashion in practice.[18]

Some countries have gone further, however, by introducing additional standards of intervention. More particularly, in Germany a 2017 Act against Restraints on Competition creates a lower standard in national

---

[17] J. Tirole, *Economics for the Common Good* (Princeton University Press, 2017).
[18] OECD, *Rethinking Antitrust Tools for Multi-Sided Platforms* (Paris: OECD, 2018).

legislation than that adopted in EU competition law on abuse of dominance. It introduces the principle that for a distortion to take place, absolute market power may not be necessary if there is a material difference in relative market power that creates a situation of economic dependency. This is illustrative of a multiplicity of other proposals of this kind, few of which have been enacted.

Breaking Up the Largest Platforms

It would be virtually impossible to break up Facebook by sending the 2.5 billion users of its main platform off in different directions: this would destroy the current positive network effects. Facebook, however, owns several different networks, and some of these could be passed into other hands. Exactly this happened in the analogue world in 2008 when the UK competition authority made a ruling with the effect that the company owning the three major airports serving London and the South East sold off two of them to separate buyers.

This approach, to be accomplished by unwinding previous take-overs by Facebook of Instagram and WhatsApp, was proposed in 2016 by US Senator Elizabeth Warren.[19] Alphabet, Amazon, and Apple would have to do the same for some of their own acquisitions. To the extent that the firms thus created competed with their previous parent firm, this would increase immediate competition, notably in the markets for digital advertising. Equally, the separated firms could enter the market in which Facebook continued to operate. The increase in competition would be expected to increase innovation. As a result, excessive prices would fall and service quality would rise. The prospect of such action, however, does create an incentive for firms to integrate their portfolio of services more fully.

At the same time, Senator Warren proposed that the owner of any large platform (with annual global revenues in excess of US$25 billion) would be prohibited from trading on those platforms. This is designed to avoid the conflicts of interest which might lead to the favourable treatment of services affiliated with the platform owner. This would require Amazon to spin off its own brands and Apple to cease offering its own mail and maps on its App store. We noted in Chapter 7 that the same separation solution

---

[19] Senator Elizabeth Warren, 'Reigniting Competition in the American Economy', https://www.warren.senate.gov/files/documents/2016-6-29_Warren_Antitrust_Speech.pdf. On the two take-overs by Facebook mentioned, see Levy, *Facebook*.

has been applied in relation to physical distribution networks, to keep natural monopolies out of potentially competitive markets.

These break-up solutions are broadly consistent with the ordinary processes of competition law: they enhance competition to solve the problem at hand. An alternative approach would assimilate the regulation of the digital platform to the category of natural monopolies requiring utility-style regulation, similar to physical local distribution and other assets discussed in Chapter 7 on the regulation of traditional utility networks. As in the case of those networks, the owner can be either a private sector or a public sector body.

That earlier discussion noted the obstacles to innovation and incentives for inefficiency associated with price control regulation, and the attempts to introduce different forms of competition in order to solve this problem. In the case of a fast-moving sector like digital platforms, where both technology and customer tastes may change, it is questionable whether a solution based on confirming and 'dealing with' a monopoly would work well.

Partnering Competition Law with a Regulator

There are a lot of options to consider under this heading, but almost all of them involve significant interventions beyond anything that currently takes place under traditional competition law. This requires us to consider which activities are best left to competition law and which are best dealt with under sector-specific regulation.

The difference between the two forms of intervention is most simply described as being that competition law operates across the whole economy by forbidding certain practices in advance, and is applied after the fact. Normally it applies structural remedies (allowing mergers subject to divestitures or disallowing them outright, for example), which do not entail long-term supervision of the firms in question. Regulation, on the other hand, is both more prescriptive, biased in favour of operating before the fact, and specific to particular sectors. As shown in Chapter 7, a regulator, unlike a competition authority, is often in near permanent contact with the firms that it regulates.[20]

A strong but not universal feature of the discussion in this section is that much of the analysis and many of the recommendations are driven by

---

[20] This is clearly an over-simplification. See N. Dunne, *Competition Law and Economic Regulation: Making and Managing Markets* (Cambridge University Press, 2015).

specific features that have now been identified in the digital platforms which have recently emerged, and which are not applicable to the economy as a whole. This is accompanied by a recognition of the need for a speedy response by the relevant authority, in order to avoid long-term harm. Thus the Furman proposal for codes of conduct permits the enunciation of enforceable principles-based regulatory rules before the event.

It is also apposite to mention that competition law, as an area for policy-making and practice, is a fairly conservative and closed world, containing many practitioners who, with their clients, may have a general interest in avoiding any extension to its scope. The Stigler Centre Report (p. 31) concluded that US competition law and its application by the courts over the past several decades have reflected the now outdated learning of an earlier era of economic thought, so that they appear in some respects inhospitable to new learning. This has led to under-enforcement. It is not obvious that the same is true in other jurisdictions, but if there are advantages in intervening in digital platforms on the basis of special legislation, a specialized agency may be able to act within those rules more promptly than would be the case with a competition authority.

Conclusion

There is little doubt that digital platforms—having been a 'new frontier' for massive if uneven wealth creation—now play a centre-stage role in discussions of regulation. The two 'poster children' of the sector, the fabulously successful Facebook and Google, rely for most of their revenues on genuinely two-sided platforms, the benefits and potential costs of which we now understand much better as a result of the advances in economic analysis that have been made in the last fifteen years.

Amazon (primarily a cloud provider and e-commerce firm) and Apple (most significantly, an equipment manufacturer) are caught up in the platform slipstream. Uber and Airbnb are also subject to considerable controversy. We should also note the existence of multiple smaller platforms and expect the emergence of many more as digital transformation proceeds.

Recent reports by and for governments and regulators, and by independent academic researchers, exhibit widespread agreement that the largest digital platforms—in addition to the very large benefits which they offer—can also cause harm to consumers, through their combination of the two classic abuses of market power: exploitation of customers and exclusion of rivals. Those who continue to oppose regulation increasingly focus their warnings upon the risk of throwing out the innovation baby with the excess profit bathwater.

There also seems to be mounting consensus about the kinds of remedies that are required. The list includes the following (some of which may be alternatives, others complements):

- Limiting larger platforms' abilities to engineer default options for end users and others which are advantageous to the platforms.
- Considering remedies which give providers of personal data a monetary reward.
- Tougher policing of acquisitions by dominant platform firms.
- Imposing specific rules on dominant platforms in relation to data exchange and interconnection with less powerful rivals.
- Using quicker 'soft law' *ex ante* remedies such as enforceable codes of conduct, whether brokered privately or in the context of administrative review by a regulator.
- Considering reversing the burden of proof on larger platforms, requiring them to show that they do no harm.
- More radical options such as unwinding completed mergers, preventing larger platforms from trading on them, and controlling their revenues.

All of these remedies are likely to require legislation, which has already been passed in some jurisdictions. Decisions have to be made about the institutional framework for enforcement of the new regulations.

Because the larger platforms are generally global, the most impactful legislative arenas for dealing with competition problems are likely to be the USA and the European Union. As always, coordination between these two jurisdictions will be a testing task. The European Commission has recently appointed an Executive Vice President 'for a Europe fit for the Digital Age'. Other jurisdictions are likely to act too. It looks as if the next few years will be a period of trial and error, from which we expect a clearer understanding to emerge of how the adverse effects of digital platforms can be avoided, but their undoubted benefits retained.

The notion of positive regulation emphasizes that the self-regulatory capacities of platform providers should be harnessed to the maximum extent feasible. The difficulty with such platforms, however, is that they are structured and operate in ways that incline them to certain core activities that bring negative consumer consequences. This explains why most of the control proposals noted above involve strong 'command' based interventions.

As regards the need for awareness, intelligence, and dynamism in the control of platform providers, the above discussion emphasizes that regulators and regulatory reformers need high levels of these characteristics in assessing such matters as the extent of the indirect network effects encountered in this area. Positive regulation stresses, moreover, the central importance of anticipating and responding to the dynamism of new technologies and offerings in this sector.

9
How to Prevent Regulatory Disasters

The model of positive regulation suggests that regulators perform poorly when they fail to demonstrate the appropriate levels of awareness, intelligence, and dynamism in setting objectives, delivering outcomes, or meeting procedural expectations. Thus, the regulatory failures associated with the financial crisis of 2007–8 involved at least: a lack of awareness of the risks associated with the sale of securitized subprime mortgages; a failure to develop information systems to evaluate the systemic risks associated with such sales; and a failure to respond effectively and rapidly enough to the newer kinds of securitized products that were flooding into financial markets.

When regulators fail to satisfy expectations about the objectives they pursue, or about the processes they employ, they will often have failed to appreciate, or deliver on, certain stakeholders' particular conceptions of appropriate regulatory aims, or their appetites for explanation, transparency, and openness, or their conceptions of fair procedures. Such failures can often result from weaknesses of awareness and intelligence—or dynamism where there is an inadequate response to a change of relevant expectations.

Failures to deliver desired substantive outcomes such as safer workplaces or cleaner environments can often result from a number of deficiencies. A lack of clarity on objectives can undermine delivery as can a lack of cost-effective implementation of strategy. In the case of the latter, poor performance often flows from weaknesses in discharging the various sub-tasks that make up the broad behaviour-influencing and enforcement processes. Thus, problems (e.g. of non-compliance or undesirable behaviour) may not be detected; the rules, strategies, and intervention tools employed in response to targeted risks or problems may be imperfect; or the application on the ground of those rules, strategies, and tools may be lacking. The regime, furthermore, may lack performance sensitivity (and hence direction) because it fails to assess whether current controls are working, and the system may be unresponsive in so far as it fails to address failings or new challenges that have been picked up. All such kinds of failure will tend to be associated with weaknesses of awareness, intelligence, and dynamism.

Case in point: The Child Support Agency

The Child Support Agency (CSA) was set up in 1993 to implement the Child Support Act 1991 so as to ensure that all parents who were liable to pay child support to their partners would do so. It is, however, the agency that is most frequently cited as a failed regulator.

It was heavily criticized for its failures of management and communication, the poor quality of its information, and its lack of fairness and effectiveness in enforcing maintenance payments. Particular complaints about CSA administration focused on delays, errors, and failures to take action.[1]

In November 2004, the head of the CSA resigned following widespread criticism and, in 2005, Tony Blair admitted that the CSA was 'not properly suited' to its job, amid reports that for every £1.85 that was delivered to children, the CSA spent £1 on administration.

In 2006 the UK Government announced that the CSA was not working and as a result would be axed and replaced by a 'smaller, more focused' body. A new system of child maintenance, the 'Child Maintenance Service', began operations in 2012 and the CSA was closed progressively in the period to 2018.

In the case of the CSA, criticisms related to all three of the elements of awareness, intelligence, and dynamism and weaknesses were evident across the tasks of setting objectives, delivering outcomes, and meeting procedural expectations.[2] The CSA was said, for instance, to have had little control over its objectives and targets (which were imposed externally). As for delivering outcomes, it did not produce results for a host of single parents (case backlogs were huge) and its decisions were subject to the delays, errors, and inactions referred to above. Nor did it meet procedural expectations with awareness, intelligence, and dynamism: it was accused,

---

[1] See https://www.independent.co.uk/news/uk/politics/child-support-agency-chief-quits-as-criticism-mounts-533573.html.

[2] See C. Irigoyen, *The UK's Child Support Act* (London: Centre for Public Impact, 2017), https://www.centreforpublicimpact.org/case-study/child-support-act-uk/.

for instance, of being weak on awareness of stakeholder concerns and of having insufficient intelligence on these (there was little research regarding parents' stances on maintenance issues). In addition, decisions were said to be made inconsistently; criteria for actions were often unclear; and the Agency was charged with not operating adequate communication and consultation procedures.

Case in point: The Financial Reporting Council

In late 2018 the Kingman Review of the Financial Reporting Council was published.[3] This independent examination echoed two earlier Select Committees in its adverse appraisal of FRC performance and in identifying a number of key weaknesses. Failures of awareness and intelligence were revealed in numerous findings: the FRC, for instance, had not been sufficiently aware of its need to change approach, nor had it amassed a full range of evidence on such matters as audit performance. In addition, both its scale of monitoring corporate reports and its reviews of its own processes were found to be low by international standards. Nor was FRC dynamism up to scratch—thus its legal powers were deficient but it had not responded by making the case for change.

General failings of approach were reflected in multiple shortcomings of delivery. Objectives, for instance, had not been set with clarity, precision, or sense of purpose. Outcomes, such as assurances of audit quality, had not been delivered with credibility and work to ensure robust corporate reporting had been hindered by cumbersome enforcement actions. Procedural expectations had not been met because FRC processes had been inconsistent, had not dealt well with conflicts of interest, and had been subject to leaks. In addition, the FRC had not engaged meaningfully with stakeholders, and its work in reviewing corporate reports was marked by a lack of transparency.

The Kingman Review recommended replacing the FRC and, in March 2019, the UK Government announced that the FRC would be disbanded and a new regulator established.

---

[3] See https://www.gov.uk/government/publications/financial-reporting-council-review-2018.

When regulators fail, the root causes of their deficiencies can be explained in a variety of ways. Different approaches to explanation will emphasize different factors. *Institutional* explanations come in many versions but commonly emphasize the degree to which regulatory failures can be explained by looking at either the forces that act within organizations (intra-institutional versions) or the structured relationships, and frictions, between different agencies, governmental and non-governmental (inter-institutional versions). Institutionalists of the latter variety might, thus, stress that the 2007–8 financial crisis cannot be fully explained without understanding the interdependencies of the financial regulators, the central banks, and the credit ratings agencies. More generally, such theorists would emphasize the degree to which regulatory tasks tend now to be spread across different layers and types of governmental body—a practice that leads to a host of coordination issues and potential deficiencies of collective performance. In the case of the Child Support Agency, for instance, the finger would be pointed at a lack of coordination between different government departments and the CSA regarding the aims, objectives, and targets appropriate for the child maintenance regime.

Interest-based explanations may take different forms. The 'public interest' approach typically assumes that regulators are pursuing public goals, and regulatory failures tend to be put down to different kinds of ineptness of delivery. In contrast, the 'private interest' approach stresses the extent to which regulators, firms, and other actors engage in self-interested behaviour. Economic versions are likely to 'follow the money' and point out the degree to which economic interests impact on regulation. A clear example of the 'economic theory of regulation' is associated with University of Chicago economists. This can crudely be summarized as the proposition that regulation is a means of wealth transfer, in the course of which regulators enrich themselves by selling their control of this power to the highest bidder; that bidder being almost invariably the concentrated and heavily-invested producer interest rather than the diffuse and isolated consumer interest.[4] The posited result is that the economically powerful will exert control over a regulatory regime so that there is a re-orientation of objectives (in favour of the capturers), or a failure to enforce so as to secure mandated outcomes, or a procedural distortion that favours the voices of the powerful.

---

[4] For a fuller discussion, see C. Veljanovski, 'Economic Approaches to Regulation', in R. Baldwin, M. Cave, and M. Lodge (eds.), *The Oxford Handbook of Regulation* (Oxford University Press, 2010), pp. 17–38.

More simply, it may be argued that many regulatory failures are caused by budgetary constraints, which stem, in turn, from the broad resistance to regulation of economically powerful interests. (On capture see further below.)

More political versions of *interest* accounts will stress that regulatory failures often stem from the exertion of political power—as in suggestions that the regulatory failures leading up to the global financial crisis of 2008 are best explained by the political imperative to engage in 'light touch' and 'business-friendly' modes of regulating rather than any regulator's lack of awareness of risks.

Ideas-based accounts will focus on beliefs, worldviews, or intellectual positions, as when it is contended that the financial regulators' systems were not aware or intelligent enough to appreciate the risks associated with the securitized products being traded in the lead-up to the 2007–8 financial crisis.

Case in point: MAFF and mad cow disease (BSE)

In late 1994, a number of people began to show symptoms of a neurological disease that would go on to be identified as Variant Creutzfeldt-Jakob disease (vCJD). This occurred primarily in younger people and was caused by eating meat infected with bovine spongiform encephalopathy (BSE).

In 1995 the UK Government continued to emphasize the safety of British beef. It was not until 20 March 1996 that the UK Government announced that vCJD was caused by eating BSE infected meat. By 2014, deaths from the disease numbered 177.

The 2000 Phillips Inquiry into BSE and vCJD strongly criticized the regulator, MAFF (Ministry of Agriculture, Fisheries and Food), for its lack of foresight, and level of relevant information on these diseases: there was said to be a failure to understand the nature of transmission of BSE that stemmed from the regulator's failure to consult experts.

The 'institutional', 'interest', and 'ideas' accounts of regulatory failure often tell part of the story only, and the best explanation in any instance may be achieved by drawing on different narratives as and when the evidence suggests that a contribution to the explanation may be made by a particular mode of analysis.

Preventing Regulatory Disasters

Regulation is largely conducted by human beings working in an institutional framework created by a political or legislative process. How then, can they avoid the errors and omissions to which an individual or a team regulators may be systematically prone?

Here it is worth looking at three major causes of regulatory failure and considering avoidance strategies. They are the three C's: culture, capture, and cognition, each of which would be a focus of the three varieties of explanation just noted. Culture would be a special concern of institutional theory, capture is central to interest theory, and cognition issues would be stressed by ideas theorists. Failures of culture, capture, and cognition can all impact on the awareness, intelligence, and dynamism of regulators, and, in turn, on their performance in setting objectives, delivering outcomes, and meeting procedural expectations.

Before developing our analysis of regulatory failure we offer a particular example. In this instance the (normally) regulatory function is performed by a government minister.

Case in point: How not to design a spectrum auction

Since 1994, spectrum auctions have generated nearly US$1 trillion, largely from mobile companies. In principle such auctions both direct spectrum to more efficient companies and maximize, for the public good, gains derived from the value of a scarce natural resource. But running a successful spectrum auction requires clarity of thought and some basic skill.

The auction described in this box was in fact run by an Australian Government department, not a regulator, but the diagnosis of failure would be the same. At the time, the government was seeking to balance its budget—thus to maximize auction revenues. It decided to accomplish this by raising the reserve price, the minimum bid which they would accept. This carries the risk that the some of the spectrum available is unsold and lies idle.

When this possibility was mooted, the minister responded as follows:

'The regulation of telecommunications powers in Australia is exclusively federal. That means I am in charge of spectrum auctions, and if I say to everyone in this room "if you want to bid in our spectrum auction you'd better wear red underpants on your head", I've got some news for you. You'll be wearing them on your head...I have unfettered legal power.'[5]

In the event, some spectrum was unsold, the government's revenue target was substantially missed, and the economy was denied access to a key resource. This appears to be the result of giving excessive weight to a sectional, rather than the public interest, and over-reach by the auction designer (who cannot force mobile companies to bid). This may have been complemented by a flawed internal valuation process.

What went wrong? In terms of our discussion below, this included a chaotic decision-making culture, capture of the regulatory decision by extraneous ambitions, and a series of cognitive errors based on wishful thinking.

Regulatory Culture

The ability of a regulator to reflect awareness, intelligence, and dynamism in discharging its tasks cost-effectively will be impacted significantly by its organizational culture: its shared attitudes, beliefs, values, and accepted modes of interaction. Peter Drucker has argued that, as an effect on firm performance, 'Culture eats strategy for breakfast, operational excellence for lunch and everything else for dinner.' This is likely to be as true for regulatory authorities as it is for corporations.

Case in point: Dr Shipman and a lack of dynamism at the GMC

Dr Harold Shipman was a UK general practitioner who murdered an estimated 250 patients in his care between 1974, when he entered practice, and 1998 when he was finally exposed.

The case became a regulatory crisis for the General Medical Council (GMC)—the regulator of the medical profession with responsibility for ensuring that doctors registered to practice were fit to do so.

Continued

---

[5] http://www.coleago.com/australian-spectrum-auction-failure/.

Continued

> The GMC had increasingly been criticized for a culture that was over-protective of doctors and it had been operating in a climate of growing dissatisfaction for some years. Extensive reforms had been proposed but progress on them was perceived to be slow.[6]
>
> Shipman committed suicide on 13 January 2004, one day prior to his 58th birthday, by hanging himself in his cell at Wakefield Prison.

One of the few anthropological studies of a regulatory body reveals the importance of organizational culture in shaping agency behaviour and performance.[7] This research on the then UK telecommunications regulator, Oftel,[8] points out that from the outside 'culture is visible only as it comes out in organizational behaviour, for example in a disposition to prosecute or invoke sanctions; but from the inside perspective, culture is what regulates regulation and hence is all-important to understanding the process'.[9]

The study concludes that culture served as a regulator of Oftel's work in defining meanings, setting boundaries, and keeping contradictory attitudes and beliefs in tension:

> Some of this was deliberately contrived by management, which was trying to impose a project management structure which challenged traditional civil service working practices. But some of it was spontaneous, unintended, dysfunctional or all three. The underlaps between the rival microcultures...created gaps in information transfer... [A]ccordingly it seems safer to conclude that the cultural regulation shaping Oftel's behaviour was a mixture of consciously-contrived management-engineered culture and a deeper set of attitudes, beliefs and working practices that were rooted in coping strategies, inheritance, inertia and reactions against change.[10]

Culture was said to determine how decisions were taken at Oftel—in three identifiable styles, characterizable either favourably or pejoratively as shown in Table 9.1.

---

[6] B. Hutter and S. Lloyd-Bostock, *Regulatory Crisis: Negotiating the Consequences of Risk, Disasters and Crises* (Cambridge University Press, 2017).

[7] C. Hall, C. Scott, and C. Hood, *Telecommunications Regulation: Culture, Chaos and Interdependence Inside the Regulatory Process* (Routledge, 2000).

[8] Replaced by Ofcom in 2003.

[9] Hall et al., *Telecommunications Regulation*, p. 5.

[10] Hall et al., *Telecommunications Regulation*, pp. 56–7.

Table 9.1 Decision-making styles at Oftel

Favourable description	Pejorative description
1. Cartesian	Bureaucratic
2. Diplomatic	Bargaining
3. Adhocratic	Chaotic

In the first, decisions can be taken on the basis of a pre-set objective, but either well and 'scientifically' or badly and bureaucratically, within a strictly hierarchical pattern of decision-making. We return to this later.

The regulator uses the diplomatic/bargaining approach to resolve inter-operator disputes, for example, but it can degenerate into bargaining with different groups of producers, to the detriment of their customers (or even to something akin to capture, discussed below).

In relation to the third approach, the adhocratic/chaotic variant is implemented within a flexible, adaptable, and informal form of organization defined by a lack of formal structure—the very antithesis of bureaucracy. The process may entail a degree of path-dependency, based upon an unstable and shifting process, partly driven by intuitive responses, learning, and doubling back. Chaotic has the normal meaning.

A contrast between the between the first and the third mode is well illustrated in the study by the conduct of a price control in UK telecommunications in the late 1990s. The task was to set a trajectory of retail prices offered by the former monopolist BT. This was the third such review by Oftel, so that precedents existed, which formed the basis for an analysis along standard modelling (i.e. Cartesian) lines, using standard bureaucratic procedures: work was divided into parts, which were then re-assembled within a decision-making hierarchy.[11]

Adhocratic/chaotic elements were, however, introduced by the agency's director-general, who felt that the staff's method would repeat previous over-rewarding of the incumbent operator. To do this he set aside the convention of choosing values for the calculations in the middle, rather than at the extreme of the supposedly feasible range. 'He floated in and out of decision-making in an unpredictable fashion, or by allowing his staff to reach a conclusion before he reopened the issue and introduced new variables or actors. His staff hated it.'[12] In the event, despite these adjustments,

---

[11] Hall et al., *Telecommunications Regulation*, pp. 127–39.
[12] Hall et al., *Telecommunications Regulation*, p. 111.

the company substantially over-performed even against the higher targets it was set as a result of the process.

Most regulatory authorities now have a board rather than an individual at the apex of decision-making. In the case described above, a skilled regulator with extensive private sector experience had an acute understanding of the potential cost savings available to the company, which triumphed over the negotiated conclusions of the tribes of economists, lawyers, and policy-makers which made up most of the team involved in the decision.

Let us consider the difference between a bureaucratic and an adhocratic/chaotic culture in a little more detail. When a regulatory process has lapsed into the bureaucratic version of culture, it will tend to exhibit the characteristics set out below:

- Hierarchical organization.
- Formal lines of authority.
- A fixed area of activity.
- Rigid division of labour.
- Regular and continuous execution of assigned tasks.
- Officials with expert training in their fields.
- All decisions and powers specified by regulations.

The adhocratic/chaotic approach, by contrast, exhibits:[13]

- Highly organic and non-bureaucratic structure.
- Little formalization of behaviour.
- Shifting areas of individual activity.
- Roles that are not clearly defined.
- Little or no standardization of procedure.
- Job specialization not necessarily based on formal training.
- All members have authority, in coordination with other members, to make decisions and to take action.
- Use of liaison devices to encourage mutual adjustment within and between teams.

In our terms, the principal regulatory failure associated with the 'bureaucratic' version of Oftel was its lack of dynamism. That deficit was partly, but not fully, made up in the event.

---

[13] See R. Waterman, *Adhocracy: The Power to Change* (Norton, 1990) and H. Mintzberg, *Mintzberg on Management: Inside Our Strange World of Organizations* (Free Press, 1989).

Regulators can today be observed trying to inject that necessary dynamism. The vocabulary of management science in the private sector has moved on, and has for some years focused on the concept of agility. This is partly a response to the digital transformation which, having initially conquered the communications sector, is now increasingly affecting almost every act of production, consumption, and social interaction.

An agile approach is characterized by a combination of clear goals and a leadership which both enables and disrupts.[14] A range of practices calculated to achieve these ends has been developed. Within regulatory bodies, so far this thinking is more reflected in plans than in attainments. For example, the 2019 *Strategic Narrative* published by the UK energy regulator Ofgem states:

> We now aspire to adopt a more agile regime, which is more project-based and less durable in structure, with teams forming and reforming more often, retaining professional specialisation where necessary and exhibiting multi-disciplinary ways of working. With a changing energy sector, we need to combine our existing expertise and specialisms with new skills…We expect such agile teams to operate in a more decentralised way and with more autonomy, sharing knowledge and joint internal decision-making. The data function in Ofgem will need to play a much greater strategic role in changing working practices across the organisation.[15]

Some regulatory actions, such as licence enforcement, may lend themselves less well to such approaches. However the design of regulatory policy, especially in sectors such as energy and telecommunications, which are characterized by substantial technological change, imposes new challenges, in terms of speed of process and a need imaginatively to consider new options. In an increasing number of cases, regulatory design is closely connected with digital transformation, and the greater use of data analytics. This juxtaposition increases the benefits of more dynamic and flexible approaches. It is for this reason that some regulatory agencies are making strenuous efforts to introduce cultural change into their organization via programmes designed to increase agility.

---

[14] M. Bazigos, A. De Smet, and C. Gagnon, 'Why Agility Pays' *McKinsey Quarterly* (December 2015); B. Waldock, *Being Agile in Business* (Pearson, 2015); ; S. Hayward, *The Agile Leader* (Kogan Page, 2018).
[15] Ofgem, *Strategic Narrative 2019–2023*, p. 24.

Regulatory Capture

In so far as regulators pursue private ends that are not within the terms of their legitimate objectives, this will rule out proper attempts to deliver outcomes and to meet procedural expectations (such as fairness). 'Positive regulation' will be undermined in a fundamental way. Such capture can, as noted, be explained in different ways but, in this section, we focus on the strand of regulatory capture theory that stresses the tendency of political considerations to divert regulators from the pursuit of mandated ends.

This approach is well demonstrated by Paul Joskow, who describes the regulator's predicament as follows:[16]

> In terms of the objectives of the firms being regulated, there is little question about the fact that they "like" profits...The objectives of regulatory commissions are naturally less clear and probably more complex than those of regulated firms...Given this fairly large amount of flexibility [for regulatory agencies] the general view taken here is that [they] seek to limit conflict and criticism appearing as "signals" in the economic and social environment in which they operate.

A more recent contribution by Clare Leaver uses the vivid descriptive phrase 'minimal squawk behaviour' to convey broadly the same hypothesis, where the regulator is assumed to seek to quieten criticism by giving way to those with loudest voices.[17] In more detail, this account suggests:

- Regulatory decisions are taken to keep interest groups quiet and to keep mistakes out of the public eye.
- Informational asymmetry is pivotal: the regulator knows its limitations; interest groups have private knowledge of the state of the world, which they can reveal or disclose.
- An able regulator has an incentive to gain reputation by pursuing the public interest: a less able one buys off squawk by generosity to noisy interests.
- This account is distinct from the economic theory of capture in which regulatory favour is universally sold to the highest bidder.

[16] P. L. Joskow, 'Inflation and Environmental Concern: Structural Change in the Process of Public Utility Price Regulation', *The Journal of Law and Economics* 17(2) (1974): 291–327 (296–8).

[17] C. Leaver, 'Bureaucratic Minimal Squawk Behaviour', *American Economic Review* 99(3) (2009): 572–607.

Leaver's study involves an empirical investigation designed to test the hypothesis that longer tenure of utility regulators will reduce the concerns of (weak or poor) regulators about the long-term reputational effects of squawk. (This hypothesis, it can be noted, contrasts with the 'economic' theory of regulation, which would indicate the opposite.) Citing US data, Leaver suggests that electric utility rate reviews are more likely to result in falling costs when regulators enjoy longer rather than shorter tenure.

What measures can be taken to combat this tendency for a regulator lacking self-confidence to put up the white flag and allow regulated firms to profit at the expense of their customers? A good start would be to choose better regulators who have greater awareness of their abilities to withstand political pressures and 'squawks'. Failing this, the regulator could deploy procedures that are designed to ensure that the squawking it hears is better balanced. It might, for instance, keep logs of the voices that it listens to, and it could encourage breadth and fairness of input by setting up access arrangements and information flows in ways that will encourage the expression of view by consumers' organizations and other parties who are financially less well-placed to make noise.

Cognitive Failings

Positive regulation requires awareness and intelligence, but these qualities may be difficult to supply when a regulator is afflicted with the kinds of cognitive failings that behavioural scientists have highlighted in recent years when analysing individual and group decision-making. When regulators look outwards, they often use behavioural insights to identify ways in which agents—usually individuals, but sometimes firms as well—depart from the full rationality of an ideal economic decision-taker. For example, householders fail to save adequately for retirement or to switch energy supplier when doing so would generate large bill savings.

But will regulators themselves be similarly afflicted? Cooper and Kovacic discuss this possibility,[18] and note that the time taken by regulators to make decisions is more likely to place them in the Kahneman and Tversky category of slow rather than fast thinking.[19] That fact, however, may not be enough to immunize regulators from the list of cognitive failures to which

[18] J. Cooper and W. Kovacic, 'Behavioral Economics: Implications for Regulatory Policy', *Journal of Regulatory Economics* 41 (2012): 41–58.
[19] D. Kahneman, *Thinking, Fast and Slow* (Penguin, 2012).

other agents are subject, including such familiar ones as biases induced by: errors in assigning weights to different sources of evidence; misconstruing the likelihood of possible outcomes; optimism; and myopia. Other failings may be due to a status quo, availability, or confirmation bias, to inertia, or to a propensity to engage in imitative or herd-like behaviour.

Case in point: Setting the allowed rate of return on network assets

We saw in Chapter 7 how the regulator typically has to set an allowed rate of return on network assets, with the calculation using a model that is populated with a variety of forward-looking financial data which depend crucially on a forecast of the risk-free rate—the real rate of interest on government bonds.

As the global financial crisis unfolded in 2008, this rate fell roughly from 2 per cent to minus 1 per cent. How would the UK regulators react? Would they incorporate the new lower figure as a semi-permanent feature or would they, as regulated firms proposed, assume a quick recovery to earlier, higher levels?

This issue arose sharply in 2011–13, as a number of near simultaneous price controls were set in several UK sectors. In the event, the various regulators made a very limited adjustment only.

In 2013, however, the regulatory appeals body, the Competition Commission, when hearing its first regulatory appeal for many years, signalled that it favoured a downward adjustment of the historic figure. This reduction gathered significant momentum in subsequent price control decisions, some regulators acknowledging that earlier rates were set too high.

As Max Weber noted, if we observe a bunch of people at a street corner putting up their umbrellas, they may be engaging in imitative social behaviour; or it may have started raining.[20] It is not possible to know how each individual decision was made, and whether it was a case of herd-like behaviour. But regulators are encouraged to communicate with one another over the cost of capital.

Increasingly, regulators are avoiding the need to predict the different components of the cost of capital into the future. Instead they can apply formulae to calculate the relevant companies' price ceilings into which observed market rates can be slotted as the period of the price control unfolds. This should make a 'squawk-minimizing' regulator less timorous.

---

[20] Max Weber, *The Theory of Social and Economic Organization* (Free Press, 1947), p. 114.

By way of illustration, a regulator, like a consumer, may pay excessive attention to readily available data (the 'availability' bias), or give excessive salience to one facet of a situation (in a market analysis, for example), or misconceive the probability of one outcome or another (a representativeness bias). Optimism and myopia are self-explanatory, and status quo bias and confirmation bias are well-understood concepts: people are reluctant to contemplate change or to depart from an earlier judgement, and this distorts their calculations.

Herd-like behaviour arises when individuals do what others are doing instead of making independent decisions. It may arise because (each) individual assumes that others have better information at their disposal and follows suit, or because the individual wants to avoid exposing herself as an outlier.

What can be done to reduce these risks of cognitive failure? If a distinction is drawn between what can be done before or while a regulatory decision is made, and what can be done afterwards, the following options can be identified.

Ex ante actions:

- Better mechanisms for selecting regulators—for example investigating pre-existing implicit biases and examining choices made by candidates in previous regulatory settings.
- Requiring publication of clear reasons for decisions, and specifications of underlying assumptions.
- Challenge groups within or outside an agency, or other anti-groupthink measures.
- Institutional arrangements which do *not* reward dysfunctional behaviour.
- Long tenure, ensuring that the regulator sticks around not just to see the publication of the regulatory decision, but to take responsibility for what eventuates.
- Use of sunset clauses for regulations, which triggers a necessary rethink and may diminish status quo and confirmation bias.

Ex post actions:

- Enhancements of the accountability of regulators for outcomes, to parliamentary or other institutions.

- Systematic auditing of outcomes, decomposing divergences from expected outcomes into false assumptions, mis-calibration of regulatory instruments and exogenous events.[21]

Conclusions

The temple of the oracle at Delphi had the phrase *gnothi seauton* or 'know thyself' carved on the portico. According to some accounts, the priestess (the Pythia) delivered oracles in a frenzied state induced by vapours rising from a chasm in the rock, speaking gibberish which priests of the temple then interpreted as enigmatic prophecies, and turned into the hexameters preserved in Greek literature.

Modern regulatory pronouncements may sometimes be obscure, but are not generally disseminated in this fashion. But the precept on the temple, defined by Socrates as an instruction for self-reflection, continues to be sage advice.

This chapter has suggested that regulators go wrong through a lack of awareness, intelligence, and dynamism, as well as an inability to deliver on the key tasks of regulation. These failures are systematic. A central way to reduce them is to work on awareness, intelligence, and dynamism. Thus, when regulators develop their awareness and intelligence systems, this increases their self-reflection and consciousness of their own fallibility, which can reduce the likelihood that mistakes will be made or repeated. Similarly, an emphasis on dynamism fosters the more agile regulatory systems that are especially needed in sectors marked by rapid technological and other changes.

As for responses to the specific causes of failure that are discussed above, the positive regulator will be alive to the need to re-examine its organizational *culture* in the face of changing circumstances. The self-awareness of such a regulator will make it conscious of the risks of *capture* or quasi-*capture* when regulated firms pile public pressure on the regulator at key junctures, for example at moments in the construction of a price control when the allowed rates of return are being set. Forearmed by

---

[21] A good example of such *ex post* quantitative analysis relating to energy regulation in the UK can be found in a report prepared for the relevant regulator examining the disparity between allowed and realized rates of return enjoyed by energy networks over the period 2013–17. See CEPA, *Review of the RIIO Framework and RIIO-1 Performance* (March 2018), https://www.ofgem.gov.uk/system/files/docs/2018/03/cepa_review_of_the_riio_framework_and_riio-1_performance.pdf.

this knowledge, the positive regulator will ensure that less well-represented interests groups are heard both within the regulatory body and more generally in public discourse.

With regard to potential *cognitive* failures, the positive regulator will engage in the kinds of counter-measures that have been noted above. Many of these measures are designed to improve the intelligence system that underpins action, and to ensure that regulatory decisions are made on the basis of the soundest available evidence, the optimal analysis and use of such evidence, and the avoidance of incentives and pressures that may lead to perverse or unsupportable decisions or policies.

10
Can National Regulators Solve Problems?

In a host of areas national regulators play only a limited role in dealing with issues, risks, and problems. In the environmental field, for instance, new risks relating to such matters as climate change and marine pollution have emerged with global reach and, as discussed in Chapter 6, responses to carbon emissions, and an array of issues have to be resolved on the international as well as the domestic stage.[1]

Economic globalization and the rise of the multinational corporations are factors that have also encouraged a movement towards harmonized control systems that facilitate trading, are not located in particular states, and rely not so much on laws and commands as on less coercive and more flexible controls. In this shift of approach state-based regulatory bodies have tended either to combine with, or give way to, networks of transnational institutions and to complex mixtures of private and public organizations that are positioned at a variety of governmental levels. Spheres in which transnational networks play an important role include financial services, banking, accounting chemical safety, insurance, fisheries, and product safety.

Julia Black has emphasized that such regimes are often 'decentred' or polycentric and lack a central locus of authority—they are marked by five central notions: complexity, fragmentation, interdependencies, un-governability, and the rejection of a clear distinction between public and private.[2]

Veerle Heyvaert has argued that, in the environmental area, there are five main reasons for resort to transnational regulation: 'to confront environmental problems that cannot effectively be governed at local level; to facilitate trade; to make up for absent or insufficient state regulation; to

---

[1] See generally V. Heyvaert, *Transnational Environmental Regulation and Governance* (Cambridge University Press, 2019).
[2] J. Black, 'Constructing and Contesting Legitimacy and Accountability in Polycentric Regulatory Regimes', *Regulation & Governance* 2 (2008): 137–64.

manage private sector risks; and to enhance the effectiveness of national environmental regulation.[4] To expand on the first of these points, local level action may not suffice because many pollutants traverse borders, state-based controls may be undermined by incompatible policies elsewhere (as when protected birds are shot when they migrate across a border), and because national regulations may be vulnerable to free-riding by third countries. These challenges will very often call for a coordinated regulatory response from numbers of countries and kinds of organization.

Case in point: Logging

Transnational regulation is encountered in the control of illegal logging.[3] National and international laws apply to harvesting, processing, transporting, buying or selling timber but a key role is also played by a transnational initiative: the EU Forest Law Enforcement, Governance and Trade Facility (FLEGT). The facility is hosted by the European Forest Institute (EFI), and was established in 2007. It supports the implementation of the EU FLEGT Action Plan, at the heart of which are Voluntary Partnership Agreements (VPAs) negotiated between the EU Commission and developing countries to create export licensing regimes.

Those regimes operate on the basis of jointly defined standards, requirements for monitoring, performance reviews, and third-party verifications. They incorporate acceptable logging standards as negotiated by the Commission, countries, and stakeholders against the background of EU and national legal requirements.

When regulation is conducted by means of such complex networks, special challenges arise in discharging the key tasks of setting objectives, delivering outcomes, and satisfying representative values. The following discussion focuses on transnational regimes, which tend to involve more complex networks than domestic systems but, even when risks and problems are more distinctly located within national boundaries, many of the below challenges are echoed when, as is commonly the case, national regulators operate within control regimes that are polycentric and involve networks of bodies that are located at different levels of government (local,

---

[3] Heyvaert, *Transnational Environmental Regulation and Governance*, pp. 10, 40.
[4] Heyvaert, *Transnational Environmental Regulation and Governance*, p. 55.

regional, national, and supra-national), that have different characteristics (public, private, state, non-state), and exert different kinds of influence (binding, non-binding).

Setting Objectives

In complex transnational regimes the identification of regulatory objectives is a particular challenge. Individual state regulators may be clear about their own aims but their influence on the broader regime may be limited and the aims and intentions of other regulatory actors may be unclear or even inconsistent. As was seen in Chapter 6, greenhouse gases have to be restricted by governments and regulators who have to act in the face of conflicts of interest between nations—whose positions often reflect different income levels, different levels of reliance on carbon-generating activities, and different levels of responsibility for past emissions. Such conflicts of national interest similarly impact on the regulation of digital platforms. We saw in Chapter 8 that the world's five most valuable corporations are digital platforms that are all based in the US. Developing agreed transnational policies on controlling their market power and on where and how much tax they should pay thus raises considerable problems.

In polycentric regimes, the reasons why different bodies may be willing to come together in pursuing a certain set of goals may also vary, as may their envisaged ways of operationalizing their aims. Thus, some public bodies may aim to control certain risks in a legally binding manner but they may be working with private organizations whose priorities are to use measures that are only aspirational in order to manage the risks presented to, or the reputations of, the industries they represent. As discussed when looking at sustainability in Chapter 6, there may be organizational divergences on not merely the content and meaning of objectives but also their force and range of application.

A further difficulty that afflicts the setting of objectives is the complexity of issues that may have to be addressed transnationally. Thus, as indicated in Chapter 8, the regulatory agenda relating to internationally dominant digital platforms, such as Facebook, covers a range of both social issues (such as hate speech, harmful material, and political chicanery) and a set of familiar economic problems (such as abuse of market power and anti-competitive conduct). The more extensive and sensitive this agenda, the more there is scope for nations to take divergent positions that are difficult to resolve.

Numbers of control processes may also have to be coordinated if objectives are to be agreed and steps taken to implement them. Thus, the geographical spread of the largest digital platforms is global and this places a premium on finding common (or at least compatible) remedies to counter the consumer detriments that are encountered or can be anticipated. (As noted, these remedies may take the form either of *ex ante* sectoral regulation or of amendments to competition law.) This may, however, require coordination between, amongst other things, the larger competition and regulatory authorities of the EU and the USA. Various international fora exist to facilitate such coordination in the field of competition law, notably the Organisation for Economic Co-operation and Development (OECD) and the International Competition Network (ICN). Regulatory interventions, on the other hand, have traditionally been specific to a sector and a country (or group of countries such as the EU), and are thus both more adaptable to local conditions and susceptible to national (or regional) control. The challenge of coordination (on both objectives and modes of implementation) is all the greater when the geographical bases, agendas, processes, priorities, and schedules of regulators and competition authorities diverge in so many ways.

How can direction be established in such networks? A common route within national governmental systems lies through hierarchical controls in which a body with central authority lays down rules and policies to give direction to inferior institutions. This method is not available in transnational polycentric regimes that lack any definitive legal framework or stipulated layering of authority.

An alternative mode of coordination is through community-based actions. Such processes operate when bodies recognize each other's common interests and involvement in relation to an issue. Within a 'community' mode, regulatory actors will engage in a variety of interactions that are designed to identify common aims and methods of furthering these. The difficulty in many transnational regimes is that there will be too many divergences of interests and objectives to bring parties together by engaging in such discourses and agreeing solutions. Thus, in the case of greenhouse gases, the chosen process for coordination centres on annual UN Climate Control Conferences (COPs or Conferences of the Parties) at which national commitments are sought. The 2019 conference in Madrid (COP 25), however, produced no great step forward and critics attacked the glacial pace and convoluted nature of the talks.

The kind of consensus-seeking processes that were seen in Madrid often encounter another difficulty. This is the tendency for 'lowest common denominator' decision-making and the development of objectives and control systems that are unambitious enough, or sufficiently lacking regulatory bite, to satisfy the least committed actors.[5]

A third approach to coordination is network management—in which a lead body takes positive steps to generate coordinated aims and processes across the network. This will commonly involve the facilitation and steering of negotiations and interactions so as to foster the pursuit of shared objectives and the building of consensus. (United Nations efforts on climate change exemplify this approach in so far as the UN works, *inter alia*, to broker international agreements on action over climate change; to build the scientific consensus, and to place the issue higher on the agendas of the world's media, governments, and businesses. In this respect, responses to climate change involve a mixture of 'community' and 'managerial' modes of coordination.)

A more modest version of network management occurs when a given body manages a particular aspect of the control regime and this role is be accepted by other institutions in a manner that yields some commonality of approach. Thus a body may develop detailed technical standards and these may gain general currency within the regime even though they are applied in different ways by different bodies.

Overall, the success or failure of the managerial approach will often turn on the technical skill and the resourcing of the network managers, the complexity of the network, and the extent to which genuine divergences of interests are encountered in the group and are amenable to resolution.

In the face of such coordination challenges, transnational regulatory regimes very often rely on the use of highly flexible requirements, such as broad principles and standards, that give different bodies a high level of interpretative freedom and scope to take their preferred approach to control. In such arrangements there is often high-level agreement on the values and objectives to be furthered but this may conceal very different approaches, and even tensions, at the level of implementation—as can be seen, again, in the climate control area.

What is clear is that, whatever mode of transnational coordination is employed, there are many areas of regulation in which state regulators will have limited abilities to exert control over the precise objectives being pursued in networked systems.

---

[5] See Heyvaert, *Transnational Environmental Regulation and Governance*, p. 59.

Delivering Outcomes

Transnational regimes face significant challenges in producing rules and principles that can be applied in a manner that changes behaviour effectively. For a start, the absence of a definitive source of legal authority and the lack of any regime-wide mechanism for enforcing prescriptive rules are factors that make traditional command and control strategies difficult to apply. Mechanisms for applying penalties for non-compliance are rare and mandatory prescriptions tend to give way to the language of persuasion. Transnational regimes commonly rely on mixtures of 'soft' laws, self-regulatory and self-assessment systems, voluntary guidelines, reporting requirements, and cooperative mechanisms. These instruments may be produced by private bodies, and state authorities will not be able to compel addressees to comply with privately sponsored frameworks. Controls rely routinely on indirect actions, steering mechanisms, and informal regimes of influence. The voluntary nature of such controls brings the associated risks that the public and consumers will lack trust in the system; that this will produce business-unfriendly uncertainty; and that free-riding non-compliers will undermine the regime.

Transnational regimes can also lack dynamism where deliberative efforts to secure consensus stand in the way of regulatory action. Factors extraneous to the regulatory project may impact on efforts to secure such consensus—as when concessions are demanded by some parties in order to further the prospects of trading freely. One way to respond to the dangers of regulatory stagnation is to delegate tasks to specialist implementation or expert bodies. Another is to avoid the use of precise and binding instruments and to exert control (at least partially) through non-binding mechanisms such as flexibly drafted advisory documents, guidelines, blueprints, and recommendations. Here it can be alleged that there is a trade-off: the price for securing broad inter-institutional agreement is the move towards 'weaker' forms of controls that are to be observed on a voluntary basis. There is, however, a limit to this argument. Strategies based on commands and deterrence also have their limitations (as noted in Chapter 3) and it should not be assumed that the use of other modes of influence will always prove ineffective in changing behaviour—much will depend on political contexts as well as the nature of the organizations, firms, and individuals that are addressed by those seeking to exert influence.[6]

---

[6] Heyvaert, *Transnational Environmental Regulation and Governance*, p. 177.

Meeting Procedural Expectations

Satisfying procedural expectations is especially challenging in regulatory networks that mix state and non-state bodies, public and private actors, as well as formal and informal controls. Significant amounts of power are often exercised by a variety of non-state or private organizations and lines of responsibility will be unclear where mixes of controls operate concurrently or where decisions and policies are traceable not to a single source but to a constellation of national, supra-national, and public and private bodies. These varieties of influencing bodies will, moreover, operate with quite divergent systems of accountability and they will engage in their own specific kinds of communications with multiplicities of stakeholders. Matters may also be rendered more complex because certain bodies, such as non-governmental organizations, may carry out regulatory functions at the same time as campaigning or lobbying activities. Non-governmental bodies may even lack a central organizational structure and they may engage only in certain regulatory functions such as standard-setting or information dissemination or monitoring.

The often-expressed worries about such regimes are that their mandates are not clear and it may not be obvious who they represent or to whom they render account—or for what. They are free from accountability through standard international law mechanisms and treaties, they are not transparent in the way that state regulators tend to be, and they provide limited forms of access and consultative processes. They are, moreover, said to be weak in providing redress procedures and those affected by their controls are both excluded from decision processes and unable to challenge these through such procedures as judicial review.[7]

Viewing transnational regulation more positively, it can be argued that accountability and legitimation mechanisms do exist in complex regulatory networks—but not on the traditional model associated with legally hierarchical domestic regimes. Thus, it can be said that complicated, and often messy, mixtures of processes, claims, and counter-claims typically provide means by which bodies are both embedded in transnational networks and render account to, and interact with, a host of other bodies in a variety of ways. Such processes may include the exchanging of explanations, information, and justifications as well as interrogations, opinion-giving,

---

[7] Black, 'Constructing and Contesting Legitimacy and Accountability in Polycentric Regulatory Regimes'.

auditing, performance measurement, legal review, and inspection. The legitimacy and authority of bodies in such a network becomes manifest in the willingness of other organizations, firms, or individuals to accept their influence and to adjust their behaviour accordingly.[8] A dilemma for many organizations, however, is that there may be tensions and contradictions between the demands, values, and expectations of the bodies that they are networked with. Demands compete and it may not always be possible to satisfy all of these concurrently. Justifying actions to regulated firms, for instance, may involve processes and actions that will not keep consumers or other stakeholders happy; demonstrating dynamism of action to certain parties may not satisfy those who demand high levels of procedural justice.

Overall, then, it can be argued that legitimacy claims and modes of justification are hard to establish and sustain in transnational networks of regulators. The lack of clear mandates rules out a key avenue of justification, levels of expertise may vary hugely across the network, accountability is fragmented, complex, and obscure, performance assessment is challenging, and fairness has to be searched out in a host of locations. This is not to say that such legitimacy claims and justifications cannot be made to carry weight, but it is to suggest that a non-traditional model of accountability and justification has to be worked with.

Regarding the potential of national regulators to deal with problems, it can be seen that there are a host of reasons why transnational controls and influences are needed in a world of increasingly globalized challenges. It should not be forgotten, however, that state-based regulators are not wholly passive receivers of influence. There are often deep interdependencies between state and non-state bodies, and national regulators frequently have considerable impact on transnational regimes. State-based actions, moreover, are central to enforcement and other regulatory processes in many areas (such as threats to the environment).

Conclusions

Can transnational networks (or polycentric domestic regimes) regulate positively? Pessimists would point to the challenges of coordinating such

---

[8] Black, 'Constructing and Contesting Legitimacy and Accountability in Polycentric Regulatory Regimes'.

complex and messy regimes so as to ensure lowest-cost yet effective systems of control. The more optimistic view is that the very diversity of such networks brings advantages. Thus, awareness can be fostered in regimes involving multiple players. This, it could be argued, reduces the dangers that a dominant, incumbent regulator will fail to appreciate challenges—certain network agents will stimulate others so as to bring new issues on to agendas. Information-gathering may be galvanized, and intelligence improved, when data flows around the network from many sources, and dynamism may be encouraged when the most responsive bodies push others to make changes to come to grips with a changing world. Whether such advantages can be realized will turn on the degree to which divergences of interests and approaches stand in the way of collaborative actions. None of this, however, detracts from the need to aim for the most positive approach to regulating that can be achieved in the given context. Our two examples of regulating climate change and digital platforms demonstrate the importance of getting this right.

11
Regulating for Future Needs

This book has argued for taking a positive approach to regulation and for seeing regulation as part of the core process for furthering both business success and social welfare. If regulation is to develop in a way that meets future needs, as well as current ones, it will be necessary to develop the key attributes of positive regulation. This involves a predisposition to maximize the degree to which objectives (substantive and procedural) can be achieved by harnessing corporate capacities to behave well. Such a minimalist approach to 'taming the corporation' implies that enabling and flexible modes of influence should be the first choices of regulators, rather than restrictive control mechanisms. Realism, however, demands that regulators take on board the inclinations and capacities of regulated firms to behave well and that they act firmly with corporations and individuals that are not likely to deliver desired outcomes without strong forms of external stimulation.

Positive regulation delivers results by building on the qualities of awareness, intelligence, and dynamism as applied across the core tasks of regulation. When setting objectives, delivering desired outcomes, and meeting procedural expectations, positive regulators will thus be lively to challenges, strong on evidence, and responsive to changes in their worlds. They will be aware, as noted, that some corporations will be more capable and trustworthy than others and some will be more in need of taming than their peers. The positive regulator's ability to discern the nature of those parties to be regulated is thus vital to choices of regulatory strategies, intervention instruments, and enforcement approaches.

Positive regulatory delivery also has at its heart the identification of all opportunities for producing win-win outcomes. Such outcomes are a high point of regulatory success when the wins extend to not merely regulators and businesses but to consumers, the environment, and society generally. As was seen in Chapter 2, though, the conditions under which win-win can be achieved may be limited but this should caution us to avoid excessive optimism rather than to abandon the search for win-win results.

Strategically, positive regulation demands an awareness of, and willingness to deploy, the full range of control strategies, ranging from 'command' approaches and incentive mechanisms to disclosures and nudges. As discussed above, each of these mechanisms has strengths and weaknesses and the key to successful, positive use is an awareness of these qualities and also knowledge of the conditions under which different tools bring the best chances of producing desired outcomes. Important, again, is regulatory intelligence concerning the attitudes and capacities of the firms and individuals whose behaviour is to be influenced. It is essential, for instance, to be able to distinguish between firms that can be trusted to control risks on their own account and those that cannot. Awareness and information on corporate attitudes and capacities is central here and this is especially the case in relation to strategies of self-regulation, meta-regulation, self-assurance, and collaborative regulation.

Moving from choices of broad strategy to matters of implementation and enforcement, regulating positively calls for an awareness of those measures that can be used to stimulate compliance with rules and that will encourage behaviour consistent with the achieving of desired outcomes. Again a regulator that has awareness and intelligence regarding the firms and individuals it deals with has an important input into its choices of intervention instruments. When combined with data on the kinds of risks involved in firm activities, this offers a framework for identifying the least costly and intrusive intervention tools and the levels of regulatory intensity that are appropriate in a given scenario—as was seen in the GRID approach discussed in Chapter 4.

In seeking to target regulatory interventions, risk analyses are used widely around the world, but it was noted in Chapter 4 that risk-based regulation informs regulatory decisions more readily than it provides neat quantitative determinations of decisions. There is more art in regulation than the purveyors of risk-based regulation have often drawn attention to. Risk analyses tell regulators only a very limited amount about the best ways to bring about behavioural changes and identifying the key risks to be evaluated and focused upon is not a simple or uncontentious matter. Positive regulation calls for a realistic approach to risk-based intervention, one that involves awareness of potential pitfalls but also recognizes the value of the risk analysis as an input into decisions on priorities.

As for choices between precise rules and broadly stated principles, the importance of intelligence on firm characteristics comes to the fore again. Operating through principles rather than rules tends to bring success with well-intentioned and high capacity firms but works less effectively in relation to firms with poorer attitudes and lower capacities. A key challenge for positive regulators is, accordingly, to devise intelligence systems that will allow them to assess the intentions and capacities of firms as well as the levels and kinds of risks that are posed by the activities in which they engage. Intelligence systems that are sensitive to changes in intentions, capacities and risks will also be a feature of positive regulation.

Regulating for future needs places dynamism at the heart of the qualities to be demonstrated by positive regulators. As seen in Chapter 5, high quality regulation involves an ability to respond to new challenges and risks and to negotiate evidential uncertainties so as to make effective regulatory decisions and policies. Regulators also have an important role to play in encouraging business innovation, and in stimulating the development of new ways to address such problems as global warming and the need to maximize the net benefits of digital platforms. These ends will sometimes be served by regulatory strategies and intervention approaches that give firms the flexibilities to develop new operational methods and technologies. On other occasions, the regulator will have to take the lead and demand that changes are made.

Yet again, an awareness of the kinds of firm being dealt with will be crucial in choosing strategies that will actually encourage innovation. Intelligence on the potential of innovations to solve existing problems will also be important. If regulation is to be used to foster innovations, the regulators will have to develop the information-gathering and research capacities that are needed to identify and act on the opportunities offered by technological and other innovations. Similarly, the positive regulator will aim to encourage business innovations by implementing necessary regulatory adjustments in the least costly ways—and in order to do so, they will be aware of, and choose from, the full array of possible methods of implementing and managing changes in their regimes.

Regulating to foster sustainability is central to future needs and yet it was seen in Chapter 6 that the challenges of doing so are considerable, with many difficulties flowing from the indeterminacies associated with the notion of sustainable development.

We have argued that, to meet these challenges 'sustainability regulators' need to be especially aware, intelligent, and dynamic so that they recognize and deal with the numerous and often acute problems that they face. They need to render their projects feasible and coherent—often by acting creatively to translate their mandates into understood and realizable missions. Substantive outcomes must be delivered by building on an awareness of relevant corporate intentions and capacities and the ways that these are likely to impact on strategic choices—such as whether to seek to extend the use of best available technologies, or to drive improvements in such technologies, or to stimulate radical transformations in production methods. Procedural expectations have to be satisfied by negotiating a path through complex institutional and informational landscapes as well as changing expectations and regulatory environments.

On the pre-eminent issue of decarbonization, regulation needs to be at its most positive. Governments and agencies need to be highly aware of the complex sets of expectations and institutional frameworks within which they have to act. They need to operate with systems of intelligence that provide the data and evidence with which they can deliver decarbonization effectively, assess their own performance, and meet the procedural expectations of a host of affected parties—particularly with respect to finding solutions which are perceived as being sufficiently fair to all parties to win the allegiance of the public to tough climate change targets. They need to operate dynamically so that they can react to changes in such matters as: markets, costs, technologies, emissions sources, stakeholder expectations, and political constraints.

Two further and contrasting applications of the idea of positive regulation can be found in the discussion in Chapters 7 and 8 of, first, regulation of traditional physical networks in the utility and related industries, such as energy and telecommunications access networks, and, second, the more recent issue of how to regulate digital platforms, such as Facebook, Google, and Uber.

The challenges of regulating traditional physical networks have arisen under both public and private ownership, and stem from a combination of the natural monopoly properties of some of the relevant companies' assets, and the essential nature of the services they provide to their customers. The problems have proved to be systematic. Their solution may be aided, if not fully resolved, by increasing digitization, which permits a more varied range of options competitive with what the incumbent network operator provides. These will increasingly be exploited by intelligent and dynamic regulators.

Now in train is the process of using regulation to address the adverse effects created by the massive growth of certain dominant digital platforms (effects that are matched, of course, by the clear benefits that they have also generated). Like traditional physical networks, these digital platforms are often characterized by persistent market power. There is some convergence on the solutions needed to resolve the resulting problems of unequal exchange between the platform and the households and other agents with which it interacts. It looks as if action of a regulatory nature will soon be taken to resolve some of these issues.

The other side of regulating for success is avoiding regulatory failure. In Chapter 9 we argued that poor performance tends to be associated with a lack of awareness, intelligence, and dynamism in performing the key regulatory tasks and that the root causes of such failings can be explained in different ways: as due to institutional factors (within the regulator or external to it), or contests between interests (as in capture theory), or due to errors of understanding (as in 'ideas' theories). Responses to such problems, we suggested, should focus on addressing root causes by attending to matters of culture (an institutional and 'ideas' issue), capture (central to interest theory), and cognition (ideas).

All of the above regulatory challenges are rendered more complex in the very many areas in which regulators respond to mischiefs that cross national borders ('risks sans frontières') and do so by acting within networks made up of state, non-state, and public and private bodies. As noted in Chapter 10, this world of 'decentred', polycentric, and, often highly fragmented, regulation incorporates formal and informal, legal and non-binding modes of influence so that the challenges of setting objectives, delivering outcomes, and meeting procedural expectations are severe (and, to a degree, echoed in complex, polycentric domestic regimes). The hope lies in seeking to build on the positive aspects of such networks. This can be undertaken by taking such steps as: building awareness by using multiple viewpoints to identify issues and create feedback systems; stimulating intelligence-gathering by encouraging data flows across the network; and encouraging dynamism by using the most responsive bodies to drive forward the changes that are needed to come to grips with a changing world. State-based regulators, moreover, can encourage these positive actions: they often have considerable impact on transnational regimes and routinely play key roles in such regulatory actions as enforcement.

In transnational regulation, as in domestic regulation, the way to regulate for success is to aim for the most positive approach that can be achieved in the given context. To return to our mantra: the basis for a productive stance on regulation is to move away from the 'red light' conception and to see regulation as part of the process for promoting both business success and social welfare.

Further Reading

General reading

Many of the issues discussed in this book are dealt with in greater detail in:
Baldwin, R., Cave, M., and Lodge, M. *Understanding Regulation: Theory, Strategy, and Practice* (2nd ed., Oxford University Press, 2012). (Hereafter *Understanding Regulation*)

Collections of useful essays on regulation

Baldwin, R., Cave, M. and Lodge, M. (eds.) *The Oxford Handbook of Regulation* (Oxford University Press, 2010). (Hereafter *The Oxford Handbook of Regulation*).
Drahos, P. (ed.) *Regulatory Theory: Foundations and Applications* (ANU Press, 2017).
Levi-Faur, D. (ed.) *Handbook on the Politics of Regulation* (Edward Elgar, 2011).

Also useful

Gunningham, N. and Grabosky, P. *Smart Regulation: Designing Environmental Policy* (Clarendon Press, 1998).
Heyvaert, V. *Transnational Environmental Regulation and Governance: Purpose, Strategies and Principles* (Cambridge University Press, 2019).
Hodges, C. *Law and Corporate Behaviour* (Hart, 2015).
Lodge, M. and Wegrich, K. *Managing Regulation: Regulatory Analysis, Politics and Policy* (Springer, 2012).
Morgan, B. and Yeung, K. *An Introduction to Law and Regulation: Text and Materials* (Cambridge University Press, 2007).
Sparrow, M. *The Regulatory Craft: Controlling Risks, Solving Problems, and Managing Compliance* (Harvard University Press, 2000).

Readings relevant to specific chapters

Chapter 1
Understanding Regulation Chapter 2.
The Oxford Handbook of Regulation Chapter 1.
Feintuck, M. *The Public Interest in Regulation* (Oxford University Press, 2004).
Prosser, T. *The Regulatory Enterprise: Government Regulation and Legitimacy* (Oxford University Press, 2010).
Singer, J. *No Freedom Without Regulation: The Hidden Lesson of the Subprime Crisis* (Yale University Press, 2015).

Chapter 2

Understanding Regulation Chapter 3.

Albrizio, S., Botta, E., Koźluk, T., and Zipperer, V. *Do Environmental Policies Matter for Productivity Growth? Insights from New Cross-Country Measures of Environmental Policies* (Paris: OECD Economics Department Working Papers No. 1176 (2014) (ECO/WKP(2014)72)).

Ambec, S., Cohen, M. A., Elgie, S., and Lanoie, P. *The Porter Hypothesis at 20* (Washington, DC: Resources for the Future Discussion Paper No. 11-01, 2011).

Ashford, N., Ayers, C., and Stone, R. 'Using Regulation to Change the Market for Innovation', *Harvard Environmental Law Review* 9(2) (1985): 419–66.

Coglianese, C. *Achieving Regulatory Excellence* (Washington, DC: Brookings Institution, 2016).

Porter, M. and van der Linde, C. 'Toward a New Conception of the Environment–Competitiveness Relationship', *Journal of Economic Perspectives* 9(4) (1995): 97–118.

Chapter 3

Understanding Regulation Chapters 7, 8, 10.

Ashford, N. 'Government and Environmental Innovation in Europe and North America', *American Behavioral Scientist* 45 (2002): 1417–34.

Baldwin, R. 'From Regulation to Behaviour Change: Giving Nudge the Third Degree', *Modern Law Review* 77(6) (2014): 831–57.

Baldwin, R. and Black, J. 'Really Responsive Regulation', *Modern Law Review* 71(1) (2008): 59–94.

Black, J. 'Forms and Paradoxes of Principles Based Regulation', *Capital Markets Law Journal* 3(4) (2008): 425–58.

Cabinet Office. *Regulatory Futures Review* (London: Cabinet Office, 2017).

Coglianese, C. 'The Limits of Performance-Based Regulation', *Michigan Journal of Law Reform* 50 (2016): 525–64.

Coglianese, C. and Lazer, D. 'Management-Based Regulation: Prescribing Private Management to Achieve Public Goals', *Law & Society Review* 37(4) (2003): 691–730.

Coglianese, C. and Mendelson, E. 'Meta-Regulation and Self-Regulation', in *The Oxford Handbook of Regulation*.

Driesen, D. 'Alternatives to Regulation? Market Mechanisms and the Environment', in *The Oxford Handbook of Regulation*.

Fairman, R. and Yapp, C. 'Enforced Self-Regulation, Prescription and Conceptions of Compliance within Small Businesses', *Law and Policy* 27 (2005): 491–519.

Gunningham, N. and Grabosky, P. *Smart Regulation: Designing Environmental Policy* (Clarendon Press, 1998) Chapter 2.

Gunningham, N. and Holley, C. 'Next Generation Environmental Regulation', *Annual Review of Law and Social Science* 12 (2016): 273–93.

Heyvaert, V. *Transnational Environmental Regulation and Governance: Purpose, Strategies and Principles* (Cambridge University Press, 2019).

Hodges, C. and Steinholtz, R. *Ethical Business Practice and Regulation* (Hart, 2017).

Lessig, L. *Code and Other Laws of Cyberspace* (Basic Books, 1999).

Lodge, M. and Wegrich, K. 'The Rationality Paradox of Nudge', *Law & Policy* 38(3) (2016): 250–67.

Mashaw, J. and Harfst, D. 'From Command and Control to Collaboration and Deference: The Transformation of Auto Safety Regulation', *Yale Journal on Regulation* 34 (2017): 167–278.

Murray, A. *The Regulation of Cyberspace: Control in the Online Environment* (Routledge-Cavendish, 2006).

Parker, C. *The Open Corporation: Effective Self-Regulation and Democracy* (Cambridge University Press, 2002).

Richman, E. 'Emissions Trading and the Development Critique: Exposing the Threat to Developing Countries', *Journal of International Law and Politics* 36 (2003): 133–76.

Stern, N. *The Economics of Climate Change: The Stern Review* (Cambridge University Press, 2007).

Thaler, R. and Sunstein, C. *Nudge: Improving Decisions about Health, Wealth, and Happiness* (Harvard University Press, 2008).

Tietenberg, T. *Emissions Trading* (2nd edn.) (Washington, DC: Resources for the Future, 2006)

Chapter 4

Understanding Regulation Chapters 11–14.

Ayres, I. and Braithwaite, J. *Responsive Regulation: Transcending the Deregulation Debate* (Oxford University Press, 1992).

Baldwin, R. and Black, J. *Defra: A Review of Enforcement Measures and an Assessment of their Effectiveness in Terms of Risk and Outcome* (London: Defra 2005).

Baldwin, R. and Black, J. 'Really Responsive Regulation', *Modern Law Review* 71(1) (2008): 59–94.

Black, J. *Risk-Based Regulation: Choices, Practices and Lessons Being Learned* (Paris: OECD, 2008).

Black, J. 'The Role of Risk in Regulatory Processes', in *The Oxford Handbook on Regulation*.

Black, J. and Baldwin, R. 'When Risk-Based Regulation Aims Low: A Strategic Framework', *Regulation and Governance* 6 (2012): 131–48.

Diver, C. 'The Optimal Precision of Administrative Rules', *Yale Law Journal* 93(1) (1983): 65–109.

Dutch Ministry of Justice. *The Table of Eleven* (The Hague, 2004).

Gunningham, N. 'Enforcement and Compliance Strategies', in *The Oxford Handbook of Regulation*.

Gunningham, N. and Grabosky, P. *Smart Regulation: Designing Environmental Policy* (Clarendon Press, 1998).

Hampton, P. *Reducing Administrative Burdens: Effective Inspection and Enforcement* (London: HMSO, 2005).

Hood, C., Rothstein, H., and Baldwin, R. *The Government of Risk: Understanding Risk Regulation Regimes* (Oxford University Press, 2001).

OECD. *Reducing the Risk of Policy Failure: Challenges for Regulatory Compliance* (Paris: OECD, 2000).

Parker, C. and Lehmann Nielsen, V. 'Compliance: 14 Questions', in P. Drahos (ed.), *Regulatory Theory: Foundations and Applications* (ANU Press, 2017), pp. 217–32.

Royal Society. *Risk Analysis, Perception, Management* (London: Royal Society, 1992).

Shavell, S. 'The Optimal Structure of Law Enforcement', *Journal of Law and Economics* 36 (1993): 255–87.

Sparrow, M. *The Regulatory Craft: Controlling Risks, Solving Problems, and Managing Compliance* (Harvard University Press, 2000).

Sparrow, M. *The Character of Harms: Operational Challenges in Control* (Cambridge University Press, 2008).

Chapter 5

Ashford, N., Ayers, C. and Stone, R. 'Using Regulation to Change the Market for Innovation', *Harvard Environmental Law Review* 9(2) (1985): 419–66.

Baldwin, R. and Cave, M. *Regulatory Stability and the Challenges of Re-regulating* (Brussels: CERRE, 2013).

Deloitte. *A Journey through the FCA Regulatory Sandbox* (London: Deloitte, 2018).

FCA. *Regulatory Sandbox* (London: FCA, 2015).

Levy, B. and Spiller, P. *Regulations, Institutions and Commitment* (Cambridge University Press, 1996).

Shrader-Frechette, K. *Risk and Rationality: Philosophical Foundations for Populist Reforms* (University of California Press, 1991).

Chapter 6

Berners-Lee, M. *There is No Planet B* (Cambridge University Press, 2019).

Black, J. 'Constructing and Contesting Legitimacy and Accountability in Polycentric Regulatory Regimes', *Regulation & Governance* 2 (2008): 137–64.

Black, J. 'Decentring Regulation: Understanding the Role of Regulation and Self-Regulation in a "Post-Regulatory World"', *Current Legal Problems* 54(1) (2001): 103–46.

Brundtland, G. *Report of the World Commission on Environment and Development: Our Common Future* (Brundtland Report) (Oxford University Press, 1987).

Ellerman, A., Joskow, P. L., Schmalensee, R., Montero, J. P., and Bailey, E. M. *Markets for Clean Air: The U.S. Acid Rain Program* (Cambridge University Press, 2000).

Heyvaert, V. *Transnational Environmental Regulation and Governance: Purpose, Strategies and Principles* (Cambridge University Press, 2019) Chapter 4.

Nordhaus, W. *The Climate Casino: Risk, Uncertainty, and Economics for a Warming World* (Yale University Press, 2013).

OECD. *Sustainability in Impact Assessments* (Paris: OECD, 2012).

Stern, N. *Why Are We Waiting? The Logic, Urgency, and Promise of Tackling Climate Change* (MIT Press, 2015).

Tol, R. *Climate Economics: Economic Analysis of Climate, Climate Change and Climate Policy* (Edward Elgar, 2019).

Chapter 7

Alexiadis, P. and Cave, M. 'Regulation and Competition Law in Telecommunications and Other Network Industries', in *The Oxford Handbook of Regulation*.

Decker, C. *Modern Economic Regulation: An Introduction to Theory and Practice* (Cambridge University Press, 2015) Chapters 2, 4–6.

Florio, M. *Network Industries and Social Welfare: The Experiment that Reshuffled European Utilities* (Oxford University Press, 2013).

Hauge, J. and Sappington, D. 'Pricing in Network Industries', in *The Oxford Handbook of Regulation*.

Meeus, L. and Glachant, J. (eds.) *Electricity Network Regulation in the EU: The Challenges Ahead for Transmission and Distribution* (Edward Elgar, 2019).

Chapter 8

Allcott, H., Braghieri, L., Eichmeyer, S., and Gentzkow, M. 'The Welfare Effects of Social Media', *American Economic Review* 110(3) (2020): 629–76.

Auletta, K. *Googled: The End of the World as We Know It* (Penguin, 2009).

Australian Competition and Consumer Commission. *Digital Platforms Inquiry—Final Report* (July 2019).

Chicago Booth Stigler Center. *Stigler Committee on Digital Platforms: Final Report* (September 2019).

Competition and Markets Authority. *Online Platforms and Digital Advertising Market Study: Interim Report* (London: CMA, December 2019).

Cremer, J. et al. *Competition Policy in the Digital Age: Report to Commissioner Vestager* (Brussels: EC, April 2019).

Evans, D. 'The Economics of Attention Markets', *Review of Industrial Organization* (February, 2019).

Evans, D. and Schmalensee, R. *Matchmakers: The New Economics of Multisided Platforms* (Harvard Business Review Press, 2016).

Levy, S. *Facebook: The Inside Story* (Penguin, 2020).

OECD. *Rethinking Antitrust Tools for Multi-Sided Platforms* (Paris: OECD, 2018).

Prat, A. and Valletti, T. 'Attention Oligopoly', Working Paper, 19 June 2018. Available at http://dx.doi.org/10.2139/ssrn.3197930.

Tirole, J. *Economics for the Common Good* (Princeton University Press, 2017) Chapter 14.

Unlocking Digital Competition. Report of the Digital Competition Expert Panel (Furman Report) (March 2019).

Chapter 9

Cooper, J. and Kovacic, W. 'Behavioral Economics: Implications for Regulatory Policy', *Journal of Regulatory Economics* 41 (2012): 41–58.

Hall, C., Scott, C., and Hood, C. *Telecommunications Regulation: Culture, Chaos and Interdependence Inside the Regulatory Process* (Routledge, 2000).

Hayward, S. *The Agile Leader* (Kogan Page, 2018).

Hutter, B. and Lloyd-Bostock, S. *Regulatory Crisis: Negotiating the Consequences of Risk, Disasters and Crises* (Cambridge University Press, 2017).

Jennings, W., Lodge, M., and Ryan, M. 'Comparing Blunders in Government', *European Journal of Political Research* 57(1) (2018): 238–58.

Joskow, P. L. 'Inflation and Environmental Concern: Structural Change in the Process of Public Utility Price Regulation', *The Journal of Law and Economics* 17(2) (1974): 291–327.

Kahneman, D. *Thinking, Fast and Slow* (Penguin, 2012).

Mintzberg, H. *Mintzberg on Management: Inside Our Strange World of Organizations* (Free Press, 1989).

Waldock, B. *Being Agile in Business* (Pearson, 2015).

Waterman, R. *Adhocracy: The Power to Change* (Norton, 1990).

Chapter 10

Auld, G., Betsill, M. and VanDeveer, S. 'Transnational Governance for Mining and the Mineral Lifecycle', *Annual Review of Environment and Resources* 43(2018): 425–53.

Baccaro, L. and Mele, V. 'For Lack of Anything Better? International Organizational and Global Corporate Codes', *Public Administration* 89(2) (2011): 451–70.

Bernstein, S. and Cashore, B. 'Can Non-State Global Governance be Legitimate?', *Regulation and Governance* 1(2007): 347–71.

Black, J. 'Constructing and Contesting Legitimacy and Accountability in Polycentric Regulatory Regimes', *Regulation & Governance* 2 (2008): 137–64.

Black, J. 'Mapping the Contours of Contemporary Financial Services Regulation', *Journal of Corporate Law Studies* 2 (2002): 253–88.

Bomhoff, J. and Meuwese, A. 'The Meta-Regulation of Transnational Private Regulation', *Journal of Law and Society* 38(1) (2011): 138–62.

Braithwaite, J. and Fisse, B. 'Self-Regulation and the Costs of Corporate Crime', in C. Shearing and P. Stenning (eds.), *Private Policing* (Sage, 1987).

Gehring, T. and Krapohl, S. 'Supranational Regulatory Agencies between Independence and Control', *Journal of European Public Policy* 14 (2007): 208–26.

Gunningham, N. and Rees, J. 'Industry Self-Regulation: An Institutional Perspective', *Law and Policy* 10 (1997): 363–414.

Heyvaert, V. *Transnational Environmental Regulation and Governance: Purpose, Strategies and Principles* (Cambridge University Press, 2019).

Pattberg, P. 'The Institutionalization of Private Governance: How Business and Nonprofit Organizations Agree on Transnational Rules', *Governance* 18(4) (2005): 589–610.

Pattberg, P. 'Private Governance and the South', *Third World Quarterly* 27(4) (2006): 579–93.

Rees, J. 'Development of Communitarian Regulation in the Chemical Industry', *Law and Policy* 19(4) (1997): 477–528.

Vogel, D. 'The Private Regulation of Global Corporate Conduct', in W. Mattli and N. Woods (eds.), *The Politics of Global Regulation* (Princeton University Press, 2009).

Index